How To

Raise The Dead

+ A Practical Guide to Resurrection Power +

By Tyler Johnson

This book is for You, Heavenly Father.
We have misunderstood You.
May we step beyond the torn veil.

Acknowledgements

Mom, thank you for your perseverance in proclaiming God's goodness, even in the face of death and loss. Everything good that God has done through me can be traced back to the foundation of love that you laid in my life. I am grateful for you and dad, and I love you.

Dad, I love you! I cannot wait to dance with you in joy on streets of gold. The wisdom and grace that you lavished upon me was a seed that blossomed into a tree, now rooted into the soil of my heart, making me stand strong, as an oak of righteousness. You were God to me, embodying His likeness, gentleness, and humility. I miss you.

Christine, being a forerunner isn't always easy, but it is so much easier when you are by my side. If forced to choose, I would rather be bread to a remnant than palatable to the masses. Thank you for standing with me in my convictions about God's goodness, for you have strengthened me. You are exactly what and who I need and want in a wife. Thank you for not calling me crazy when I would come out of prayer with a new revelation that seemed contrary to everything we had ever learned in institutional Christianity. You are beautiful, and I love you.

Marc and Lydia, thank you for having a *big* God that was inexhaustible in His goodness, and for always wanting more of Him! I love you two, and am honored to call you parents. You have backed us through thick and thin, and I am grateful. Thank you for loving our children, for always speaking life over us, and for being such a source of encouragement and guidance. I love you. Jean, you will always me our blissercessor.

Brian and Cindy, your wisdom, genuineness, generosity, and freedom have richly blessed us. Thank you for being our out-of-state parents. Your insight, guidance, and love is deeply appreciated. You are family. Steven, your chapter titles were hilariously amazing. You will find them at the end of this book. Love you buddy.

Adam, you are my best man! Thank you for being a pillar in my life, for your laughter, your prayers, your passion, your brotherly kisses, and your love. You are a diamond in the crown of God, and I cherish you as David did Jonathan.

Sung, thank you for believing in a good God. I wish more people were as violent as you are in living grace and preaching it. God's favor is upon you. Greatness is yours. I love you and am so thankful for your friendship.

Bill Johnson, thank you for taking up the mandate of revealing the goodness of God to the nations. I love the story of the time the Lord thanked you for telling people that He is good. I join Him in the thanks He gave you.

David Hogan, you have been the remnant in the West to obey Jesus in His command to raise the dead. In a season of history when raising the dead was rare, you steadily continued in the fullness of the Gospel. Your obedience has resulted in an unseen worldwide breakthrough; Dead raising is becoming a norm for those that desire to obey God to the fullness. That which was impossible and out of reach has become more than a possibility because of your example. Thank you.

Mike Bickle and the IHOP staff, may the fire continue to burn. Your lifestyle of prayer and worship, centered around the adoration of His beauty, is a fountain to drink from daily. We would live in the prayer room if we could, but tents aren't allowed.

C.S. Cowles and Richard Murray, thank you for your insights into scripture and the revelation of the nature of God found in the Christ. Many have benefited from your pioneering the way in the theological realm pertaining to God's goodness. Your hearts are pure; you see God.

John Crowder, we are so thankful for you. History reveals that the mark of a true forerunner is impedance by those that you would expect to support them the most. Your freedom, love, and willingness to give away what God has given you, though it may be controversial to some, is beautiful. Thank you for obeying God rather than pleasing man. Your reward is great. Mark Twain said it best; "In the beginning of a change, the patriot is a scarce man, brave, hated, and scorned. When his cause succeeds, the timid join him, for then it costs nothing to be a patriot."

TABLE OF CONTENTS

Every cell in the dead body of Christ ground to an utter halt in the grave. His cold corpse grew rigid, the muscle fibers still and stiff in the lock of a seemingly hopeless and utter finality. No more breath. No more life. Cold. Silent. Numb.

By all accounts, the hands that had healed and the feet once kissed were now abandoned to a waterless, wasting atrophy in the earth. It was a real death. It was a complete death. Everything was over.

Fluids ceased to flow. Nerve endings ceased to spark with vitality. The eyes that once wept and sparkled with joy were now glazed over, vacant and dried. Pressed close perhaps, they saw nothing as his senseless, bloodless torso was left alone. No fire was needed in that tomb to warm Him – no food to sustain Him. There would be no more eating and drinking. No more dancing. Quiet and darkness fell around it. For He was no longer there. The corpse lay lifeless and alone. Emotionless, its heat and appetites had slipped away into the night. Its *essence* had drifted away, committed into another's hands.

Have you ever pictured yourself there? You were up close and personal for this whole affair. Not merely a spectator – you were a participant. Has anyone ever told you that you died a very *real* death on that day? Despite all the cliché talk about "death to self," it is not a lifelong process of abstinence, as some would lead you to believe. It was a *finite point*. In fact, you were lying right there in the cold Earth with Christ. You were planted together in the garden of His grave. The nails went through your hands when His were pierced. The spear sliced through *your* side, when they checked just to make sure the job of dying was finished.

You were wrapped up, rolled into that dank hole in the ground. You were left there as the living carried on with their lives and conversations. You hung on the tree with Him. For mystically you were *in Christ* that day. Crucified together in utter finality, you were united to Him in His death. Every cell, every functioning component of what made you a sinner – all your sickness, disease and corruption – came to a complete, decisive closure. The *curse* itself died – not partially, not just in *principle,* but completely. It all fell motionless like the engine of an old car left to rust in the grass along some forgotten country road of antiquity.

But that wasn't all ...

Surely death itself died that day. Within Christ's body, the governing entity of sin and all its ramifications died, and you died with it. That body sucked up every drop of darkness, every speck of sin. In fact, he carried the entire world down into that black hole of His sufferings. *For God was in Christ, reconciling the cosmos to Himself.*

But then something began to flutter ...

We don't know what it looked it like. Our eyes were still tacked shut. Nor do we quite recall what it sounded like ... for no one remembers the conversations of the midwives when they are born. And yet somehow – in some way – we have *seen* and we have *heard.* Somehow, we *remember* and can therefore testify of what we ourselves have touched and handled that day.

In that forgotten closet of Earth, something began to *move.* Deep in the core of those silent membranes of flesh, a *stirring* began. Perhaps it started with a hum. Perhaps it happened with a flash, a bang or a thunderclap. But one by one, each and every individual cell in that lifeless body began to vibrate. Those cells began to bounce and bend again. They started to twirl and dance and sing and come *alive.*

We don't know where it comes from, or exactly where it's going. But this ever-coursing torrent of *resurrection power* got its hands on us that day. It snatched us clean up from that cold stone slab. It shot through us like an ethereal voltage – running solvent through our clotted veins and putting goose bumps back on our clammy skin. It's the *energeon* that holds us together this very moment.

The limp frustration of mortality was swallowed up in immortality. In an instant, everything had changed. Sorrow was eclipsed by ecstasy. A holocaust became a holiday. A fast turned into a festival. When the last curtain call came in, we found that light really did have the power over darkness. That life is indestructible. Love is unquenchable.

Why should it be thought a thing incredible with you, that God should raise the dead?

God Himself is the Breath of Life. The unstoppable flame of charity. The *joie de vivre*. The flat announcement of the gospel is that we don't have to die unless we want to. For love is as jealous as the grave. Death's sting has been rendered impotent. And the saints can live *forever*.

In "How To Raise The Dead", Tyler sets forth a gamut of revelation, varying from practical "how to" aspects of raising the dead, to deeper, more meditative truths. Surely, the keys presented in this book provokes the reader to walk in resurrection power, but more importantly causes their gaze to be put back upon Christ time and time again. Central to the message of this book is Jesus. Enjoy!

John Crowder, Sons Of Thunder

INTRODUCTION

This book is about how to raise the dead. Literally. You will learn principles to live by in this book that will lead you into inevitably raising a dead body to life. As Jesus commanded in Matthew 10:8, "*...raise the dead*", so you will fulfill.

It is understood by the author that the topics discussed in the pages of this book are generally topics that are not being conversed about with much regularity within Christianity. A long time ago I decided that if I was forced to choose, I would rather be bread to a remnant than palatable to the masses. Jesus seemed to have exemplified this same value. Though there is little money, fame, and honor in proclaiming where the Church is headed, it nonetheless gives me a deep joy to do so.

It is a very easy thing to teach people what they already know, to say it in a new way that captivates them, and in doing so, to walk paths that others blazed years ago. It is a whole other matter to teach people on subjects that are altogether new to them. There are countless teachings on healing, evangelism, and other topics that relate to following Jesus, but teachings on dead raising are a rare thing.

Dead raising is generally viewed by western Christianity to be a radical, even bizarre concept. Nevertheless, Paul's words in Acts 26:8 still ring true today, "Why should it be thought an incredible thing that God should raise the dead?" In reality, God is presently making dead raising a common happening for anyone that desires to believe. Want to raise the dead? Read on.

Resurrection power is closely related to a spirit of revival. The dictionary defines revival to be "the recovering of life". God is in the business of not just bringing dead bodies to life, but breathing life into *anything* that is dead. This includes your heart, your ministry, your finances and any other facet of your life that has died. Revival is an all-encompassing way of life. It is the posture of a man's spirit; an overcoming and victorious paradigm. This victorious paradigm is not stumbled upon through happen chance, but becomes raw instinct when the correct foundation is laid in the heart and mind of a follower of Christ. A person cannot avoid raising the dead and living triumphantly when the groundwork of love and faith is laid properly. Hence, this book lays a foundation of the goodness of God, righteousness by faith, intimacy with Jesus, and the power of the tongue before delving into the topic of resurrection power. Without these imperatives in place I am convinced that one may work miracles for a time, but that inevitably burnout and compromise will follow shortly behind.

For the reader, this book is a shortcut. The revelations of the nature of God found in these pages can save you years of seeking answers to questions that have yet to be settled in your heart. The included insights are not typically taught in the Body of Christ and are much needed in order that a person walks in resurrection power. In part, this book is a preverbal kick-down of a few of the sacred cows that oppose the authenticity of God's goodness. He wants us to be sure, to the point of conviction, of His goodness and love. Only then will we have true faith to consistently raise the dead.

We can't drink milk forever. He is targeting your sacred cows, so prepare for some fresh meat. The gun is in your hands, in the form of a book. Pull the trigger; turn the page.

Tyler Johnson

+ PART ONE +
THE FOUNDATION
TO RESURRECTION POWER

"There comes a time when one must take a position that is
neither safe, nor politic, nor popular, but he must take it
because his conscience tells him it is right."
-Martin Luther

ot only is intimacy the fulfillment of the first commandment, but it is *the* purpose of our lives. Loving God is the most pleasurable, most exciting, most gratifying experience in existence. In order to be people that walk in resurrection life on a continual basis, the love of Jesus must first touch our heart in an emotionally moving way. Once our hearts have been captured, we become like a battering ram against the gates of hell. Dead raisers are people that have fallen in love with the Source of Life; Jesus. Intimacy with Jesus will be what keeps you fueled to continue to step out in faith to raise the dead. Without intimacy, you will burn out, guaranteed.

We can love the Father in a beautiful, intimate way by receiving His love as a child. We can worship and adore the Holy Spirit for His mystery, wonder, power, and comfort. In this chapter we are going to be highlighting the relationship between Jesus and ourselves.

It needs to be clear from the start that this chapter isn't merely about loving God; this is about being romanced and pursued by a passionate Bridegroom. Even the word "intimacy" is an understatement to what God desires you to experience with Him.

A bridal paradigm of God is a powerful conduit through which to connect with God. Though it is mentioned numerous times in scripture, it is widely neglected in the Church. And though a majority of the worship songs that we sing in services are derived from a bridal paradigm, it is rarely taught or even mentioned in times of teaching.

Intimacy with Jesus makes a person bold, secure, and humble. It is directly related to fruitful ministry, and is the prerequisite to stewarding the power of God that He desires to pour out in the life of every believer. If you get Him, you will get power.

Enjoying God and allowing Him to delight in us is the foundation from which ministry is built upon. Without such a revelation of God's love, people are not confident enough to approach the throne boldly. Instead they cower away in the corner, confused about God's will, what He desires to give His people, and how close He wants to be to us.

If we want the church to be discipling nations, we must teach the church how God really views Her. Once we do that, we will see the slim, weak, Body of Christ feast on His love, and she will grow strong. Intimacy with God is the better way, the high road, and the narrow path.

In this chapter we will learn that intimacy with God is all that matters, the trump card, the finality, the eternal, and the goal. Nothing is superior, nothing is more rewarding, nothing is more powerful, nothing more effective pertaining to ministry, nothing is more pleasurable and full of bliss, and nothing is more impacting upon eternity.

Faith and hope will fall away, but love will never fade away. We will not need faith or hope in heaven. Love, on the other hand, will always be our aim, vision, and goal. Love is the currency of heaven.

+ THE YEARNING OF EVERY HEART +

If a person takes a look at the shelves at their local bookstore, the shows that litter the daily schedule of television programs, and the movies that pass through cinemas all over the world, they find that a major genre in all of these arenas of culture is romance. The human heart has been wired with a deep need for romance. To know and to be known and to love and to be loved are built in necessities for every person on the planet. God, in His wisdom, created man with a need for romance, but did not intend for that need to be fulfilled by the opposite sex alone. He created man with a need for intimacy with the Divine. Suddenly, the tenacious drive in teenagers to engage the opposite sex is explained by more than just an increase in hormones, but by an opportunistic season of their life when they can pursue God with a passion for romance.

Because a majority of the world does not know Jesus as a Bridegroom, they worship anything that hints to providing the least bit of romance. The Church has been largely deficient in revealing Jesus as a Lover, thus we witness a world stuck in a form of idolatry that flows from a God-given need. Each facet of God's character meets a need that we have; Healer, Savior, Lord, Friend, Father, and Lover.

Intimacy and commitment are both starting and lasting points in a relationship, but romance is a reality that involves the depths of the heart. Romance is the mutual involvement of emotions, vulnerability, and passion. It is the ecstasy that every human heart yearns and searches for. Though commitment may keep the relationship from completely disintegrating, without romance love grows cold. The "first love" that God desires for us to live in is a love enhanced with the aspect of romance.

Want to reach a world that is hungry for romance? Enter into a romantic relationship with Jesus and experience the answer to the question that billions are asking and seeking after everyday. He is the desire of the nations.

+ WE LOVE HIM BECAUSE HE LOVES US +

In 1 John 4:16-5:2 we are given a wonderful insight into the nature of love and how it functions. In verse 19, John tells us that, "We love because He first loved us." This is not a statement simply indicating that the source of our love for Him is because He first demonstrated His love to us through sending Jesus. This passage is not only trying to specify that we did not seek Him out but that He sought us out, though that is true.

John is telling us that we cannot give away what we don't have. We cannot assume that we will be able to love the Lord before we first receive love from the Lord. To think that we have anything that He didn't first give us is arrogance. Anything good we ever have comes because He first imparted it to us. A person cannot sit down and deeply love God until the fact that God loves them is a fresh reality in their heart. What we do that does not come from His enablement is usually borne out of striving and performance. God still accepts this offering, but it is not refreshing for the person to offer. On the other hand, love that is given because it is first received is the most revitalizing, invigorating, stimulating activity in all of existence.

We need to learn that worship starts with Him loving on us first. Imagine worship services, revolutionary in nature, where we just allow God to love us rather than trying to get a "breakthrough" in our emotions and the second heavens by offering praises from our own strength. What if we let Him love us instead of trying to offer Him something we don't always possess? What if we simply laid down in humility and let Him adore us? What if we stayed on the ground until His affection filled us to such an extent that we could no longer hold back the flood of love that was breaking forth from our hearts, and we exploded to our feet in undignified praise?

The Glory cannot help to show up when we simply open the doors of our hearts to His love. When He sees open doors to the heart of man He bounds from His heavenly throne and dives to Earth to fill the void. There is no place that He would rather be but in the hearts of men, loving them to life. We just need to let Him.

John clarifies himself in 4:10 by telling us, "This is love, *not that we loved God*, but that He loved us…" Notice that this scripture makes it clear that love is *not* us loving God. Love is God loving us. This is not to say that what we offer Him is impure or not desirable to Him. A father delights in anything his child gives him, even if it is bit of food that the child already took a bite out of. The fact that child wants to give to the parent is what is beautiful. God receives whatever we want to give Him. If only we would do the same towards Him!

This scripture is saying that the love we give to God did not originate from us, but came from Him first loving us. Love is not us loving God because we have no love to give if He didn't first give it to us. This is love; that He loved us.

You can't make this kind of love well up within your heart. You must let Him love you to the point of eruption, where you cannot hold back your affection any longer. Man has no capability to love God in this way on his own accord.

If we try to feel feelings towards the Lord that we haven't first felt from Him towards us, we will find that our prayer times will feel like striving, and we will find ourselves more sapped of energy than when we began. The fatigue that comes from trying to scrounge up emotions that are not present should bring us to a place where we just give up and let Him have His way with us.

Let Him love you before you *try* to love Him. It is the order of heaven, and the desire of His heart. He simply wants to love you; no strings attached. The only thing that God wants to take from you is delight. He isn't concerned what you have to offer Him, because He knows His love will cause you to love Him back.

+ Four Commands In Two +

When Jesus was asked which was the most important commandment in Mark 12:28-31 He replied with,

"Love the Lord your God with all your heart and with all your soul and with all your mind and with all your strength. The second is this: 'Love your neighbor as yourself.' There is no commandment greater than these."

Obviously, loving the Lord is our first priority, but we have just established that before we are able to love Him we must receive His love. You cannot give away what you do not have. Inherent in telling us to love God, Jesus was communicating to first receive God's love, then to steward the presence of that Love in our hearts rightly and give it back to Him.

Secondly, Jesus tells us to love our neighbor as we love ourselves. The implication to this statement is that you will only be able to love those around you to the degree that you are comfortable with who God has made you to be. If you don't like yourself, you will treat the majority of those around you in the same way. But if you love who you are because you love how God has uniquely expressed Himself through your personality, body, and heart, you will be able to love every person that crosses your path to the same degree.

That leaves us with two prerequisites that must be fulfilled before being able to walk out the commandments to love God and love our neighbor. First, we must allow God to love us to such a degree to which we possess enough love to give it back to Him. Secondly, we must allow Him to love us enough to convince us that He is right in saying that we are beautiful and delightful. Once we agree with Him, we begin to like ourselves because He likes us, and the door is opened to enabling us to love our neighbor.

We are in error in thinking that we will last very long in loving God or our neighbor without first being ruined by His love. Start with loving God and never leave that place, for the fulfillment of every other commandment in scripture flows from the reality of loving God.

There are four commands given in two, to be lived out in the following order; 1) *Be loved* so that you are able to 2) *Love Him* 3) which enables you to *love yourself* as He does 4) which allows you to *love your neighbor* as you love yourself. It all starts and ends with loving God.

+ THE FIRST COMMANDMENT FIRST +

In chapter 1 John 5:2, John tells us how to know if we are loving others, "This is how we know we love the children of God: by loving God…"

If you want to rest assured that you are loving others and producing fruit in ministry, simply love God. The second commandment will always naturally follow the first if the first is truly fulfilled. But if we focus primarily on the second commandment rather than the first, we will most definitely run into problems. Jesus said that Mary had chosen better than Martha.

St. Augustine is known to have said on more than one occasion, "Love God and do whatever." Mike Bickle said it well when he said that there are lovers and there are workers, but lovers get more work done. Be a Mary.

+ INTIMACY, NOT JUST FOR WOMEN +

A typical hindrance for men when it comes to intimacy with Jesus is the fact that we are referred to as the Bride. As pictures flash through the mind of a man of them wearing a white wedding dress, terror and confusion strikes, hilariously and understandably so. Not only is it hard to relate to something so unfamiliar as imagining oneself as the opposite sex, but it is disturbing, reminiscent of emasculation. Men rest assured; removing masculinity in hopes to discover the depths of Christ's love is not the path to intimacy. If John the Baptist (a real man's man), who hunted and killed animals, wore their skin, ate insects, and got his head cut off because of his boldness and courage, could call himself a bride (John 3:29), surely we can.

Intimacy with Jesus is not primarily intended for women because Christ's love transcends gender. The needs of every human heart, whether woman or man, are always the same; to be known, to be valued, and to be thrilled. Christ's love dives past the shallow regions of need that differ in man and woman that are mere symptoms of the foundational needs found in both sexes. His love goes deep enough to meet the needs that are shared between men and women.

He calls us a Bride not to feminize us, but to help us understand the way in which we can relate with Him. He is God, and without some kind of grid from which to approach Him and to relate with Him, we wouldn't know how to function in relationship with Him. Therefore, He uses natural, Earthly relationships that we understand to help give us an idea of how we are to relate with Him.

One example can be seen in how God calls Himself Father and us His children. He doesn't primarily do this because are His literal children. After all, He didn't have sex with our mother. It isn't that He is literally our father, but that we relate with Him in a way that reflects an Earthly relationship that most of us understand. He calls us His children because He wants us to understand what our relationship with Him can look like. He wants us to know that what is His is ours, that He loves us, that He will always provide for us, that He cheers us on, that He will protect us, that He always wants the best for us, that He always wants to heal us, and so on. We understand God by looking at the characteristics that govern our Earthly relationships that have given us life, then apply them to God, but a million fold in goodness.

He calls us a Bride to get us to understand that He wants to passionately pursue us, loves us completely, is impacted by our love towards Him, will destroy anything that tries to harm us, and that He feels strong emotions towards us. These are normal characteristics of a relationship between a husband and wife on Earth, therefore appropriate to apply to our relationship with God. Men, He is not trying to make you more feminine by calling you a Bride, He is helping you understand how you can relate with Him.

Lastly, His love isn't sexual in nature, though it is extremely full of pleasure. Men have a hard time picturing intimacy with Jesus simply because the word "intimacy" sometimes reminds them of physical intimacy. But sex isn't the pinnacle of intimacy; that is why the heart of a man is not profoundly touched when he sleeps with a prostitute. If stewarded rightly, sex is a bi-product of intimacy in a Earthly relationship, not the finale. He calls us a bride because the earthly relationship between a husband and wife most typifies the nature of the His pursuit of us. In being called His bride, we are being encouraged to feel the way a bride feels towards her lover; passionate, committed, vulnerable, secure, and safe.

+ THE GREATEST PROPHET +

In Luke 7:28, Jesus tells us this about John the Baptist,

"Among those born of women there is no one greater than John..."

Anyone that knows the Bible is taken back by this statement when it is first read. Elijah called down fire from heaven and raised the dead. Ezekiel saw astounding visions. Daniel virtually ruled a kingdom. But no angelic visitations followed John the Baptist's ministry, no signs and wonders that we know of, and even his own followers left him to follow Another. So what would cause Jesus to call John the greatest of the prophets?

John did two things that set him apart from all of the other prophets. First, He was given the honor of preparing the way of the Lord. He had the insight and discernment to recognize the Lord when He appeared among us. This is an amazing accomplishment, and is what the Pharisees failed to do. The Pharisees prayed for God to move but they missed the Move of God because they couldn't recognize God when He showed up.

The second thing that set John apart and could be why Jesus called him "the greatest prophet" was that John knew that Jesus was a Bridegroom. Right when John enters the scene, he starts ranting and raving about God being a Bridegroom (John 3:29). Isaiah hinted to this revelation, but never overtly stated it as literally as John did.

John had a different paradigm of God. He didn't merely interact with Him on the basis of servant and master, or even father and son. John had a bridal paradigm. He viewed life and his relationship with God through bridal "lenses". He interacted with God as a bride does with her bridegroom. John knew intimacy with God. What else would drive a man to live in the desert other than finding something incredibly satisfying in that place of solitude?

There are many references in the Bible to our identity before God as the Bride, but the book in the Bible that most consistently illustrates this reality is the Song of Songs, also called the Song of Solomon.

But sadly, much of the Body of Christ does not know how to read the book of Song of Songs in a way that draws them closer to Jesus. Whether it is the poetic language causing confusion, or the recent emphasis of marital love when reading this book, the present day Church hasn't been able to deeply enjoy, value, and rely upon this book. If this pertains to you, know that you are not alone. Though in the distant past the Church grasped the depths of this book, its revelations have been largely lost by modern-day Protestantism.

The Song of Songs is one of the most profound books in the Bible. While different books in the Bible highlight different aspects of ministry and relationship with God, there is no book in the Bible that more accurately captures the *emotions* of God's heart towards man as the Song of Songs. The book of Acts reveals the work of the Holy Spirit through normal people. The Gospels show us the life of Jesus, God on Earth. Psalms open our eyes to the aspect of worship and adoration. The Song of Songs on the other hand, gives us an inside perspective of how God *feels* towards *you*.

Did you know that God has emotions? While some emotions are destructive, many emotions were not only produced in the heart of God and imparted to mankind when He created man, but are feelings He is experiencing right now.

You know that God loves you, but do you know how He *feels* towards you? God is a very emotional person, especially when He thinks of you. His emotions are never harmful or unloving, but always extensively kind, warm, and joyful. He is a happy guy, and He is wildly in love with you. He doesn't just love you; He is *in love* with you.

There is an enormous release of power, confidence, and revelation that spills forth in the life of the believer that receives from the love that is captured in the verses of the Song of Songs. It is fabulous.

Many of us grew up being taught that the Song of Songs is a reflection on a marital relationship between man and woman. While this isn't inaccurate, it is a very new trend in the Body of Christ. For 2800 years the Body of Christ has read Song of Songs as an interaction between God and His bride, and only in the last hundred years has the literal marital interpretation grown in popularity. While this natural view isn't unhelpful, it doesn't facilitate intimacy between the reader and God. Even the rabbis realized this, and for thousands of years read this book through the lenses of God romancing His people. Though it is acknowledged that the natural interpretation of Song of Songs is valid and beautiful, this chapter will emphasize the interpretation style that focuses on intimacy with Christ.

If you want to experience more of what the Song of Songs offers, at the end of this book is an appendix called "Loved by Love" that will lead you into that desire. Part study and part prayer, this appendix helps the reader further understand the prophetic language of the Song of Songs.

Now that an especially brief groundwork is laid pertaining to the importance of experiencing intimacy with Christ, we can start feasting on the meat of His word.

I would venture to say that most of the following revelations will be new to you, and could possibly make you uncomfortable. Love does that. It is beautifully invasive, revealing, and accepting, which are all things that human beings naturally keep at bay.

If His love hasn't reached a point in your life when it has made you thoroughly uncomfortable, you need to let Him love you as much as He desires to. Allow the walls of your heart to drop, choose to trust Him, and let Him into your most deepest, darkest places. He is safe, and will speak beauty over the areas of your heart that you are most frightened to face. You will know when you have reached a place of depth in the love of Christ when He speaks something to you that is absolutely and totally wonderful and good, yet it makes your cower back in fear and disbelief. His words may even make you mad because He is so relentless in His grace and love. If the words, "This is too good to be true…" haven't crossed your mind at some point when you are with Jesus, buckle up. He has much more to give you. His love will astound you.

The enemy does not want you to learn and experience the following truths. Many times he will attempt to avert our eyes from Jesus and back to our problems so that we miss what God is showing us. But do not let shame, guilt, self-hatred, and condemnation hinder you from receiving what follows. Try to be "irresponsible" in your receiving of condemnation. Receiving love and grace is often more hard than receiving condemnation because it doesn't feel like what we deserve.

The remainder of this chapter will consist of revelation after revelation having to do with God's heart of love towards you. The following truths are progressive in depth, starting with more fundamental truths and ending with the ecstasy of being wholly loved and cherished. I exhort you to lay open your heart before Him, let Him have His way with you, and slowly read each section as you apply it to your own life. Sit back, relax, and receive.

+ YOU ARE HIS FAVORITE +

In Song of Songs 1:8, Jesus calls you the "...most beautiful of women". The use of "most beautiful" in this passage conveys comparison. God actually compares you to the rest of humanity and the outcome is that *you* are His favorite. You are the *most* beautiful to Him.

Think of your heroes and those you look up to in life. Think of those you feel you could never be like because of their greatness, and then realize that God calls you His favorite, even over them. You are more beautiful to Him than anyone else.

When a person realizes that they are God's favorite, competition, jealousy, and insecurity go out the window. God heals competition and jealousy not by calling off the race, but by deeming both as the winner.

When we aren't sure if we are God's favorite, other people's successes and blessings feel threatening, as though they took our piece of the pie. But when you know that you are God's favorite, you will rejoice with your brother when he succeeds, is promoted, or is blessed, because you will know that there is always enough love and favor to go around. You will know that God has His own blessings in store for you, and that there is no reason to be jealous of someone else.

Song of Songs is virtually line upon line of Him affirming you in the reality that *you* are beautiful to Him, over and over again.

"...Most beautiful..." 1:8

"How beautiful you are, my darling, Oh, how beautiful you are! Your eyes are like doves." 1:14-16

"...Arise, my darling, my beautiful one..." 2:10

"'...Arise, my darling, my beautiful one...'" 2:13

"How beautiful you are, my darling, how beautiful you are!" 4:1

"You are altogether beautiful, my darling. There is no blemish in you." 4:7

"How beautiful is your love, my sister, my bride!" 4:9

"You are as beautiful as Tirzah, my darling, As lovely as Jerusalem, As awesome as an army with banners." 6:4

"'Who is this that grows like the dawn, As beautiful as the full moon, As pure as the sun, As awesome as an army with banners?'" 6:10

"How beautiful are your feet in sandals, O prince's daughter!" 7:1

"How beautiful and how delightful you are, My love, with all your charms!" 7:6

As you read these verses, remember to read them as though God is saying them to you as a Bridegroom that is completely overcome with love. He loved His bride so much He died for her. When you read these verses, read them with an awareness of His passion for *you*.

For example, listen for the emotion in His voice for you as you read this verse;

"How beautiful you are, my darling. Oh, how beautiful you are!" 1:14-16

Could you hear it that time? Did you hear the sigh of longing that He has for you as He started the second sentence? This is how God feels about you. This is how He sees you.

If we were to hear God's voice as scripture portrays, we would have already won the world to Jesus because of the power and love that we would be walking in. We would believe we were beautiful. We would be secure and confident. Every lost soul would be instinctively drawn to us.

The fact is that most of the church is not yet convinced in their heart of the passion and love that God has for them. Though they may confess God's love for them with their mouth, their hearts second-guess the authenticity of God's love towards them because the majority of the church has not experienced the *emotions* of God. Once a person experiences His emotions they are forever changed into a carrier of revival.

If we were to hear His voice as scripture portrays, we would hear His affirmation more than condemnation. In fact, we wouldn't hear condemnation at all. He calls you beautiful. Break the mold; let His emotions become real to you.

Typically, when we speak of "the Presence of God", we are referring to a reality of the manifestation of the Holy Spirit upon a person or filling a geographical place. The presence of God seems to be something that descends from Above, or rises up from within like a spring of water. You can actually feel the presence of God; it has substance to it that can be perceived through the natural senses.

Though, in normal life apart from our faith, we use this same statement of "presence" to communicate to others that *we were around a person*. The emphasis is more on the person than on the atmosphere around them. For example, if we were to meet Bono of U2 in Starbucks, we may tell our friends, "I was in the presence of a rock star." In doing so, we are communicating that we were *near* Bono.

When it is taken literally, the statement "the presence of the Lord" refers to the fact that the person of God is nearby. The presence of God points to the fact that God Himself just showed up. A person dictates a presence.

He will never leave you or forsake you (Joshua 1:5, Hebrews 13:5). You are also seated in heavenly places with Christ, literally (Eph 2:6). You are on Earth and in heaven at the same time. That means that Jesus is seated next to you, and that is the farthest He will ever get from you. He is always within reach. Because the Presence of God is dictated by the nearness of God, you are always in "His presence."

Never question if God is nearby. He is not a distant God. Even if things feel dry, as though you are in a spiritual desert, God would never put you in a place where you would die of thirst. Though you very well may be in a desert season, there is always living water within reach. You may have to dig to find it, but it is there.

He is not merely available, but is seated next to you. When you sit down to dinner, He sits beside you. When you lay down to sleep, He lays beside you. He is always with you. You not *feeling* His presence doesn't change the fact that He is undeniably near. He must be; He is bound by His Word. You unavoidably live in the presence of God.

I have a friend who lives a lifestyle of love towards the Lord. One morning she woke up and went out to her kitchen to have a cup of tea. As she prepared her tea, she realized that Jesus may want a cup as well, so she poured Him one. One cup sat in front of her, while the other cup sat on the opposite end of the table in front of a seemingly empty chair. As she communed with the Lord and drank her tea, the teacup across the table from her miraculously emptied, sip by sip. He is always present, ready to interact with you, ready to show you His affection.

+ HE WANTS TO SERVE YOU +

During His life on Earth, Jesus exemplified that a true leader is revealed by his desire to *serve* those that he leads (Luke 22:27, Matthew 20:28). Jesus illustrated a completely different set of values in leadership than present day dictators. Rather than domination and control, Jesus led as a humble servant.

A husband is the leader of his house. This means that a husband and father's main role is not to be the one in control, but to be the first to serve his family. I thought I knew all of this until a day I met Jesus in a vision while in prayer.

In the vision I was laying on a couch or bed. Jesus came to me and as soon as I saw Him, I began thinking what I could do for Him and how I could serve Him. He is our King and we are His people, ready to adore, worship, and serve Him.

But because He is our husband, and a husband is the leader, He began to do something that caught me off guard. He brought me grapes and a fan, and began to wait on me. It was as though my wish was His command. He was serving *me.*

I quickly grew uncomfortable with what was taking place. Wasn't I the one that was supposed to be serving Him? He is the King, I am the servant! This was backwards!

He calmed my thoughts by saying, "It is true that I am your King, but I am also your husband. Any good husband first thinks of how he can first serve his wife before having her serve him. I am out to serve you firstly, not to be served."

Are you letting God serve you? Are you letting Him wait on you, feed you, enjoy you, and fan you as you rest? Are you letting Him treat you like royalty? You are married to the King of all Kings, surely you are expected to enjoy it.   Rest in His affections, in His desire to motivate you through delight, not control. Let Him serve you to His heart's content. He enjoys doing it. As you allow Him to serve you without doing anything in return, something will shift in your heart. You won't serve Him any longer out of duty, but desire. That desire will well up in your heart and ambush your life with wholehearted devotion. Your joy will be determined by His happiness.

+ BACKWARDS IS FORWARDS +

I used to think that allowing character to be refined was the chief priority in the life of a believer. Now I know it is faith expressing itself through love, which when genuine, naturally produces character without effort. Because of my misled belief about character, I was always striving to be changed by the Lord and become purer in character. It felt as though I got more of the Lord by doing this, so my prayer life consisted of digging deep into my heart and finding motives, actions, and thoughts that didn't line up with heaven. Once these undesirable things were found, I would allow Him to change me. I called it dying to myself. I wanted to have every issue in my character ironed out. I submitted my heart to God's scalpel on a daily basis in order that He perform surgery on me and remove anything not of Him.

One day while in prayer, God quietly spoke something to me that shocked me. He simply said, "I don't want to change you. I just want to love you."

Everything in me recoiled when I heard this statement. How could He not want to change me? I was me! I had problems, and had need of change.

My mind began to swirl at the implications of His statement. I couldn't quite grasp the fullness of what He was showing me, so moments later He gave me a vision.

I was standing before Jesus, desperate for more of Him, holding my heart in front of me. In a desperate attempt to receive more of Him, I shot out my hands and heart towards Him in a gesture that communicated the surrendering of my heart. I was giving my heart to Him so that He could mold it in anyway He pleased, and in turn, I would receive more of Him.

To my surprise, Jesus wildly knocked my hands aside as He embraced me. He didn't want me to offer my heart to Him for another inspection. He wasn't concerned about the problems I had. He just wanted to love me.

I was stunned. Who is this God that is more concerned with loving us than fixing us? Who is this God that isn't as worried about our sin as we are?

Love is always His priority. He isn't searching to find your problems then convict you of them. He just wants to love you as you are. He is sure that when you let

Him love you, the issues that are present will take care of themselves.

Though it took me a few years to process what He told me that day, I slowly began to live and pray differently. When I would pray, instead of searching for all the places that could be refined in my heart, I began to think upon how much God loved me despite the fact that I didn't have it all together. This way of approaching God is much more fulfilling, gives joy, and will instigate a deep gratitude for the cross. Instead of feeling noble about my most recent painful surrender to God, I began to feel good about who I was, and began to feel more and more affectionate towards God. You cannot help but love someone that delights in you just as you are, but it is work to love someone that is constantly pointing out your areas of imperfection. You will find that as you sit in His delight of your whole person, everything that needs to be changed will naturally be transformed.

Did you know He is more concerned about you not receiving His love than the issues that you are struggling with? God knows that true change only comes through being loved, so change isn't His priority, love is. It isn't that He isn't concerned about us growing; it is that He knows the best way for us to grow is to be loved.

In addition, God sees us as righteous already. Most of the time it is ourselves or the enemy that is highlighting our imperfections, not God. He already knows your problems, and calls you a saint in the midst of them.

+ FLAWLESS +

It may come as a shock to some, but God isn't concerned about changing you. In Jesus, we are already beautiful to Him. Even more than beautiful, He takes it up a notch and calls us flawless. He says this not once or twice in Song of Songs, but three times.

"All beautiful you are, my darling; there is no flaw in you." 4:7

Let this reality affect your emotions. God does not see a flaw in you. Allow yourself to think about the things you do not like about yourself, though they may be hard to admit, even to yourself. Think about the things in your body, in your heart, in your personality that you think are less than perfect, even unappealing. Now receive His heart about those same things. Let His thoughts and feelings trump your thoughts and feelings. He says that you have no flaws. Agree with Him.

In case you didn't catch it (or believe it) the first time, He reaffirms His heart;

"...my darling, my dove, my flawless one." 5:2

Wait, you thought you were undesirable in some way? But that cannot be. He says you are flawless. Truth is not determined by how you view things, but how *He* views things. In case your mind is still trying to resist His love, He tells us third time, just to drive the point home;

"...my dove, my perfect one, is unique...." 6:9

This is the pinnacle of affirmation. God views you in such a redemptive way that He actually thinks you are perfect. You can't argue with it...it is the Word of God. Say it out loud and declare it. Next time you notice something about yourself that you don't like, ask Jesus how He sees it. You will be surprised at what He delights in. He delights in things about us that we are totally convinced are undesirable. In fact, He *especially* loves the things you hate about yourself. He is blinded by love, and cannot relent in His obsession over your beauty.

+ Just A Strand of Hair +

Once while in prayer the Lord spoke something to me that was very difficult for me to accept for a period of time. He told me that just one strand of my hair was more important to Him than anything in creation, like an entire mountain range.

I couldn't understand this until I experienced it myself. Years ago I was involved in a prayer room that functioned in Night and Day prayer. We would pray 24 hours a day for our community, and I had the midnight to 2am shift. A young woman that I had recently met took the shift before mine, so when I would get into the prayer room I would find her hairs on the ground. I began to fall in love with this woman from afar, but I publicly kept my distance. Secretly though, behind closed doors of a prayer room, I would gather her hairs like gold. I would just stare at them as butterflies rose inside. I was well aware of the oddness of the whole thing, but it didn't matter; I was in love. Those hairs were a part of her, and because they were a part of her, I loved them. If I had needed to, would have even *paid* for those strands, because they meant that much to me. They were all I could have of her at the time.

Though I married that young woman and now have her as my best friend that I can talk to and spend time with whenever I like, I still keep her hair in my Bible to this day. Those strands of hair serve not only as a reminder of my love and affection for her, but also how and why God would value one strand of our hair over something as majestic and breathtaking as the Alps.

Your worth is inexpressible. Jesus doesn't just love you, He likes you. He adores every facet of you to such a degree that He would give the whole created Earth for just one little piece of you. In fact, He went one step further and gave Himself.

+ THE VALUE OF YOUR LOVE +

At the beginning of Song of Songs, in the second verse of the book, the Bride declares a truth that the majority of the church is yet to discover.

"...for your love is better than wine."

It is a simple statement, but much is contained in these few words. Wine is the drink of celebration and joy. In saying that God's love is better than wine, she is highlighting the fact that God's love is better than anything in existence that causes us to rejoice and celebrate. Anything that brings gladness to our heart, happiness to our lives, or pleasure in our bodies pales in comparison to experiencing the love of God. Family, drugs that produce a fading high, physical intimacy, spiritual blessings, abundant finances, intellectual abilities, athleticism, etc. The list goes on and on, but nothing can be set on par with the love of God. In this verse the Bride is beginning to understand this reality. She declares it, then seeks God until it becomes something that she has experienced.

The love of God is incredibly satisfying, but what is even more marvelous is found in chapter four, verse ten. Jesus tells His bride the same thing we just witnessed her declare about Him.

"How delightful is your love, my sister, my bride! How much more pleasing is your love than wine."

Remember that wine represented anything that causes celebration? It is still true in this passage. Jesus is revealing to the Bride something extraordinary. He is telling her that He enjoys her love more than anything else in existence.

You are His drink. He is intoxicated on you. He gave it all for you. You are His source of pleasure. You are His reward, which He bought on the cross. You are His inheritance.

God has experienced and is experiencing the highest level of pleasure and happiness of any being that has ever lived. Nobody is as satisfied, fulfilled, and content as God. God had the pleasure of creating the earth and man, is worshipped by cherubim, lives in a city with streets of gold, and is constantly living in glory. These are all things that bring immense pleasure to Him. In fact, He is enthroned in pleasure. Yet, all of these things pale in comparison to the pleasure He experiences when you offer your love to Him. He craves your love just as you crave His. Your love is better to Him than any pleasure He has ever experienced.

+ YOU ARE UNIQUE +

Being called unique, especially by God Himself, is one of the highest compliments a person can be given. Jesus tells His bride in Song of Songs 6:9,

*"…but my dove, my perfect one, is **unique**…"*

Things are given worth by the frequency or infrequency of their existence. For example, steel is common, therefore inexpensive compared to platinum. Gold is valuable not because of its appearance, but because it is rare. Likewise, diamonds have incredible worth because there aren't many of them on Earth. If rubies laid in abundance on every beach and field on Earth, they would have no monetary value, for they would no longer be rare.

Uniqueness though, is even more exceptional than something being rare. Something being deemed "unique" means that it is the only one of its kind, thus its value is inestimable. This is what God is communicating to *you* when He calls you unique.

There is nobody that talks, walks, laughs, or acts like you, and He delights in each one of these aspects of your person. He can't delight in anyone like He does in you, because you are unique.

More importantly, nobody loves God like you do. The way you love Him is unique to everyone on Earth. In fact, there is a place in God's heart that only your love can fulfill. If you don't give your love to Him, nobody else will meet that place in His heart, because it is designed to be fulfilled by you alone.

My wife's love fulfills a place in my heart that only she can fulfill. She does this by simply being herself, in all of her beauty and wisdom. Simply the way she smiles gives my heart life. Nobody loves me in the way she does. If she didn't give me her love, a place in my heart that only she can fulfilled would remain empty. Other friends could never meet the need in my heart for the love that my wife gives to me, because her love is unique to me.

+ ONE GLANCE +

In the forth chapter of the Song of Songs, Jesus makes an incredible statement;

"You have stolen my heart, my bride, with one glance of your eyes…" 4:9

This is one of the grandest statements in all of history. Other translations also use the words, "captured", "ravished", "charmed", "beat faster", and "conquered" in the place of "stolen". They all convey the same truth; that *we* can capture the heart of the God with a mere glance of affection. This is absolutely phenomenal.

To most of us, it takes quite a lot for us to feel that God is pleased with us, and even more for us to feel that He is jumping with joy over our actions and the state of our heart. But that is not the picture of God that is set forth in scripture. According to these scriptures, all it takes to completely ruin God with our love is to glance at Him.

He is not a God that has made it hard to impact Him emotionally. Welcome to relationship. He has allowed Himself to be *easily affected* by our love, to such a degree that He feels ravished by our mere glance. Our weak love easily causes Him to be overwhelmed with deep and pleasurable feelings and emotions.

This is not any god we are talking about. This is the God that created the heavens and the earth. This is the God that is seated on the throne, in total holiness and power. This is the God that is unconquerable by any demon in hell, *yet* your love conquers Him. Our love is weak compared to His towards us, but it makes no difference to Him.

It does not take you saving souls, healing the sick, starting a huge ministry, or bringing whole nations to the knowledge of God in order for you to capture God's heart. You already have, but you may have not known it until now. Every time you have turned the affections of your heart to God, even for a brief moment, you have won Him afresh. Every time you told Him that you love Him, His has heart melted. You make His knees weak when you give your affection to Him. He is so enthralled about the fact that you love Him that He allows Himself to be impacted by your love.

God is the center, the focal point, of heaven. Everything that happens there is a result of what He is doing and who He is. When you give your love to Him, He is stunned by joy and pleasure. Frozen by delight and awe, He gasps as the company of heaven stands still. When He recovers from His faintness over your offering of love, heaven slowly begins moving again, no longer stationary. He brags about you to the angels, saying, "Look at that lover of mine. Despite the filth and darkness that is all around them, they glanced at Me in love! It is victory! It is what I went to die for!"

He absolutely drinks up every drop of love that you pour out to Him, so never again devalue the love you give Him.

+ WORDS SWEET LIKE HONEY +

A few years back I was in the Middle East, planting a church among Muslims. We had three short months to gather a group of Muslims, fellowship and worship with them regularly, and bring them to a place through discipleship where they could follow the commandments of Jesus in the Bible on their own. More than one person told us that what we wanted to do was impossible.

God did succeed at this task, but there were points during the trip that were very challenging. One such morning, I was spending time in prayer on a very large beach. I began asking the Lord if He was answering my prayers, let alone even *heard* them. I was doing my best to worship and try to enter into His Presence, but I wasn't doing too well on that front, wondering if He heard or accepted my praise either.

After some time, God whispered to me to read a verse in Song of Songs, so I turned to the chapter and verse that I sensed Him leading me to. I turned to chapter 4, verse 11:

"Your lips, my bride, drip honey…"

I read this verse over and over, trying to understand what God was communicating to me through it. As I pondered the verse, two things became clear to me. First, that our mouth is the place our prayers and praise pour forth from, and second, that honey is sweet and fulfilling. As I combined the two realities, I began to understand that the Lord was telling me that He not only heard my prayers and praise, but that they were overwhelmingly sweet unto His ears. He didn't just put up with my prayers, He delighted in them and feasted upon them. My prayers weren't something He filed away in the cabinets of heaven, but words that were sweet and fulfilling unto His heart, thus were given the utmost attention and value.

As soon as this truth became clear to me I began to question its validity, because my circumstances didn't seem to reinforce what the Lord was telling me. I didn't feel like He heard my prayers at all! I told Him that my heart needed more affirmation in order to be convinced. Mentally, I then moved on and began thinking about other issues that were unrelated to what He was talking to me about.

I was sitting fifty or so yards from the sea, with around 200 yards of sand behind me. There was very little foliage on this beach if any at all; at the most there were a few strands of grass here and there. Most definitely, there were no flowers as far as the eye could see.

You would think that bees would stay remotely close to flowers, but in spite of this, a bee suddenly landed on my right arm. In fear that I was about to be stung, I instinctively flicked it off my arm as quickly as it had landed. It died and fell into the sand next to me. I sighed with relief, and continued my reading and prayer.

Ten minutes later, something clicked in my head. I realized that bees produce honey, and God had given me a verse about honey a few minutes before the bee had landed on my arm. What was even more interesting was that the bee landed on me only seconds after I told God that my heart needed more confirmation in order to be convinced of what He was telling me.

I looked down at the spot on my arm where the bee had landed, and was shocked to see a large drop of liquid. In disbelief, I thought to myself, "There is *no way* that is honey." Bees carried pollen when they fly, not honey. Nonetheless, I dabbed the drop of liquid with my finger and touched it to my tongue. I was astounded to find that it was in fact honey as its sweetness flooded my mouth with taste. I was wordless.

God sent me a bee, loaded down with honey, to prove me to that He not only hears my prayers and my songs of love, but delights in them more than I can understand. Ecstatic, I got up and started wildly dancing up and down the beach in worship. That day I learned that God doesn't just hear our prayers and praise, but He is enchanted by them.

We seem to forget how easy it is to gain God's approval and to make Him proud of us. Simply by praying we are exerting faith, because it takes faith to speak to a Being that we cannot see. And because you can only please God by faith, God is pleased whenever we pray. (Hebrews 11:6)

He hears every prayer. He would never delight in our prayers then not take action. If you have asked for healing to manifest, do not lose faith; He has heard you and is answering your prayer. In fact, He heard it before you ever prayed it and sent Jesus to the cross in response. If you have been praying for family members to know Jesus, be sure that salvation will gain access and overcome your loved one. If you have been praying about an area of your life that you struggle with and can't seem to triumph, don't lose hope. God is a God that frees those that are bound. He is working on your behalf.

It took twenty-one days for an angel to come to Daniel because a principality held up the angel, but God had heard Daniel's prayer when he first started praying, and and immediately took action.

"Since the first day that you set your mind to gain understanding and to humble yourself before your God, your words were heard…" Daniel 10:13

Never again question if God hears your prayers and your praise. He does, drinks deeply of it, then moves in action for your benefit. God is for you.

+ THE VULNERABILITY OF GOD +

A few years after the "bee encounter", I was in a prayer room, studying the same verse (Song of Songs 4:11). I was thinking about how God had spoken to me through an insect, and as bizarre as that is, I was thanking Him for it. I will never recover from the fact that the God of the universe interacts with *me*. The bee was amazing, but the bee points to a greater reality…that God is mindful of *me*. That the God of the universe interacts with *us*, let alone care at all, is absolutely astounding.

As I thought on the verse and the instance at the beach with the bee, I began asking the Lord what the latter part of verse eleven meant:

"…milk and honey are under your tongue."

I heard a loud buzzing sound coming from the inside of my shirt. Unbelievably, a bee suddenly crawled out of my shirt near my neck. I again swatted the bee to the ground, and stood over it with my jaw in my lap, blinking my eyes in disbelief. I thought I was imagining the bee, but there it was.

I had been at the prayer room for about an hour before this bee crawled out from my collar. I hadn't been riding a bike that day, or been riding in the car with the windows down, thus I couldn't figure out a way that the bee got into my shirt! It wasn't a coincidence that in the very moment I was thinking about the first time God sent me a bee, another one crawled out of my shirt.

When things happen like this, I assume Heaven is trying to tell me something. I could have just continued in my prayer time as usual, but I drew the conclusion that God wanted to illuminate this verse to me, so I drew aside and listened for His voice to help me understand this verse.

It became clear to me that milk and honey represented *provision* in the Bible. The Promised Land was repetitively referred to as "...flowing with milk and honey." This statement was attractive to the Israelites because it conveyed to them that their needs would be met once they possessed the land.

It occurred to me that "milk and honey are under your tongue" meant that provision was in my speaking. The words that I speak to God provide *for Him*. But how? How did my weak words of love provide for an all powerful God that doesn't need anything?

The reality is that God has an emotional need like any other being in existence. He created you with an ability to give to Him, and He has made Himself vulnerable to such a degree that He allows you to offer Him something that drastically affects the emotions of His heart.

Your words are provision for the needs of the heart of God. Though He has no lack, He has made

Himself vulnerable to you by letting you love Him. You actually feed His heart with His love.

Don't misunderstand me; He didn't create humans to fill a need in His heart. Ultimately, He doesn't need us and could exist perfectly well without us. But He has come into an intimate relationship with us that presupposes vulnerability. Intimacy cannot take place outside the existence of vulnerability. And a necessary part of any intimate and vulnerable relationship is the facet of allowing another being to give to you and meet a need. God is no different.

The priests of old understood an element of the life of faith that the church has largely forgotten; ministry to God Himself.

"But the Levitical priests…shall come near to   Me   to minister to Me…" Ezekiel 44:15

According to the dictionary, the word "minister" means to give help to someone in need. Inherent in the word "minister" is the assumption that one party allows the other party to give them something they need. The fact that God would use this word in describing how we can interact with Him is astonishing. There is place in relationship with God where He allows Himself to be ministered to by *you.*

Have you ever thought about the fact that God has love languages just like any one of us? He enjoys gifts, quality time, acts of service, physical touch, and words of affirmation. And unlike us, He is good at receiving all of the five love languages. He is good at receiving them, and very good at giving them.

You are the provision for his heart. His provision is in our praises. Milk and honey are under your tongue. The needs of His heart are met in the words of love that we give to Him. After all, *you* are His Promised Land, for He sold it all to by the field.

+ THE LOVE LANGUAGES OF GOD +

Once we have received the love of God towards us, we are able to recognize and respond to the voluntary need that God has made available in His relationship with us. "The Five Love Languages" don't apply to just natural relationships in life, but also to your relationship with God!

First, God loves verbal affirmation. This is commonly referred to in the Bible as praise and worship. Ultimately, it is simply recognizing who God is and sharing it with Him verbally. He loves to be verbally affirmed and even has a need for it that He has voluntarily made an actuality, but He won't ever make His needs something that He will force you to fulfill. He won't push His needs upon you or pressure you in any way. In fact, He doesn't want you to try to meet the needs of His heart unless you truly want to, so He won't even mention them. He knows that when you are overflowing with enough love, you won't think about His needs as a duty to fulfill, but a delight.

Secondly, God loves to be touched. You can touch Him in the visionary realm, as well as literally touch Him through visitation and encounter. Additionally, you can touch Him by allowing the all of your affection of your heart to touch His heart. He loves to be touched.

Thirdly, He loves gifts. A well thought out gift speaks volumes to the receiver. God loves your gifts, such as your finances given to the Kingdom.

These things are very hard for people to hear without thinking, "But I need to do that anyways." That is partly true, but God wants to take you out of a duty driven relationship into a desire driven relationship. He wants to bring you to a place where your actions are not driven in the least bit by what you think you *need* to do, but what you *want* to do. Some of you may need to stop giving God gifts until you can learn how to *want* to give again out of affection and true love, instead of it being a duty-driven action. Have you ever given money to the Lord in the same way you would give a material or financial gift to your spouse or best friend? The gift is a token of your love, well thought out and done without the least bit of hesitation, not something that you had to muster up in order to give. You *wanted* to give it, and it gave you joy to watch them unwrap the gift. Their smile gave you joy. Their joy determined yours. This is where God wants to bring us in relationship with Him!

Forth, God loves quality time with Him. Quality time is time spent alone, devoid of any agenda but to focus on each other. He loves to simply be with you, with no expectations set upon you to *do* anything. Just sitting before Him and *being* with Him fills the needs of His heart. You are a human being, not a human doing. Be a Mary, not a Martha.

Lastly, God loves your acts of service to Him. He does not desire your duty driven acts of charity, but your acts of service that are a genuine response of the heart to His love. You will know the difference between the two because one will give you joy and will fill you life when you do them, and the other will drain you, stress you out, and burden you.

Here is a bold statement; don't *do* anything for God until you really want to. Until then, just let Him love you. Christians fear that the Great Commission won't happen if we don't get off our rear ends and do something, but this is backwards thinking. The *first* commandment is to love God. Since it is *first*, lets make it *first*. More is completed, attained, and accomplished for the Kingdom through one person simply receiving the love of God and giving it back to Him than all of the crusades in all of history that were borne out of the "have to because He said so" mentality. In the end, it is all about love. If you really live in love, you will not be able to avoid influencing whole nations.

With this in mind, do you ever ask God if you have touched or affirmed Him verbally enough lately? Do you ever ask Him how His heart is feeling, wondering if He feels like He has gotten what He needs lately? If He lets you know that He could use more love, don't think you should fulfill it. Start with receiving His love in the same way He said He needs it. Eventually, you will become the answer to the need because He will fill you with Himself to such a degree that you simply become the middleman. The only way to stay full is to enter His delight of Himself.

It takes confidence to boldly approach the throne. Most likely, you won't raise the dead unless you have the confidence that comes from knowing that you are completely righteous in Christ. Then and only then will you ask God, the Lord of All, to move on your behalf in miraculously astounding ways. Do you know you are a righteous saint and that God is on your side, or are you begging God to move on your behalf as a groveling sinner?

Righteousness is a term we throw around in church and pious circles, but what exactly does the Bible teach on the subject of righteousness?

Webster's dictionary defines righteousness as "considered to be correct or justifiable." Righteousness refers to our position before God. We are either in a right place with God, or a wrong place with Him. If we are in a wrong place with God we cannot have a relationship with Him.

Without righteousness, we cannot enter the Kingdom of God (Matthew 5:20). That means that without righteousness we will not spend eternity in heaven, but also that we will be unable to bring the reality of the Kingdom of God to Earth in this life through supernatural demonstration.

The Bible tells us that without Jesus we are all unrighteous, or not in right standing with God. Because of this, God uses His law (standards of right and wrong) to reveal to us how much we fall short of His expectation of righteousness, purity, and holiness. The law's purpose is to show us our need for a savior; our savior revealed the nature of the Father. Jesus is that savior, and He saves us from our own sin by His sacrifice on the cross. Once we allow Him to do this, we are made righteous before the Father because of Jesus.

+ RIGHTEOUSNESS IS BY FAITH +

Righteousness is determined by faith, not through works. This is stated plainly in the New Testament, which we have been reading for two thousand years, but we still don't understand it. Luther even went to bat for this revelation five hundred years ago, yet we still haven't grasped the implications of this profession. We can see this to be true through the way we treat ministers that stumble into sin, the legalism that still resides within our church walls, and how unbelievers aren't attracted to the majority of Christians, but repelled.

If we truly begin to grasp why we are righteous and how we stay righteous, the lost will be drawn to us. If we begin to understand righteousness, we will understand grace, and we will not confuse punishment with correction when dealing with a fallen minister. Legalism will be naturally uprooted from our churches, and Christians won't think it is an odd or radical thing to spend the weekends in bars. We must be in the bars, because how else will the drunks be reached? A bar is simply a future church.

Because our righteousness is completely found in Jesus and not in ourselves, righteousness is by faith (Gal. 2 & 3, Romans 3:21-22, 9:30). This means that your righteousness is not determined by what you do, but by your ability *to believe* that God has made you righteous through Jesus. In the new covenant, faith is the ONLY way we obtain righteousness. In fact, when we seek to establish our own righteousness in any way other than by faith, we actually work against true righteousness becoming our own (Romans 10:3-4).

Righteousness is by faith. Colossians 1:22-23 says that you are, "…holy in His sight, without blemish, and free from accusation – if you continue in your faith." The "if" in that sentence is telling us that the state of our righteousness is conditional upon our ability to believe that you are righteous.

Faith is believing something is a reality when there is nothing there, but in believing, it becomes a reality. For example, heaven is a place that has to be believed in to be seen. Likewise, if you don't believe in this place that you have never seen, you will never see it. Righteousness is similar in nature. You must believe Christ has made you righteous in order to become righteous.

It is ingrained in our thinking as the Body of Christ that we are righteous and holy if we live righteous and holy. The Pharisees believed the same lie. They believed they had it together because they lived stringently by the law. They followed the law to the last detail. They believed that their actions made them righteous, but they were sadly mistaken. Their performance to earn righteousness actually led them away from God. They became so enthralled with their self-righteousness that they actually gave themselves over to the devil and received him as their father (John 8:44). Their rules and traditions were their savior instead of letting Jesus play that role. Even worse, they didn't just reject Jesus; they killed Him. Believing that our actions make us righteous is the quickest highway to hell.

When you are a born again believer, you cannot earn righteousness by your good actions, and you cannot lose your righteousness by your bad actions. Thank God! You are still righteous in the midst of your confessed sin.

While we are righteous aside from what we do or do not do because righteousness is by faith, God still tells us to live a holy life. He knows that a holy lifestyle is truly best for us, while a life of sin will lead us to depression, death, loss, compromise, disease, regret, wasted time, and division. He wants what is best for us, because He loves us. This is why He encourages us to live rightly, according to His Word.

But also, God knows that our ability to be righteous is determined by our ability to believe He has made us righteous. Righteousness is by faith. God tells us to live rightly because if we are living in sin it is very hard for our hearts to not feel hypocritical. If our actions are unrighteous and God says we are righteous, we start to feel a contradiction in our life. If we continue in our sin, shame enters our heart because we feel like a hypocrite. Righteousness and shame cannot both exist in the same space, so when shame enters, we can no longer believe that we are righteous in our heart. The moment we stop believing we are righteous, our connection with the Lord is significantly harmed. He does not cut you off, *you* cut yourself off through unbelief. We begin to sever our connection with the Lord when we start to believe in our heart that we aren't righteous.

God wants your heart to be confident in the righteousness that we have in Christ, not only because of your faith in Jesus that brings righteousness, but also because your actions line up with what God says about you…that you are righteous! Your heart will stay confident that you are righteous if your actions are righteous. *God doesn't want you to sin because it harms your ability to believe that you are righteous.* Because righteousness is by faith, if you lose that faith, you lose your ability to stand as one who is righteous before the Father. God doesn't change his view of you; you change your view of yourself.

This is why shame is such an opponent to righteousness. When we stumble, shame comes knocking at the door of our heart, asking for entrance. We can either allow it to enter our heart, or we can leave it on the doorstep because we know that we are righteous. Shame causes us to hide our face from God. It quietly destroys relationship, for true intimacy cannot function in the presence of shame. When we do not feel righteous because of shame, we cannot have a genuine relationship with God until we believe we are righteous again.

Many people get themselves to feel righteous again by punishing themselves or by performing in special ways for God. This makes people feel like they are right with God again. Any kind of penance is an example of this. But God doesn't want us to feel like we need to do anything to be righteous again. He just wants us to have faith; faith that we are righteous because we have received Jesus' sacrifice on the cross. When you continue to believe that you are righteous in the midst of stumbling and choose to receive grace instead of punishing yourself, you are honoring Jesus. You are honoring His incredibly, costly sacrifice on the cross. And likewise, when we choose shame and punishment for ourselves, we are insensitively disregarding and dishonoring what Jesus did on the cross.

Lastly, while your righteousness is determined by faith and cannot be taken from you despite your actions, your faith is validated by your actions and lifestyle. This is the clarifier and balance to the fact that righteousness is by faith alone. The book of James is thorough on this subject.

+ ABRAHAM'S FAITH +

Abraham is an excellent example that righteousness is by faith alone. Christ came to Earth and died, ushering humanity out of the covenant of law. But long before this happened, Abraham grasped the earth-shattering imperative of the value of faith.

"Abraham believed God, and it was credited to him as righteousness." Romans 4:3

Abraham prematurely tasted of the coming covenant of bliss... through faith. Did you know that righteousness was available to mankind even before Christ came to Earth, not through offerings and sacrifices, but through faith? Noah tapped into this realm of faith as well,

"By Noah's faith he...became the heir of the righteousness that is by faith." Hebrews 11:7b

This should confound every aspect of our performance mentality before God. The Gospel is a wonderfully illogical paradigm of grace. It stumps the mind and enlivens the heart.

+ THE RIGHTEOUS WILL LIVE BY FAITH +

Is faith, or is righteousness the greater priority in the Kingdom? Most would say righteousness, but the reality is that righteousness comes by having faith. Our works mentality is so deeply ingrained into our theology and lifestyle that we don't even recognize its presence anymore.

The truth is that without faith, there is no righteousness. Hence, if you had to prioritize one above the other, choose faith. The body of Christ doesn't need more teaching on how to live holy as much as it does teachings on faith. Faith leads to holiness, because righteousness comes through believing in Christ's sacrifice. Suddenly, teachings on the miraculous or the power of God are not mutually exclusive from teachings on character.

Jesus didn't talk about righteousness nearly as much as He did faith. This was so because He didn't want people to try harder at being holy, but to believe in Him. If they believed in Him, He knew they would become holy. Likewise, the Pharisee's problem did not lie in the fact that they weren't *moral* enough, but that they had unbelief rather than faith. If they had possessed faith, they would have revered Christ to be God, and He would have made them righteous on the inside. As it was, they were left dirty on the inside because of their rejection of faith, and in turn, Christ.

The Bible makes the statement "the righteous will live by faith" many times, in different books throughout scripture so that we don't miss its importance (Habakkuk 2:4, Romans 1:17, Galatians 3:11, Hebrews 10:38). We must realize that God's way is a way that is devoid of our own performance and ability. All He asks of us is for us to believe.

+ THE LAW: NOT FOR A BELIEVER +

There is much confusion in the Body of Christ in reconciling what seems to be two different gods; the God of the Old Testament, and the God of the New Testament. One seemed to be angry most of the time, while the other seemed to be willing to give grace and forgiveness, but still a bit angry.

The Old Testament functioned on a system set up by God called the law which was a number of rules and regulations for man to abide by. The law fueled a works-based mentality; what you did determined your holiness, your sentence, and the favor you received.

More than giving us guidelines as to how to be able to have a relationship with God, the Law's greatest purpose is to reveal to mankind its need for a Savior. Nobody did all that well at keeping the spirit of the law, therefore it showed man what a mess he was. The Law's purpose was to reveal sin, which alerted mankind for its need for Jesus. The Old Testament was more about pointing to a need for Jesus than it was about rules and regulations. The Old Testament was simply getting mankind ready for God's next step in His unfolding plan for mankind; Jesus.

Law was good, but Grace is a more superior truth, and it is what was ushered in by the death and resurrection of Jesus. A lot changed when Jesus died. The new covenant of Grace is what the New Testament is based upon. Instead of based upon our works, our righteousness is given to us through faith in Jesus. In the New Testament, Jesus paid for our punishment so that we would never be punished, and we have the same favor as Jesus did because He imparted it to us through His death.

1 Timothy 1:9 tells us that the law is made not for the righteous, but for the unrighteous. Romans 3:20 says, *"Therefore no one will be declared righteous in his sight by observing the law; rather, through the law we become conscious of sin."* The Law's purpose is to reveal our need for a savior, prior to knowing Jesus. Once we have gained that revelation and received Jesus, we are righteous, despite our struggles we may have in our moral life, and we do not live according to the law and punishment, but we live according to the leading of the Holy Spirit, the guidance of the Word of God, and by grace.

Continuing to live by the law once we have been saved is detrimental to a believer's ability to grow in an intimate relationship with God. Many people continue to live by the rules and regulations of the Law, and in doing so, continue to live under condemnation and the fear of punishment.

Galatians 3:10 says, *"All who rely on observing the law are under a curse."* The person who lives by the Law stays under the curse of condemnation, because nobody can live up to the rigorous standards of the Law. We all fall short of the standard of the Law. This is why Jesus, the only one ever able to completely fulfill the Law, died in our place. If righteousness could be gained through fulfilling the Law, Christ died for nothing (Gal. 2:21).

If we want to have an intimate relationship with God, we cannot live by the law any longer. The longer we live by rules, regulations, and duty, the more we realize that we fall short and the more we feel like guilty sinners and failures. We begin to see God as angry, impatient, and mysteriously unpredictable, instead of a loving, gentle, compassionate, gracious, patient, always good, heavenly Daddy. Intentionally choosing to live in God's grace and love rather than condemnation opens our eyes to see Him as He really is. Then, and only then, are we able to have a genuine relationship of intimacy with Him.

God is pleased with you. He loves you. He is not blind to your stumbling, but He offers you grace in the midst of it because you received Jesus' sacrifice. He is not angry with you. He will not punish you when you stumble. His arms are open, waiting to hold you, not to condemn you.

In fact, God says that He sees you as flawless, perfect, and beautiful. This is not because we have acted perfectly, but because we have accepted the One that is perfect, flawless, and unimaginably beautiful, Jesus. In the Song of Songs, Jesus calls His Bride perfect three times (4:7, 5:2, 6:9). This is covered in more depth later on in this book. YOU are the Bride of Christ. Eph. 1:4 refers to us as holy and blameless. Colossians 1:22 identifies us as holy and without blemish. There are countless scriptures that refer to our righteousness before God in the present tense.

+ A Challenge +

If you are repeatedly struggling with something in your life, there is a challenge sounding from Heaven for you. In the midst of your stumbling, God wants you to start to declare that you are righteous.

At first this may be hard to do. Shame desires that we stay convinced that we are sinners, and declaring that you are righteous works in opposition to this stronghold.

When we stumble, we are supposed to ask for forgiveness, get back up, hit the delete button, and keep walking. If you are having a hard time getting back on your feet, start to declare with your mouth by faith that you are righteous. It feels like a contradiction, but it is a holy contradiction, one bought by the Blood of Jesus. Punishing ourselves for our sin isn't noble; it is devaluing the cross. But when we receive His sacrifice through living by grace and receiving our righteousness by faith, we are humbling accepting the gift of His death.

The enemy will try to tell you that you are a hopeless hypocrite, but continue to stand and declare the truth that you are a righteous lover of God. Soon, your declarations will leverage you up, and you will find that you are seated in heavenly places with Christ.

+ We are Saints, not sinners +

Even though there are so many verses on our righteousness, many of us still believe that we are sinners after we come to know Jesus. We have heard it said in church that, "Well brother, I am just a sinner saved by grace." We are not sinners...we are saints! It is a deception to believe that we are still sinners after we have received Jesus' sacrifice of love on the cross. Calling ourselves "sinners" implies that our identity is one who sins. That is no longer our identity because of Jesus. We are now righteous. We are saints.

If we believe that we are a sinner, we will act like one. On the other hand, calling ourselves "saints" is agreeing with how the Father sees us. If we believe that we are righteous, we will act like we are righteous. When we stumble, we tell the Lord our wrong, receive His grace, get back up, and move on. He calls us beautiful, not ugly, pure, not dirty, victorious, not overcome. God sees us through His Son.

Paul never referred to the church as sinners, but saints. Can you imagine if Paul opened up his letters to the churches with, "To the *sinners* in Ephesus…grace and peace to you in the Lord Jesus Christ"? Never! Paul always referred to the church in their true identity, as saints!

A saint has the right to do the works of God and be a minister of the gospel, a sinner does not. We are royal priests, assigned by heaven to lead others into the most holy place, where they encounter God Himself. We are called to walk like Jesus walked; to love, to preach the gospel, prophesy, disciple nations, heal the sick, raise the dead, and cast out devils (Matthew 10:8). Because you are a righteous saint, you are equipped with everything you need to be a minister of Christ.

+ No Condemnation +

Not only does God not want to condemn you because you are righteous, He *can't* condemn you. There are things that God is incapable of doing, and one is condemning a person that has received His son. There is no condemnation for those that are in Christ Jesus (Romans 8:1). It is a spiritual impossibility. Therefore, if there is condemnation in your life, it is not from God, even if the issue's source comes from a legitimate place of sin or weakness in your life. God isn't the one making you feel condemned or guilty. He doesn't work through condemnation, guilt, or shame, but rather through delight, love, and beauty.

Some only understand grace in the context of deserved wrath. But grace isn't grace because it was chosen to be given instead of wrath. Grace is grace because there was no choice; It is His instinct to give grace.

+ PRAYERS GOD WON'T ANSWER +

There *are* prayers that God won't answer. He won't answer prayers that He has already answered. Asking that God make you holy after you have already received Jesus is a contradictory, even schizophrenic, prayer. He has already made you holy through Christ.

However, praying that God aligns your desires with the reality of who you are is another matter. If you believe you are clean, you will act clean. If you believe you are dirty, you will act dirty. How you view yourself largely determines who you will become.

Let your righteousness become a *conviction* rather than an encouragement. It is not merely a heart-warming affirmation, but an essential truth. Wear this reality like a breastplate over your heart, fastened securely in place, not to be shaken in the midst battle.

If we are going to be a company of people walking in resurrection power, we must learn the power that our words have. Our mouths can be a gateway to heaven, or a portal into the realms of hell. Many people in the church do not yet understand the power they possess in their tongue. You *must* know what your words are capable of so that you can effectively work miracles and heal hearts, as well as steer clear from inadvertently cursing others. You have the ability to raise the dead with your voice, but conversely, you also have the ability to speak death and make things die. This chapter explores the power of the tongue, and some of the misconceptions we have had about God that relate to the power of the tongue.

+ ANANIAS AND SAPPHIRA +

We all know the story. Acts 5 picks up in the midst of the revival that was fueled by the outpouring of the Holy Spirit on Pentecost. The Church had just been born, and was thriving. People were being saved, healed, and delivered on a regular basis. Individual Christians were selling property that they owned in order that nobody had unmet need in the fellowship. Ananias and Sapphira sold some property of theirs, gave part of the money to the Lord while acting like they gave it all, and kept the rest. Peter calls out their sin and they fall down dead. Fear swept over the whole church and every unbeliever that heard about this event.

For as long as I can remember, the Church has been taught one general way to view this story; Why what Ananias and Sapphira did was bad enough to die for it. We are taught various reasons as to why Ananias and Sapphira's death was justified because of how evil their actions were.

Though it is was challenging the teaching of godly men that I highly respected and trusted, I couldn't shake the fact that we were reading this portion of scripture in a way that didn't reinforce in people's hearts that God is good. In fact, the teachings that men of God were giving to the Church on these scriptures seemed to contradict the very thing that God has called leaders in the Body of Christ to demonstrate and teach; that God is overwhelmingly good.

I began to seek God about these verses, asking Him to help me understand how He was good in the midst of the circumstances. I didn't want to read something into the text that wasn't there, lest I distort scripture. Distorting scripture limits our ability to learn more about various facets of who God is. If God wanted to highlight His holiness, the purity of this movement, and the Fear of the Lord, I was more than willing to embrace my discomfort and lack of understanding pertaining to these verses. There are times when we simply need to continue to trust that He is good even when we don't understand His actions, but was this one of those situations? As I sought the Lord about these verses, He began to show me a different way of reading this portion of scripture.

+A LITERAL POWER +

If you read the story carefully, Ananias and Sapphira die at the moment Peter pronounces judgment on them. He speaks and they die. Proverbs 18:21 says,

"Life and death are in the power of the tongue..." This is a literal statement. We can either use our words to raise the dead, heal the sick, and cast out devils through blessing others, or we can kill others by cursing them. The Living Bible translation of the second half of Proverbs 18:21 even says, *"...men have died for saying the wrong thing."*

In Matthew 21 Jesus commanded a fig tree to die, and it literally died. It wasn't a figurative situation, but a demonstration of the spiritual reality conveyed in Proverbs 18:21. Jesus demonstrated this on a tree, not a person, so that we could see its power without hurting anyone. Peter was the disciple to take notice of Jesus' words, and actually called it "cursing" the tree (Mark 11:21).

Immediately after cursing the tree, Jesus said, "If you believe, you will receive whatever you ask for in prayer." Typically we have quoted this verse when dealing with praying for the sick, financial provision, or anything else related to needing God to show up in our circumstances. Surely this verse does apply to those situations, but it is in the context of cursing, not blessing, that Jesus told us that whatever we ask for we will receive if we believe. This is sobering to say the least, because it means that the power that we possess in our words is far stronger and more expansive than we ever thought. It means that God has given every person the ability to exert power that manifests literally in someone's life, and chosen to trust us with how we use our words. It means that when you pray what you think someone needs into their life, it may not be God that carries out the implications of your prayers. You have power that He has given you, and it is powerful enough to do anything in that person's life (Matthew 21:22). It can even kill. Let us be careful to always pray according to God's heart, which is *always* to bless and bring life despite what someone has done. Let us leave judgment up to God, as Jesus told us to, and allow the kindness and love that we exude to lead others to repentance rather than praying curses onto their life so that they change.

+ RICE AND WATER +

Once while ministering at a church in Oregon, the youth pastor told me that he wanted to show me something in his office, so I followed him down the hallway that led to the back of the church.

On his desk he proudly showed me four sealed jars, with an equal amount of rice and water in each. He had glued a label on each jar that had a phrase written on it, with the first jar being, "Thank you". The second stated, "God bless you." The third, "You fool", and the forth, "You disgust me." Altogether there were two positive statements and two negative statements.

The youth pastor told me that he had started an experiment. Each day he came into his office he would speak the statement on each jar over that particular jar. The jar labeled with "Thank you" was thanked everyday, and the "You disgust me" jar was told on a daily basis just how repulsive it was.

I looked at the simple containers and was astounded at the outcome. The "Thank you" jar, as well as the "God bless you" jar looked almost appetizing. The rice and water had joined together, become one, and looked like milk.

On the other hand, the "You disgust me" jar did just that; it disgusted me. The rice and water had not joined together at all, as if adamantly opposing each other, and looked like a small animal's brain sitting in a jar. On top of that unattractiveness, it was brown with mold. The "You fool" jar was similar in appearance.

Our words are spirit, and they affect the natural in tangible ways. We can actually change the direction of creation by the way we steward our words, whether it be rice in a jar, or a person's life.

+ MADE IN THE IMAGE OF GOD +

We are made in the image of God. This does not refer so much to the image of our human bodies, but to the characteristics that we possess that are akin to God's.

When I was young, I remember learning in Sunday school that what proved that we were made in the image of God was that we could choose to create life through having babies. Shortly after learning this, I realized it couldn't be fully true because animals can reproduce as well. There had to be something more that dictated that we were made in God's image.

Years later I realized that God *spoke* the world into existence (Genesis 1). God can create with His words, and He imparted this ability to us as well. A major determining factor that we are made in God's image is that He has enabled us to speak. In speaking, we are inherently endowed with the ability to speak things into existence and to create.

You have a creative ability because of the power of your tongue. This means that everything you speak, good or bad, becomes an actuality, or at least instigates implications. Use this gift wisely!

+ A SHATTERING REALITY +

We have all seen the comical renditions on television of a woman singing at the top of her lungs causing windowpanes, wine glasses, and mirrors that are in her presence to shatter.

Most of us thought this to be myth, or at best an exaggeration. But recently it has been proven that humans really can break glass simply by the power of their voice. This ability is not confined only to rock stars and opera singers, but sixteen-year-old girls have been known to possess enough resonance in their voice to break glass. In fact, anyone that hollers hard enough inches from a thin wine glass at the right tone can probably shatter it.

What does this tell us? It tells us that our voices carry such power in the spirit that it is even demonstrated in the natural. The natural is a type of the spiritual. God is revealing to us in this hour the unseen power every person possesses in the use of their tongue.

+ PERFECTION +

Shockingly, James wrote that *the* way to determine if a person has "arrived" pertaining in spiritual maturity and character is by the way that they use their tongue;

"If anyone is never at fault in what he says, he is a perfect man, able to keep his whole body in check." James 3:2

God determines maturity by how someone uses their tongue. If a person can control their tongue, they have reached perfection of character and spirituality. Quite an accomplishment, and only One has done it.

The reason the tongue is so decisive in determining our actual maturity is because *"...out of the overflow of the heart the mouth speaks."* (Luke 6:45). The mouth is the measuring stick of the state of a person's heart. In fact, the tongue is such an accurate internal evaluator of our hearts that James tells us that if we can't keep a tight rein on our tongue that we are *deceived* and the worship we think we walk in is *worthless* (James 1:26). Quite a cutting statement.

Jesus took it even further than James pertaining to warning us about the power of the tongue. He not only warned us about the careless words that we speak that we think don't matter, but He went on to reveal an even more sobering reality. He told us that a chief matter that will determine the judgment we will receive from God when we stand before Him will be *the words* that we spoke in our lives on Earth. How we stewarded the use of our words will be one of the determining factors of what we will receive for *all of eternity.*

"I tell you that men will have to give account on the day of judgment for every careless word they have spoken. For by your words you will be acquitted, and by your words you will be condemned." Matthew 12:36-37

Some of us, when we hear of the tongue needing to be kept under tight reins, bridled, or controlled, we often think of that being limited to not saying vulgar words or cussing. Surely, this is a portion of what James and Jesus are communicating, for a foul mouth isn't attractive to anyone. But Jesus and James are *not* saying that if you swear that your walk with God is worthless. What Jesus and James are after is much more subtle and severe. For instance, how do you use your words when someone doesn't do what you want them to do? Do you subconsciously attempt to subtly control them with your words through manipulation or intimidation, or do bless them despite the fact that they aren't doing what you want them to do? Do you use your words to build up others and speak destiny, power, and encouragement into them, or do you use your words to get what you want?

I know of pastors that speak excellently and above reproach pertaining to vulgarity or "decency". Everything seems to be in line until a situation arises that they don't agree with...then the hidden comes into view. Though they never use any swear words, I have seen these pastors make comments that severely cripple the souls of those that they pastor, and they do so with a smile on their face, unaware of what they are saying. This is what James and Jesus were warning us of. Lets not limit the weight of Jesus' words to what can slip out of our mouths when we stub our toe.

For instance, a good friend of mine was the assistant pastor at a church. The Lord began to lead him out of this church and to a different congregation. When he informed the senior pastor and the pastor's wife of what he felt God was leading him to do, the wife said, "If you leave and God doesn't strike you down, I will!"

It is in these moments that the true, hidden heart is revealed; you leave, you die! Though she may have just been "joking" or "meant well" when she spoke, she was oblivious of the kind of destructive declaration she was making with her tongue.

During the second conversation that my friend had with the same couple, the pastor's wife said, "Life is going to be hard out there for you if you leave. You don't have the credentials to get a job somewhere else in ministry. You better stick around here." She was clueless of the manipulation and intimidation that she was spewing. This woman then proceeded to tell my friend that the devil was what was influencing his desire to minister elsewhere. Though she was oblivious of what she was really saying, she used her words to not only curse his ministry, but his very life! She planted a seed in the spirit realm, as well as in my friend's heart and mind that if he left their church God would kill him and his ministry would fail. Thank God that my friend knows God's heart as well as he does, or her words would have kept him bound where he was, and the plan that God had for him wouldn't have been fulfilled. He continued on the path

God had given him, trusting that God would come through on his behalf, despite the woman's words.

A week after his talk with the senior pastors, my friend was asked by another pastor in his city to have lunch. This minister led a congregation that was flourishing in love for God and the presence of the Holy Spirit. Without prior knowledge of my friend's situation, and despite this pastor's limited knowledge of my friend's life in ministry, he offered my friend a pastoral position in his church. My friend relocated his family to this new spiritual family, and happily continued doing ministry.

+ UNPUNISHABLE +

Most of us grew up believing that Jesus came to die on the cross for us so that God's wrath and punishment towards sin could be paid for. We were taught that the result is that we go free, never experiencing the punishment we deserve for our sins. We were told that we received Christ so that the due punishment that God desires to pour out upon sin could be shouldered by Christ. We learned that what Christ did on the cross made us unpunishable before God, and we rejoiced in this.

But is this the case, that Jesus died so that the wrath and punishment God has towards sin could be nullified in our lives? At face value this seems to make sense but it is not the full truth. Most of this is accurate of Jesus, but subtly and extremely inaccurate of the Father.

The reality is that the Father sent Jesus because He loved us (John 3:16), not because He had a burning need to purify the earth of its sin because of His holiness. He isn't that insecure; He really *is* God. He will be holy regardless if we are or aren't. God's agenda is not to destroy sin, but to love people in the midst of it. Here is the key; God isn't about dealing out punishment and wrath because of the presence of sin, satan is.

It is true that we all deserve hell because the inherent sin each of us were born into. But it is not the Father that ever issued this death sentence, it was satan. The enemy is a legalist; he loves the law because it is his only way to gain entrance into people's lives. He possesses no authority, thus he must gain it through a person's agreement with his kingdom; sin. Sin gives the enemy a *legal* right to afflict someone. This is why cities are and were destroyed; not because God wants to destroy the evil residing inside their city walls, but because the evil that goes on there invites darkness to have its way with the people of the city. We don't just walk righteously because that is the right thing to do, but because righteousness keeps the door shut that the enemy so that he has no authority in our lives to afflict us. Does this mean that everyone that is sick is in sin and needs to repent? No. But it does mean that God is on your side, and that the enemy is out to destroy you.

Did you know that you are unpunishable? Did you know that the Blood of Jesus makes you immune to receive what you deserve, which is hell? More importantly, did you know that it is not the Father that desires to give you what you deserve, but the enemy? Without Christ, punishment is our inheritance, but with Christ, we are set free from punishment and given an inheritance of grace, protection, and provision. Jesus is our everything. Without Him, the enemy can steal, kill, and destroy us whenever he pleases to.

God *never* had plans to punish us or deal out wrath to us, even when we were in sin. The devil, on the other hand, has always desired to pour out destruction and wrath upon us. He is looking for reasons to destroy mankind, and sin gives the enemy a legal right to afflict us with the wrath and hate that he has towards us. It is he that tries to punish us when we stumble. Punishment is a reality, for we live within in a legal spiritual system, where the enemy tries to give us what we deserve. The enemy loves the law, for its essence is getting what you deserve; a performance based system that is completely "fair". Yet because of Jesus we don't get what we legally deserve. The gavel dropped in your favor when He said, "It is finished."

We must remember that Jesus didn't make us unpunishable because the Father was wanting to punish us for the sin we have committed, but because the enemy wanted to. It isn't that Jesus satisfied the wrath and punishment of God on the cross, but that Christ satisfied the need for payment for our sin, which gave the enemy full right to afflict us with the wrath and punishment our sin legally earned. Jesus didn't come to keep us safe from the Father's wrath, but to shield us from the enemy's desire to destroy everyone made in the image of God. There was no need for the cross to make us unpunishable before the Father, for He never had plans to punish us to begin with.

Because we have accepted Jesus as our Lord and Savior, since the moment He announced, *"It is finished"* we were marked *unpunishable*.

+ PETER'S BACKGROUND IN LAW +

The Law is simple to explain. If you did what to said to do, you were blessed. If you did what it said not to do, you were cursed. The Law gave you what you deserved, and it was a completely fair, grace-filled, perfect way for God to engage with humanity for that time.

If you think about it, God actually didn't give us a super high standard to meet, contrary to common belief. Don't kill, don't steal, don't covet your neighbor's wife, and don't worship other gods are a few of the sins He told us to not partake in, none of them being unclear in their evil. They weren't commandments that were too immense to abide by. A good father always sets up His children for obedience by not making the standards higher than the child can be expected to meet. God didn't set us up for disobedience by setting the standards too high.

Yet despite the low standards, we still chose to partake in sin. Enter God's solution; Jesus. God ushered in a new covenant through giving His own Son unto death on the behalf of our inability to measure up to very reasonable standards. This is why Jesus is so worthy of our praise. He is exceedingly wonderful to come bail us out of a very fair situation that we messed up by choosing to sin.

Peter was born into a time in history when God was drastically renewing people's minds. For thousands of years men had learned that they got what they deserved because of the Law. Peter had read story after story in the scriptures of groups being sanctified through the killing of sinful and rebellious individuals and families within the company, cities being cleansed of sin by violent and intense measures, and prophets regaining their honor through calling bears out of the wood to kill a bunch of kids. Radical retribution seemed to be the norm.

But in Jesus there was a sudden revolutionary shift to grace. God was taking mankind out of a mindset that functioned out of a paradigm of Law and into a mindset that functioned out of a paradigm of grace. We went from depending upon our own performance to depending upon Jesus' performance.

Peter understood this new way of thinking because He had been with Jesus. Peter breathed in an atmosphere of grace for three years. Jesus repeatedly demonstrated that we have the power to give people grace that they did not earn and do not deserve. He told us to love our enemies, forgive those indebted to us, and bless those that persecute us. But this new paradigm of thinking hit home strongest when Jesus forgave Peter three times for forsaking Him three times. Peter had sinned in the worst way possible, yet because of grace, relationship was restored without the need of punishment or sacrifice.

And though Peter experienced immeasurable amounts of love and grace through being in relationship with Jesus, he still was getting used to this new way of thinking and acting. Like anyone that is trying to change, once and awhile he would revert back to his old way of thinking; law and punishment. Next is one example of a time Peter reverted back to his old way of thinking, and it cost a few people their lives.

+ No Longer Fig Trees, But People +

Towards the beginning of Acts, God gave Peter extraordinary authority that was meant to build up this newly born Body of God. Authority is the right to exercise power, and God gave Peter loads of it because he needed it in order to lead well. Paul said in 2 Corinthians 13:10 that God gives authority to build up, not tear down.

Peter had been given the responsibility of leading the newly born church. He needed to lead the people in a way that stewarded the Presence of God well, and as any good leader does, Peter probably felt the weight of not wanting the Holy Spirit grieved by what was happening in the movement.

Ananias enters the room, lays down part of the money, and Peter rightly discerns the sin that he is living in. Instead of taking Ananias aside and talking through his error with him, Peter speaks out judgment over Ananias and he dies on the spot. Sapphira comes in three hours later, Peter curses her, and she died as well.

God did not kill Ananias and Sapphira, Peter did. Peter wrongly used the authority that God had given to him to build up the newly born church. Instead of building up the church, he tore down. For a moment he forgot what covenant he was in, reverted back to that familiar mindset of Law, and used the power he possessed to destroy rather than give life. Though Peter had experienced the Lord's grace in a greater degree (when Jesus forgave him three times) than what Ananias and Sapphira's situation called for, he forgot the mode of operation of grace. It took some time, but Peter figured it out by the end.

God doesn't endorse everything people in the Bible did. Every man in scripture, excluding Jesus, was still a man with faults and weaknesses, despite the anointing, calling, and influence that God gave them. We must remember that though godly men in the Bible did amazing exploits, they were still men. They were not perfect. Being an apostle or prophet does not mean that God endorsed everything they did. Thus, just because something is in the Bible doesn't mean that God supported what happened.

+ THE DEPTH OF FORGIVENESS AND GRACE +

If God forgives rapists and murderers in our day, what makes us think that God would not have forgiven Ananias and Sapphira for something much less serious than murder? If God killed them for lying, then why aren't you and I dead?

The grievance that we cause God when we teach people that God killed Ananias and Sapphira is that we affirm in their hearts the very thing they already suspect; that God is angry with us, is quick to destroy us and judge us, and will not tolerate our stumblings. These are lies from hell, and if they are true, there is no value of receiving Jesus' death on the cross for us. Either Jesus' death is as radical and wonderful as we think it is because it revolutionized our relationship with God, or it is not.

+ DISCERNMENT WRONGLY USED +

One thing people regularly ask me after I have shared about Ananias and Sapphira at a conference or church is, "But wasn't Peter functioning in discernment? He accurately called out their sin! Doesn't that prove that God was the one that brought the conclusions about?"

It is a great question. Peter was in fact moving in discernment, one of the prophetic gifts mentioned in scripture. It is obvious that he was moving in discernment, or he wouldn't know the facts about the sin that Ananias and Sapphira were committing. But having a gift and knowing how to use it correctly are two different scenarios. Countless times in scripture we see men that have been given power, but are still trying to learn how to use it. Remember, the men in scripture were not perfect just because they were spiritually gifted. Being spiritually gifted does not prove that someone is mature, but that they are gifted.

1 Corinthians 14:3 says, "But everyone who prophesies to men for their strengthening, encouragement, and comfort." That is a very clear outline of the guidelines for the prophetic ministry in the New Covenant. Though Old Testament prophets may have ministered differently, Paul makes it clear that when *we* prophesy and minister, the motive would be to strengthen, encourage, and comfort. That means that we do not deal out judgments of God on people, nor do anything else that doesn't *strengthen, encourage, or comfort.* A mature prophetic ministry today can be recognized by their humility and kindness towards others.

A believer may rightly discern the issues in a person's life but not handle it in love. Discernment without true love is actually judgment. Judgment is a form of cursing, like what Jesus did with the fig tree. Thus, much of the Body of Christ uses their God-give gift of discernment to lead them into judgment, which is sin. They may pray a condescending, critical, judgmental prayer over the one that is struggling, or not do anything about it, both which are unloving.

We must learn how to believe the best about people in the midst of picking up on their weaknesses. Those of us that "feel" in the spirit have to be careful that when we discern sin in someone's life, that we deal with it through love and out of a desire to bless them, not to fix them, purify them, "help them grow", or any other reasons that are rooted in being offended with other people's sin.

+ A STORY OF DISCERNMENT +

Once I was in a church service and we were told to hold hands with the person next to us. The moment my hand touched the man next to me, I distinctly saw pornographic pictures flash through my mind. Not understanding discernment, I began repenting, asking God to forgive me for having such thoughts. Then I realized that I saw those pictures the moment I touched that man's hand and that pornography was not a struggle for me. I became aware of the fact that the images I was seeing were not coming from an unhealed place in me, but from the man next to me.

I didn't know what to do. He was a total stranger and I couldn't just go up to him and tell him that I knew he struggled with pornography. At least I had the sense to know that wouldn't go over well. Because I didn't know what to do, I didn't do anything. I'm thankful God gave me another chance.

Remarkably, almost a year later and two states away from where I live, I saw the same man at a small gathering. It was God saying, "Ok, get it right this time." I now knew how to handle the situation without judging the man or doing anything that may not strengthen, encourage, or comfort him. I got a chance to spend some time with him, and instead of calling out his sin, I prophesied what the Lord said about him, which was that he was pure. God calls that which is not as though it is, because of Jesus.   If you discern someone's sin, look at them through God's eyes. He will say that they are the exact opposite of what they are struggling with, because of Jesus. You must find Jesus in others, or you will always judge the sinner, the prostitute, the liar, the porn addict, or the poor. You will find no love in your heart towards them, but if you see them through the Father's eyes, you will see Jesus in them, saved or not. If they are saved, you will see them through the Blood. If they are not saved, you will see them as they will be when they are saved. Then you simply call them into their Destiny.

+ THE TRUE PROPHETIC MINISTRY +

Sometimes we may think that God is involved when a person deals out a judgment that doesn't strengthen, encourage, or comfort because it actually happens. Just because a judgment that a person speaks out happens doesn't mean that God endorsed it, or was even involved in it. What it *does* mean is that men have tongues, and a man's tongue possesses power.

I know if a minister in Africa that was highly respected by other Christians because he would prophesy when other believers and unbelievers would die or get sick because of their "resistance to the Lord". They would regularly die or get sick just as he said. People reverently feared this man.

The reality is that this man had a problem with control, and when people wouldn't do what he told them what to do, he would prophesy judgments to them. In doing so, he was cursing them with demonic declarations that would actually manifest exactly as he believed them to. It was Christian witchcraft. Whenever control is in the mix, witchcraft is assuredly present as well.

The true prophetic ministry today would never do something that doesn't strengthen, encourage, or comfort. It is much easier to just judge people and have those judgments come true than it is to love people through their problems. So, don't be impressed when you hear stories about men calling out people's sins or the day they will die because of their hardheartedness. Rest assured that God is a God of grace, uses kindness to bring us to repentance, and never ever controls us.

+ WHAT ABOUT THE FEAR OF THE LORD? +

There are two different categories of fear presented in scripture. The first is the Fear of the Lord, which is the beginning of wisdom. It is the starting place in relationship with God, because it comes with the recognition that He is Holy and we are not without Jesus. The word "reverence" is an understatement when experiencing the Fear of God. The Fear of the Lord is wonderful, and quite possibly one of the most exhilarating experiences and revelations in existence. The Fear of the Lord has nothing to do with fearing that you will be destroyed by this God of holiness, but has to do with being overcome by His exceedingly foreign goodness. He is unlike anything or anyone that we have ever encountered. He is set apart, or holy, in a way that is unfamiliar to us, as well as the total fulfillment of the desire of our hearts. We tremble because of His goodness. As Hosea 3:5 says, *"In the last days, they will tremble in awe of the Lord and His goodness."* (NLT) C.S. Lewis said it like this; "...beauty, which most of them had never seen, worked on them as a terror might work".[1]

It is important to understand that the word in Hebrew for "fear" is ירא, or yârê, and primarily means *awe*. Though religion has tried to convince us otherwise, the fear of the Lord is more about the adoration and worship we give God for His beauty than it is the dread that God will squish you for your sin. In fact, the fear of the Lord cannot be something that involves *any* feelings of fear or dread towards God rather than awe. Why? Because 1 John 4:18 tells us that when we feel fear towards God rather than awe, it is an indication that something is awry with our love towards God. Here is the verse:

"There is no fear in love. But perfect love drives out fear, because fear has to do with punishment. The one who fears is not made perfect in love."

If you feel plain fear towards God, whether subtle or overt, don't let people tell you that is a good thing. Scripture tells us that if we feel fear towards God it reveals to us that there is something that we believe about Him that is not true, and it is resulting in our love towards Him to be hindered, stunted, and halted rather than growing to its full capacity. The reality is that if you believe God is mad at you for your stumblings, or that you are scum and God can barely stand to be around you and only because of Jesus' blood, or that He will punish you for something you did or kill you for lying, the inevitable result will be that you won't want to get close

---

[1] Excerpt from "Till We Have Faces"

to Him. You may *think* you want to get close to Him while believing that, but it will be a facade, and you will be lying to yourself. You will not have the ability to be deeply vulnerable with Him, because vulnerability and intimacy can only take place in the context of trust and safety, and if you believe that the Lord will afflict you with some form of punishment, you will be unable to genuinely unfold your heart to God. Fearing God's punishment is always an indication of immaturity in the life of a believer. We have all been there.

Rather, have awe towards God. Gaze upon His beauty. Let His love undo you for how accepting it is and how unconditional it is despite your problems. *That* is the fear, or awe, of God, and *that* is the beginning of wisdom.

The Bible is clear that the fear of the Lord is the being the beginning of wisdom (Proverbs 9:10). Did you catch that? The fear of the Lord is the *beginning* of wisdom, not its culmination or conclusion. In other words, mature wisdom does not solely look like the fear of the Lord. Mature wisdom always looks like intimacy with God.

The second category of fear presented in scripture is the fear of anything other than God. It is sin, for it is borne out of a lack of trust towards God. This kind of fear is the antithesis to faith, and as destructive as idolatry. In fact, it is idolatry, because you worship whatever you fear and you fear what you worship. As believers, we cannot afford to fear anything other than God, whether it be if our children are safe or not, death, or the devil himself.

A misunderstanding that has caused us to believe that Ananias and Sapphira's death was from God is found in verse eleven, "Great fear seized the whole church, and all who heard about these events."

Typically, we have been taught that this fear was the Fear of the Lord. But what were the people that heard about Ananias and Sapphira afraid of? Put yourself in the people's shoes of that day. The people were not in the Fear of God, but the fear of being struck dead for something like not telling the truth. The church and those that heard about Ananias and Sapphira had a fear of death, not a Fear of God. They heard what Peter did and were worried that he may discern their sin and take their life as well.

Peter's mistake in how he handled the situation with Ananias and Sapphira actually introduced fear into the Church. Besides his denial of Jesus three times over, this was his darkest hour. Instead of fueling the movement of God with faith, Peter hindered the movement by introducing fear into it. *Despite this*, in His mercy God continued to work miracles through the apostles (v12). God wasn't going to let Peter's mishap stop the move of the Spirit.

+ FEAR ON FINNEY +

One man that undisputedly carried the Spirit of the Fear of the Lord was a man named Charles Finney. There are many stories from his life that pertained to the spirit of the Fear of the Lord, but probably the most impressive story took place in a factory. Charles simply walked into this factory and stood in one place, allowing the spirit of the Fear of the Lord to radiate from him. He didn't say a word, yet unsaved men began falling to their knees and repenting of sin because of the Fear of the Lord that was present.

The spirit of the Fear of the Lord does not kill men, but brings them repentance. It is a form of grace, like anything else that exudes from God. If the spirit of the Fear of the Lord killed men for the lack of genuineness in their hearts towards God or for sin, we would have stacks of bodies piled up in our churches. In a true movement of God, more people do not die for their sin, less do.

The Bible says that the Fear of the Lord is the beginning of wisdom (Proverbs 1:7, 9:10, Psalms 111:10), and wisdom is constantly referred to in scripture as something that leads to long life (Proverbs 3:2, 3:16, 3:18, 4:10). Hence, it would be quite a contradiction to say that the Fear of the Lord has a fatal element to it.

Jesus was the exact representation of the Father (Heb. 1). Take notice that while Jesus was on the earth nobody died as a result of His ministry. It sounds like an obvious point, but its implications run deep.

Men died at the hands of people's ministry before and after the life of Jesus, but *not* during His time on Earth. Doesn't this tell us something? In fact, when faced with sin that was punishable by death according to the law of the day, such as the woman caught in adultery, Jesus not only didn't kill the woman, but He surprisingly pointed the finger at those that were just trying to "follow the rules" and about to stone her to death! Jesus is the exact representation of the Father, so this should show us who the Father is pertaining to grace and sin, even more than any understanding of God that we get from the Old Testament. The life and words of Jesus take precedence over our understanding of the Old Testament because He was the exact representation of the Father. If we were to listen to the Old Testament over the words of Jesus, we could go out and marry more than one woman! Not a good idea!

Jesus IS God! He showed us who the Father is. This is why Islam relentlessly fights the fact that Jesus is God. Muslims acknowledge Jesus to be a legitimate prophet and even love Him, but refuse to believe that He is God. This is because if they acknowledge Him as God, then God can't be who they believe Him to be. Instead of an angry, condemning, violent, wrathful God, He would have to look like Jesus; gracious, nonjudgmental, and loving. Islam disintegrates at the confession that Jesus is Lord.

The point is that even after Jesus demonstrated the Father's heart through His life, the moment Ananias and Sapphira died, the church went right back to blaming God for people's deaths that were in sin. God was held as the responsible party before and after Jesus came to the earth, but not during His time on Earth because He embodied God's will and heart. The church couldn't find a way to blame the Father during the time Jesus was on Earth because Jesus *is* God. His heart was revealed as kindness and grace towards the sinner rather than anger, wrath, and punishment. If you have a belief about God that cannot be substantiated through the life of Jesus, your belief is wrong.

We have learned that because of this fear that the people experienced in Acts 5:11, their number was weeded out, and those that hadn't really jumped on the bandwagon of what God was doing were hesitant to join. But as Finney's life shows us, the Fear of the Lord causes men to be attracted to Jesus, not to be hesitant about joining up with His army. The fear of *death* would cause men to question if they wanted to join this new group of radicals, but not the Fear of the Lord. In a movement of God, more people are brought to repentance for their sin, even the fakers, not less.

It wasn't the Fear of the Lord that killed the forty-two kids in 2 Kings either. It was a curse, sent by a misled man of God. The reason we see people die when "men of God" proclaim it on them isn't because God endorses it, but because they have authority and power!

I remember the first time I read the story in 2 Kings where a group of kids are mauled to death by bears for calling a prophet bald. I felt like simultaneously laughing and crying after I read the story. Calling a person bald is exactly what I would expect a bunch of rascally kids to do, hence my impulse to laugh. But I also felt deeply grieved because of what happened to them. I visualized the kid's childish ridicule, the prophet's cursing, and the bears appearing out of the woods with speed, heading towards the now terrified children. I pictured the children running for their lives as quickly as their legs could carry them, yet the bears destroying forty-two of them despite the children's best attempt at escape.

Like the above story, prior to understanding the power of the tongue, there were instances in the Bible that confused me. I didn't understand why God would kill forty-two children for calling a prophet bald, because it didn't seem like something a good God would do to a bunch of kids that were just being kids. It is now clear that God had nothing to do with the deaths of those children, but that Elijah was the one responsible.

+ JESUS, OUR MODEL +

We must remember that Jesus is our clearest representation of God's heart. Through His life, Jesus showed us who the Father is. The only times people experienced fear in response to Jesus' three years of ministry was when He did something wonderful. These two occasions were when He raised the widow's only son from the dead (Luke 7:16, NASB), and when He healed a paralytic (Luke 5:26). Jesus' life demonstrated that the fear of God is not rooted in a fear of His wrath and anger, but a holy fear of His overwhelming goodness and love. The people that came into contact with Jesus were gripped by fear not because they were worried a lightening bolt would strike them if they didn't obey and honor Him, but because He was so incredibly beautiful in His demonstration of goodness and love. He raised the dead and gave them back to a widowed mother, healed those that were blind since birth, and made the paralytics whole. This kind of love, overwhelming and all encompassing, was terrifyingly beautiful to those that witnessed it.

The fear that was experienced through the ministry of Jesus is in stark contrast to the fear that gripped the early church when Ananias and Sapphira dropped dead. In one case people feared the Lord because of His awesome goodness. In the other case people feared the Lord because they thought He would strike them dead. We are clearly dealing with two different kinds of fears.

The Fear of the Lord is not a reality because He is angry, but because of His exceeding goodness.

"...they will fear and tremble because of all the good and all the peace that I make for them." Jeremiah 33:9 (NASB)

"In the last days, they will tremble in awe (fear) of the Lord and of his goodness." Hosea 3:5 (NLT)

Here is another way to explain it. When you really experience the love of God there will be a point where you will be forced to turn your head, to look away, to try to shield yourself from this Being of goodness. He does not relent in pouring His love out upon you despite the problems you know all too well in your life and character. This is the place of pioneering love. This is where growth takes place. This is where the capacity to hold love is expanded. But this is also the place of the Fear of the Lord. His love is so radiant, so limitlessly accepting, so holy, so terrifyingly and wonderfully intrusive, that it is impossible to not turn away. If you haven't had this experience, you haven't gone deep enough in love. It will only happen as you unveil yourself to Him completely, let

Him take the reigns, and choose to believe that no matter what He does, He only has your best in mind. Then the glory of His goodness will come and burn through you.

+ OUR MISTAKES, NOT HIS +

Some rationalize that Ananias' and Sapphira's deaths were still God's doing because He was the one to give Peter power in the first place. This isn't sound thinking.

Stewardship is a huge component in the Kingdom (Matthew 25:14-30). God gives to us in the context of trust. He gives us various things in this life that we are called to steward, and He trusts us to use them rightly.

For example, He gave us hands. We can use our hands to physically harm others, even kill, or we can use them to feed the hungry and heal bodies. God has given us this ability by giving us hands, but the fact that people sometimes misuse this power is not reflective of Him, nor does it make it His fault when someone kills another person with their hands.

It is the similar when dealing with the power of our tongue. God has given us a vast power in our tongue and scripture says that it is enough to give life or take it. He trusts us to use it rightly.

+ HERESY +

For some, to look at scripture in this new light is not only a bit risky, but borderline heretical. But ask yourself what is actually at stake if you were to give yourself to this insight? What are the worse, most heretical interpretation mistakes we could make through viewing these verses through these lenses? What are the benefits to this view?

Surely the most heretical thing we could give ourselves to *isn't* in believing something good about God; that He didn't take the life of two people that lied. There is no heresy in assuming good things about God. Heresy is assuming something about God that isn't true, like when the Pharisees said that Jesus was possessed by the devil (Mark 3:22). The worst and most heretical thing you can deduce (if you can actually call it heresy) from reading the scriptures in this way is that Peter was an imperfect man.

On the other hand, the benefits of reading these verses in this way are numerous. The most important advantage to this view is that God is not blamed for something He didn't do. In the traditional view, God is blamed in roundabout ways for killing two misled people while Peter is extolled.

If there is a choice between blaming a man or blaming God for something bad, take the safe route and blame man. Man is faulty, but God is perfect. God never lacks in His goodness, only man does. You won't go wrong to attribute bad things to man and the enemy.

After all, attributing something to God that He didn't do is far more serious than seeing Peter for less than what he was. Take your pick. Now, which view is heretical?

+ HOW PETER SHOULD HAVE HANDLED SIN +

Revival can be messy. Instead of trying to protect the move of God from imperfection, Peter should have manifested some of the fruits of the Spirit such as self-control and gentleness. All that was needed was to pull these two sinners aside and privately confront them about their sin. He could have led them into repentance for trying to deceive others, talked to them like a brother and sister, interacted with them on a relational level instead of a dictator, and sorted it out rationally.

Scripture is clear in Matthew 18 that the way we sort out issues in the Body of Christ is to go to the another person in private and communicate the ought we have with them. We do not confront them publicly at this stage. Peter was expected to follow this way of solving a problem like anyone else. Peter was probably even present when Jesus taught this spiritual protocol, but it seemed to slip his mind.

If the person continues in sin after confronting the person in private, we are to bring others with us and confront them in private again. Lastly, we confront them in public and remove them from fellowship if they continue to willfully sin. But at no point do we curse someone or judge them. Peter was *way* off in how he handled Ananias and Sapphira.

In addition, Galatians 6:1 also confirms that Peter handled the situation wrongly.

"Brothers, if someone is caught in a sin, you who are spiritual should restore him gently."

No doubt, gentleness was lacking in Peter's response to Ananias and Sapphira's sin. In doing so, Peter revealed not his superior spiritual maturity, but his spiritual immaturity.

Elijah's case is not much different. Elijah needed to calm down and realize they were just kids being kids. He needed to control himself, handle it like a man, bless them, and keep walking. But, if you like bears tearing off little kids heads and arms, reminiscent of a horror movie, so that you feel better about being called bald, go ahead and curse them, Eli. A bit sensitive about your age these days, eh?

In Acts 8 we are introduced to a man named Simon. He was a sorcerer until he saw the power of God that Peter and John had. He came to the end of himself at the realization of the limits of his power in comparison to God's power, and scripture says that he became a Christian. Soon after, he saw the apostles laying hands on others and witnessed them receive the Holy Spirit. Wanting the same gift, he offers Peter money in order that he can do the same thing. Peter rebukes him and continues on his journey with John.

Traditionally, we have read this section of scripture as though Simon was the lost one. But is that true? Was zealous, impulsive Peter at it again or was Simon the magician evil at heart and in need of a rebuke?

First off, lets look at Simon's background. He was used to sorcery, wherein you paid others to do spiritual work done for you. The sorcery he was involved in was evil and detestable in God's eyes. But Simon received Jesus and was cleansed of his sin. He was no longer a sinner, but a saint.

Naturally, because of Simon's background, when he saw the Holy Spirit being imparted by the laying on of the apostle's hands, he thought that the best way to get that ability was to pay Peter for it. This makes sense when it is established that Simon didn't know anything other than paying for spiritual abilities because of his past. This was the mode of operation to Simon.

But Peter, possibility not knowing his past, blasted Simon. This is what he tells him:

"May your money perish with you, because you thought you could buy the gift of God with money! You have no part or share in this ministry, because your heart is not right before God. Repent of this wickedness and pray to the Lord. Perhaps he will

forgive you for having such a thought in your heart. For I see that you are full of bitterness and captive to sin."

Lets breakdown what Peter is actually saying. First Peter curses Simon's life. He declares that Simon's money will perish *with him*. Perish means to die and Peter said it in respects to Simon, not just Simon's money. This isn't looking good.

Next, Peter curses Simon's ministry. He declares that Simon will have no part in "this ministry", which was the ministry that Peter was doing; the great commission and the fulfillment of Matthew 10:8 to, "cleanse the leper, heal the sick, cast out devils, and raise the dead."

Then Peter calls Simon a sinner instead of a saint by telling him that his heart was not right before God and that he was wicked. But Simon was born again and his heart had been cleansed by God. He was no longer a sinner, but God saw him as white as snow. He was a saint. Peter was not seeing Simon as God saw him.

If you aren't convinced this is what was going on in this portion, this next bit will convince you. Peter actually says, *"**Perhaps** the Lord will forgive you…"*

Notice the emphasis on perhaps. Regardless of what sin a person is dealing with, the Bible is clear that God will undoubtedly forgive us of any sin we ask forgiveness for. There is no such thing as perhaps.

We don't know what exactly possessed Peter to say these things, but he was clearly mistaken. One guess is that God was moving in a mighty way at that time and that Peter felt like the man of power of the hour, forgot his own imperfection, forgot about the grace God had shown to him in his own moments of weakness, lost his humility, and got a big head.

On the other hand, Simon's reaction to Peter's rebuke is telling of the condition of his heart. His humble, contrite reply reminds me of a man that falls to his knees in brokenness and meekness:

"Pray to the Lord for me so that nothing you have mentioned may happen to me."

Simon doesn't try to defend himself, but knows that Peter is the "man of God", and humbly submits himself to Peter's opinion, regardless of how off-based it is. Simon knows he doesn't know how Christianity works, so he places himself under Peter's rebuke. There may even be a feeling of fear in Simon's voice, and not the right kind of fear.

What is odd is that scripture doesn't record Peter praying for Simon. Immediately after Simon's reply to Peter's rebuke, scripture says that Peter and John just continued on in their journey.

✛ SIMON'S FUTURE ✛

Because Peter said these things to Simon, and because Simon didn't know that he didn't have to receive Peter's words, Peter's words manifested in Simon's life exactly as Peter prophesied.

Simon is believed to go on and start Gnosticism. Gnosticism presents an extremely destructive way of thinking and living, and was a teaching that said that salvation comes by learning esoteric spiritual truths that free humanity from the material world, which was believed to be evil. This belief system was not only misleading and hurtful to the early church, but its lies still surface with consistency in Christian thought and theology today.

Once we grasp the amount of power our words have, it is no surprise to us that Simon went on to start this heretical teaching. Peter literally cursed Simon's life and ministry, and though Simon didn't die, he never did have a part in the true ministry that every believer is invited into. He had a destiny like anyone that is born again has; infinite intimacy with Christ, signs and wonders, raising the dead, healing the sick, prophesying to others, discipling nations, and empowering the church. Simon's destiny was cut short because Peter cursed him and because Simon didn't recognize a curse when he was dealt one.

Simon should have stood up to Peter and said, "No, I am not evil. I just don't know how Christianity works. I just got born again, remember? I will have a ministry, and it will be full of fruit and truth. I will live long, and I will please God. I am a lover of God, not a hopeless hypocrite. If I can get the Holy Spirit for free, then show me how to receive Him freely!"

+ BUT DID HE MEAN IT? +

Some have questioned the genuineness of Simon's conversion because of what Peter said and because of what Simon did after he was converted. The Bible doesn't say anything about the genuineness of his conversion so we can't assume that, though it is plausible. One thing the Bible does make clear is that Peter didn't stick around to help Simon out. Simon went on to start a heretical movement, but what do we expect from someone that wasn't discipled and was left to figure his faith out on his own? They didn't have the New Testament at that time, so Simon didn't have the advantage of reading it. He was saved out of sorcery and had to fend for himself theologically, so it is no surprise that he comprised a whacked out teaching.

+ HEROD +

Not long after Peter and Simon's run-in, we witness an incident involving Herod that seems to affirm the view that God's wrath and anger still burns towards mankind.

Herod was speaking publicly to a group of people that had hopes of gaining some food from him. In an attempt to gain favor with Herod, the crowd began obsequiously shouting that Herod was a god. Herod was suddenly struck down by an "Angel of the Lord" and eaten by worms because he did not give praise to God. It was not the ending that anyone would desire.

What is going on here? Was God chomping at the bit to take out Herod? Could He not stand Herod's arrogance one moment more and finally, the hammer inevitably fell?

Though Herod was an thoroughly evil man, if God strikes down people for sin, what makes us think that when we don't give glory to God He won't smite us as well? Where is God's goodness in this situation?

There was more going on in the mind of God than the fact that Herod was an evil man. God actually loved Herod. John 3:16 says that, "God so loved the world…" God loves sinners, even unrepentant ones that choose to not submit themselves to God's way. Though some even hate God, He desires that none shall perish (2 Peter 3:9). God did not remove Herod from the earth in anger, or in a lack of love. God is *unable* to take life.

At the same time, sin gives the enemy entrance into our lives. When we sin, we open a door of the house of our life to the enemy. He can come inflict us with the "wages of sin".

Because of the Hebraic view of satan, the writer of Acts wouldn't have made much of a distinction between the devil doing something and God doing it. The "Angel of the Lord" is this passage refers to the spirit of death, or satan himself. It could not have been God's messenger because Jesus told us that God only gives life, never death (John 10:10). God doesn't have death to give (Hebrews 2:14)! Sin gives the enemy entrance, and the wages of sin is death. Live holy, not because God will strike you with lightning if you don't, but because we do not want to give the devil any legal right to afflict us.

In Herod's case, the crowd shouted words that stemmed from selfishness, in hopes that Herod would do something for them if he liked what he heard. They were using Herod. We are called to speak well of our leaders and to encourage them, but not in a way that is deceitful and manipulative through flattery.

If Herod had known the power of the tongue and the implications thereof, he would have rightly resisted the crowd's suggestion, chosen humility, and given praise to God. But because he didn't know what the people's words were doing to his heart, and because he was an evil man that had chosen to give himself to his fleshly desires, he gave into the praise of man, and opened a door for the enemy to bring upon him the "wages of sin", which is death.

Most importantly, God was not the one to kill Herod. We must plow past the basic understanding that God is good and does not do evil things.

+ BAR-JESUS +

In Acts 13:6-12 we are introduced to a Jewish sorcerer and false prophet named Bar-Jesus that was an attendant to the proconsul. The proconsul desired to hear the word of God, so he sent for Paul, Barnabas, and John. Bar-Jesus, also called Elymas, opposed Paul and his comrades in hopes of deterring the proconsul from hearing the Good News. In response, Paul verbally slams Elymas, and as a result of the power of Paul's tongue, Elymas is made blind for a time. The proconsul sees the power of God in Paul's words and as a result, chooses to believe the Gospel they are presenting.

This situation is of a different nature than Ananias and Sapphira's death or Simon's run-in with Peter. Bar-Jesus' situation took place completely within the will of God, while what happened in the cases with Ananias, Sapphira, and Simon were not. If this story isn't understood for what it is, it could be used as leverage to say that Simon, Ananias, and Sapphira's outcomes were God's doing because the situation with Bar-Jesus seems so alike to Peter's interaction with Simon.

The difference between Paul's interaction with Bar-Jesus and Peter's interaction with Simon is that Paul did not curse Bar-Jesus' destiny and life. Paul spoke out a judgment that was nonpermanent, and it was meant to bring about the fruit of repentance in Bar-Jesus' life. Bar-Jesus was hindering the Gospel, wasn't born again, and headed for hell. Paul's release of power upon Bar-Jesus was correct, gracious, and loving because Paul knew that if Bar-Jesus didn't come to repentance, he would spend eternity in hell. Paul made the proclamation with Bar-Jesus' destiny in mind, not to deter him from it. Paul gave Bar-Jesus a healthy wake-up call to the reality of eternity.

In addition, the Bible says that Paul was filled with the Holy Spirit when he spoke the words to Bar-Jesus that he did. Scripture never says that about Peter in either Simon's case or the married couple that died at his feet.

Jesus was very clear in the Gospels that we should not judge others. Christians understand this point because it is so plainly stated in scripture, though curiously the majority of Christianity generally doesn't live by that profession.

A judgment is when we make a decision about another person's state of heart or the motives behind their actions. Most of the time we will be wrong in our decision, which leads us to assume evil about another person. This kind of decision-making is detestable in the sight of the Lord.

Though they may never speak them out, most people's heart and mind are full of thoughts towards others that do not line up with what The Father says about them. The fact that their decisions about someone else are unspoken does not change the fact that they are still judgments. Anytime that we give ourselves to believing something about someone that God doesn't believe about them, we are endangering their lives and tainting the purity of our hearts through judgment. This is one reason why we are told to take every thought captive.

At the same time, in John 7:24 Jesus gave us a holy, paradoxical contradiction by telling us to make right judgments. Right judgments are judgments about others that are not made through mere appearances (the natural realm, the flesh, etc), but through love and honor (seeing people the way God sees them). What Paul did was a right judgment, hoping that Bar-Jesus would turn from his sin and come to Christ. It had love written all over it. Paul could have either loosed this blindness on Bar-Jesus, or watched Bar-Jesus waste his life and spend eternity without God.

Paul had discernment, but unlike Peter in previous cases, applied it in a way that benefited the one that he was discerning. He used his discernment to lead him to a right judgment, not a judgment that harmed the person's life.

+ BREAKING THE RULES +

There was a season of my life when I was a substitute teacher at the local public high school. At times I would have witches in my classes. I would articulate the Gospel plainly in class, telling stories of times I had witnessed God work miracles. As I would release testimonies, the witches would get out books about witchcraft and lay them out on their desks. I noticed that shortly after every time I spoke to a class with these witches present I would go through a period of dryness and depression. I started contemplating the possibility that these witches were cursing me.

My situation prompted me to ask a mentor of mine what he thought about curses. My mentor quoted the verse from Proverbs 26:2,

"Like a fluttering sparrow or darting swallow, an undeserved curse does not come to rest."

He went on to explain that if a curse is undeserved it has no authority to come upon another person, thus I should not be affected by what the young women were doing in my classroom.

But if it was as simple as my mentor made it out to be, then why was I struggling after the classes that had witches in them and not the other classes? And why were there godly people in my life that were clearly cursed if a curse couldn't rest upon someone that didn't deserve it?

Here is an example. I know a wonderful missionary family that had lived in Nigeria their whole lives. Life had been good for them, but one arbitrary day it all changed. Since that day, they had been going through hell for years, and eventually had to move off the mission field because they were under such incredible assailment. They were a holy, loving, wonderful family that was giving it all for Jesus, yet their lives had fallen apart in the drop of a hat. In a period of a few years they had been plagued with serious sicknesses, experienced deaths in their family, gotten in numerous car accidents, and been robbed at gunpoint as their children were forced to watch a family friend as she was raped. The list went on and on. Every month something extravagantly detrimental would take place to someone in their family. The way that horror pursued their lives was remarkably constant, completely removing the possibility of coincidence. They *had* to be cursed. Either they were in serious sin that I didn't know about, or my mentor's interpretation of this verse was incomplete.

It is a true statement to say that an undeserved curse doesn't have the right to manifest itself upon another person. But I have come to understand that the enemy doesn't care about having the rights to do something or not. He does not play by the rules. Unmerited or not, the enemy comes to steal, kill, and destroy. He doesn't need a reason. He is motivated by hate, not legal rights. The enemy does whatever he wants on Earth until someone enforces the law.

The law enforcers are you and I, because Christ gave us all authority over every sickness and demonic spirit (Matthew 10:1). Until we exert the authority God has given us, the enemy is free to run wild and do whatever he wants to do in the lives of people on Earth. Until we draw the line with the Blood of Christ and take a stand in the authority He has given us, curses, sickness, and death run rampant.

This is why people get sick that haven't done anything to deserve it. This is why people that live holy, God-pleasing lives become ill. If we believe people only get sick or can be cursed because of a sin that has yet to be repented of in their life, we will search their lives to find out what they are doing wrong that would give sickness the authority to attack their life. Before we know it, their healing is dependent upon performance. We find ourselves attributing to the problem by making judgments about the person in hopes of finding the foothold that has allowed the enemy to attack their life. Instead of just standing with them, we pick their life apart, convinced that if we find the right sin for them to repent of, their lives will go back to normal. We mean well, but accidentally add to the problem rather than help. We become a detective that questions the victim rather than being the law-enforcer that protects through his authority. This paradigm is born out of being more impressed with the enemy's workings than God's power. The Pharisees were doing the same thing in John 9, when they were searching for the sin that they were convinced was causing the man's blindness. Instead of judging the man, Jesus said that the blindness wasn't caused by a sin in the man's life, nor in life of the parents of the man. Then He said, "Now *let* the work of God be displayed in his life."[2] He flipped the Pharisees thinking upside down, and then revealed that their paradigm was actually keeping people from being healed!

The enemy doesn't play by the rules and attacks whomever he desires. In fact, the enemy will chase after people that are living out the fullness of the Gospel *more* than he does with people lost in sin. He doesn't need to worry about the addict taking any of his territory, but a Spirit-filled, burning lover of God causes him to have a cardiac arrest. Thus, more of his efforts to destroy are aimed in the direction of God's burning ones. And we wonder why our leaders fall.

We have the authority. He gave it to us; so don't wait for a sovereign moment of salvation out of a notion

---

[2] In John 9:3, when the Greek word, "hina" is stated as an imperative clause rather than a purposive clause, the result is a very different reading than the one we have been handed by the majority of Bible translators over the years. In the purposive it reads, "'Neither this man nor his parents sinned,' said Jesus, 'but this happened so that the work of God might be displayed in his life'", which, as we know, attributes to the origin of the blindness to God, that He would be glorified through it. Yet, in the imperative it reads, "'Neither this man nor his parents sinned,' said Jesus, 'but nonetheless, let the work of God be displayed in his life'". The latter translation of the Greek is just as valid and plausible as the former, yet in addition, consistent with the nature of God. God does not make His kids sick so that He gets more glory, thus, the latter translation is correct.

of that you are powerless. He has given you everything you need to be victorious in this life, so wield it.

+ Late Night Snack +

An example of an undeserved curse is exemplified by a story that took place one night when I was riding back from the beach on my motorcycle.

I felt an urge to stop at a fast food restaurant, though I thoroughly dislike fast food. I got off my bike, wondering why I had stopped. I was suddenly hungry, and decided to try to find something healthy on the menu of this particular restaurant. I sat down with my food, and began to read a few books that I was needing to study for school.

A very large man walked in through the door and ordered some food. As soon as I saw him, I distinctly heard the Lord say, "Go tell him that I love him."

I didn't want to. I wanted to sit there and eat my food, plus the man's unshaven face and overall size was more than intimidating. I told the Lord I wasn't going to go talk to this man. God just laughs at those kinds of "Jonah" prayers. He has a lot of methods of getting His way. Fortunate for me, I was not on a boat.

I continued reading in my book, doing my best to ignore the mounting pressure in my spirit to obey the Lord. I did my best to resist this, until I saw the heading of the next chapter that I was about to read in my book. It was titled, "Taking the Time to Talk to Your Neighbor."

I wrote it off as coincidence and hunkered back down into my world of comfort. I ignored the weight in my heart until the speakers in the restaurant starting playing a song with lyrics that said, "Go talk to the person you don't know. Love is so important."

I couldn't believe it. Regrettably, and full of joy and laughter at God's humor, I stood up and made my way over to the man.

He was eating. I interrupted his meal by saying, "Excuse me sir, I need to tell you that God loves you."

He slowly looked up from his burger and fries. My heart froze. What concerned me more than his worn face and dark bags under his eyes was that he looked very angry that I said what I had said. I thought this guy was going to pummel me, but my feet wouldn't move, so I stood next to him wearing a guise of confidence on my face.

Not just unimpressed by my one-liner but irritated, he said, "Why did you tell me that?" I responded, "Because God made it really clear that I needed to come over here and tell you that exact statement."

In one moment his face went from being cold and hard, to soft and gentle. He began shaking his head in disbelief, and told me to sit down at his table across from him. Quicker than I obeyed the Voice, I did as he said and obediently sat, still in fear of a pummeling. I didn't say much more that night, but listened to him tell his story.

He told me that six years prior to that night he had been a Christian. At that time he was dating a girl that was involved in spiritual issues that he didn't understand, but didn't ask her about what she was dabbling in. One night she told him that she wanted to put a spell on him. It sounded to him more like something out of Snow White than real life. He told her that he didn't believe in spells and that they couldn't do anything to him if they did exist, because he was a Christian. He snickered as he told her that she could whatever she wanted to. He wasn't in sin, just a lack of knowledge.

One night as he slept, she dripped black wax over his back as she murmured some words over him. That is all it took, for the next day he instantly developed an addiction to hardcore drugs he had never tried before. For the next six years, even up until the day I talked to him in the fast food restaurant, he was addicted to speed. He told me that he would stay up for three and four days at a time, renting up to fifteen movies to pass the time.

He related to me that during the past six years of living in hell on Earth, one question had continued to ring out in his in mind and spirit; "Does God still love me?" He told me that God had answered his question that night, and then ended his story with tears, not words.

The man I met in the restaurant did not give an open door to the enemy through sin, yet he was still attacked. I am not pointing this out to cause fear, but to highlight the fact that the enemy doesn't play by the rules. The enemy is as consistent in his character (steal, kill, destroy) as God is in His (good).

Curses are real. The power of the tongue is real. The enemy is real. He hates you because you are made in the image of God and full of enough power to overthrow his entire kingdom. He will try to do anything he can to destroy you.

+ What Do We Do? +

We must know what God would say and what God would not say. Then we know what words to stand against, and what words to receive. If you do not know His voice and the nature of the way that He speaks to us you will receive both blessings and curses, and they will both manifest on your life.

We are not to fear. We are not to be concerned if others curse us. Even if whole churches and covens are praying against you and your ministry, fret not. In fact,

Jesus was so unconcerned about others cursing you that He told you to bless them when they curse you (Luke 6:28).

You have all authority. You have nothing to fear. Not only because greater is He that is within you, but because God has given you the power to verbally break that which is verbally set against you. The moment you break the word curses set against you in the name of Jesus, they fall. A good verse to declare over your life is Isaiah 54:17;

"...no weapon forged against you shall prevail, and you will refute every tongue that accuses you."

You are called to stand against the enemy in the authority God has given you over him. You don't have to fight; Christ already did the warfare on the cross. You simply enforce the rules through His blood.

+ AUTHORITY OVER WORDS AND WITCHCRAFT +

God will be exceedingly victorious through you if you let Him. All it takes is believing that your Dad can beat up anyone else's dad. The enemy has got nothing on you. No man on Earth is more powerful than the Man that possesses you. No demon is strong enough to defeat the Spirit in you. We must believe that God is greater than the enemy. We must believe that God is more impressive in His goodness than the enemy is impressive in his evil. Turn off the evening news if you need to. Get grounded in what God has done, what He is doing, and what He will do.

I actually began to believe that God is greater than any other power in the world. This fact has to be grasped through faith, because life doesn't always reveal this truth. We witness death and chaos daily on the news. Nonetheless, it is true; God is greater. As I started to believe this, I began to see things shift around me.

Once, a few weeks before leaving to minister in California the Lord told me that He wanted to break the powers of witchcraft over that region. A few weeks later in California, I spoke on God's power over evil and witchcraft and gave a few testimonies of times the Lord destroyed witchcraft when it threatened my life. There was a moment in the service when God told me that it was time to destroy witchcraft, so I declared God's vengeance and wrath upon the enemy, and asked for a flood of the Spirit to invade that community. The crowd joined with me in prayer and agreement. As quickly as I had started praying, I ended, then continued speaking. We had some wonderful healings that night, and rejoiced in the Lord's goodness. I knew God had told me to do what I did, but I didn't see any specific evidence that my prayers had done anything pertaining to the enemy's power in that area. The next day we ministered again at another location, and witnessed God's love and Presence pour out again. It was over a month before I found out some of the more bizarre things the Lord did during that time.

An asteroid the size of Earth hit Jupiter around the same time we had prayed together in agreement against witchcraft. Scientists were confounded about this, mainly because they were unsure how they missed the asteroid's approach. This is crucial because years before, a certain man's first meetings were held on the top of a mountain located near the church where I spoke. This man, now passed, was the man that started the church of satan in San Francisco. Being a man of great demonic power, he influenced many to walk a path of extreme darkness and brought evil into our nation to a new degree. The mountain that this man's initial satanic meetings took place on is called Jupiter.

The Bible says that God will bring forth signs in the heavens, but also on Earth (Acts 2:19). As if the asteroid wasn't a clear enough sign of God's victory over witchcraft in that region, a fire also destroyed the forest area around the mountain at the same time we prayed at the church.

God is bigger than the enemy, and abundantly victorious. If you will begin to believe this, He will use you in your city and region to tear down that which the enemy has built in the high places. He will use you to purify the land, get the witches saved and delivered, and escort your community into the blessings that God desires to pour out on your town, city, and state. You have authority over every ill word spoken into your own life, but also the words spoken out by those that have set themselves against the plan of God.

+ RECAP +

To wrap up this chapter, lets go over few of the main points presented.

Blessing others is an extremely important facet of the Christian life. We have the authority to bless or to curse with our words. Our words carry power on them, so much so that Proverbs 18:21 tells us that, "Death and life are in the power of the tongue..." This is a literal statement. We either speak life over people by blessing them, or we destroy them with the power that God has given us in our words. We can raise the dead or fill graveyards.

The apostle Peter was given extraordinary power that was meant to build up the newly born church in Acts. The covenant of grace was a new idea to Peter, and he reverted back to a mindset of law and death when he misused his authority with Ananias and Sapphira in Acts 5:1-11. Like any good leader would do, Peter could have taken Ananias and Sapphira aside and calmly talked to them about their error in keeping some of their money from the apostles when they sold some property. In doing so, Peter's kindness would have led them to repentance and the situation would have been redeemed. Instead, he functioned out of law and punishment and spoke out words of judgment upon this couple. In doing so, Peter killed them. What Peter did is called christian witchcraft; it is anytime our declarations, words, and thoughts do not line up with the heart of God about another person. Our words and judgments about others can physically affect them (as well as emotionally and spiritually), even to the point of death.

We must read the New Testament without an Old Testament mentality about God. Jesus already paid the price for sin. No sin is too big for His Grace to cover it. No sin reaches past the realm of God's forgiveness. If God forgives rapists, murderers, and terrorists today, what makes us think that God wasn't eager to forgive Ananias and Sapphira for their sin of withholding some of their own money? They lied, but haven't you? If you believe that God struck them dead for lying, how does that help confirm in your heart that He won't strike you dead when you lie? Be rid of reading this passage through old lenses. God is love. He is good. Give Him the benefit of the doubt.

I used to read Acts 5 in a way that tried to justify God killing Ananias and Sapphira by the severity of their sin. Then I realized that God forgives rapists, child molesters, murders, and abusive spouses today, so surely He forgives people for not giving all the money that they appear to be giving. If He killed Ananias and Sapphira for a sin as small as keeping some of their own money for themselves, then you and I should be toast.

For years I thought that the fear that swept over the church after Ananias and Sapphira died was a pure and holy thing. I realize now that I was wrong. Having fear that God will kill you if you sin is not only an incorrect belief about God, but it will also never bring you closer in relationship with God. The Fear of God and the fear that God will kill you if you sin could not be further in likeness from one another. The former comes from Heaven, the latter from hell.

The unsaved world doesn't need judgment and criticism, but kindness that will lead them to repentance. After all, was it God's anger and wrath that brought you to your knees in repentance, or was it the fact that He showed His love to you by sending His son to die for you, despite your problems?

"The purpose of theology is to make love our only
option." -Richard Murray

*"Then Moses said, 'Now show me your glory.' And the LORD
said, "I will cause all my goodness to pass in front of you..."*
Exodus 33:18-19

I f our view of God isn't too good to be true, then
our view of God is most likely not true. Most of us
whole-heartedly agree with the statement, "God is good,
all the time", and would cringe if someone said anything
less. Oddly enough, people also cringe when people
overstate the goodness of God. Don't believe me? Read on.
This chapter will highlight not only the goodness of God,
but also some of the beliefs that we hold to that contradict
our confession, "God is good".

In general, modern-day Christianity has not
walked in the power that the early church possessed, nor
demonstrated the "greater works" Christ promised us in
John 14:12. Paul made it clear that the Kingdom of God
is not ministered to others through enticing words of
wisdom but by the *demonstration* of God's power (1 Cor.
2:4-5, 1:17, 4:20, 1 Thes. 1:5). It is sobering, for the most
part we no longer have a gospel that is demonstrative, but
one that is primarily talk. Paul made it clear that this
wasn't the best way to reveal God to the nations. God
desires to make Himself known through *tangible*
demonstration of His power and love. Unknowingly, we

have been holding to a form of godliness and have denied the power and love of God to flow from our lives. We have become comfortable with settling for less than what God offers to His people.

Why has this happened? Could it be that we don't *really* believe in our hearts that He is good? Though we repetitively make the profession, "God is good, all the time" when within the walls of our churches, reminiscent of a caged parrot, could it be that we aren't totally convinced that He is holistically good? If we aren't truly convinced of God's goodness there is no way that we will ever have sincere faith, thus there will be no demonstration, as the majority of believers exemplify.

Consequently, our main deficiency in reaching the world with a demonstrative gospel is rooted in our lack of understanding the goodness of God. The knowledge of His goodness must become more than a traditional guise that we wear at the masquerade of church. His goodness has to become a deeply set conviction that we carry in the reservoir of our heart. There is no better time than now to gain this precious revelation, for the world is in dire need of the Church to reveal God as He is; gentle, full of kindness, compassionate, loving, and most of all, good. The world is screaming out for someone to show them a God that is good. It is the desire of every human heart.

Thus, a true revelation of the goodness of God is the primary need for the Church. This revelation may not be found by the masses to be very palatable, as Moses showed us when he prayed for God to show him His glory. The Lord responded to Moses' request by saying that He would cause His goodness to pass before Moses, revealing that in the mind of God, His glory and His goodness were the same substance. Then the Lord had to hide Moses in the cleft of a rock, and even cover him with His hand. Why did God keep Moses from seeing all of

His goodness? It seems if anything should be held back from man, it should not be the reality of God's goodness.

Could it be that God's goodness is the most Earth shattering revelation, the ultimate offender to our traditional ways of thinking about God? Could it be that this revelation is the most dismantling revelation in the world? I would suggest that God couldn't unveil the fullness of His nature to Moses because Moses wouldn't have been able to handle it. It is as though Moses wasn't ready for it. Are you?

Faith is the result of genuinely believing that God is good. If a person believes in their heart that God is always good, faith is not a struggle but a natural, instinctive response. If you can believe that God is good, no tragedy or loss will ever be able to overcome you. With this single revelation, no demon in hell will be able to stop you. No sin will ever look enticing enough to lure you into compromise. No sickness will loom larger in your mind than the health that was purchased by Christ's costly, precious blood. No body, regardless of how long it has been without life, will be able to cause you to second-guess God's ability and desire to raise it to life.

God is good, and I don't say that as the cliché statement it has become. I say it with the knowledge that it is probably one of the most offensive declarations in history. The implications to that statement, when drawn out to their fullness, are intensely provoking to traditions and doctrines held by men. I actually mean it when I say, "God is good", with no conflicting theology behind that statement.

God is completely good. Life will try to convince you otherwise. Doctrines contrived through unbelief rather than faith will attempt to subtly undermine your ability to believe that He is good. Christians may unknowingly try to talk you out of this precious revelation. It is the key to the power of God and the secret to unlock the freedom that comes from being wholly loved. If a person can truly believe that God is good and have a way of reading the Bible that is congruent to that belief, nothing will be impossible for them. For this person, raising the dead, killing giants, saving whole nations in a day, and even literal flying are nothing more than a walk in the park.

In 2 Chronicles 5:13-14, it was when the people of God began to declare the goodness of God that the Lord showed up in His heavy, weighty glory. The cloud of God came into the temple so heavily that the priests were unable to perform their services to the Lord. God wants to convince you of His unwavering goodness to the point where you unashamedly declare His goodness, then are undone by the weighty Presence that follows. As we declare the truth about Him, He shows up. Suddenly, our agenda goes out the window, our "services" to Him become enjoying Him, and the glory of the Lord rests on our lives. To the extent that you are convinced of His goodness is the extent to which His weighty Presence and glory will rest upon your life.

✛ THE FOUNDATION TO FAITH ✛

Faith is the result of believing that God is good. The goodness of God is like the foundation that the house of faith is built upon. Without it, the house falls when the storms of adversity come. Unshakable faith is birthed out of a revelation that God is always, completely and totally, good. If you want to have true faith that can throw mountains and work miracles, you must first unwaveringly believe that He is good.

Someone being good or bad is as simple as it gets. Children play cops and robbers, picking their side according to if they feel like they want to be the bad guy that day, or the good guy. Relationships are built or dismantled by the simplistic determining factor of if someone is a good or a bad person. In fact, the most basic judgment that humans make is if someone is a good person or a bad person. You hear it being said in classrooms to courtrooms: "Oh, he is a good kid. A little confused perhaps, but a good kid." "That guy is a bad man. Who would do such a thing?" It is the most basic concept when talking about any kind of being: are they good, or are they bad?

Yet this very point is confused in the body of Christ when dealing with the nature of God. We profess with our mouths that God is good, but our beliefs contradict what we profess. We say that He is good, then we attribute to Him the bad things that happen in our lives and in the world. We see storms as an act of God's judgment upon evil cities, loved ones being taken prematurely as God's mysterious way of telling us that it was their divine time to go, and disease as a tool of refinement in the hand of God. How, when we attribute these things to God, can we turn around and profess to the world that He is good? How can we have true faith? How can we blame God for these events and say He is good in the same breath, all the while knowing that thousands of people died in the storm in question, or that the loved one that died left behind a husband and three small children, or that the disease crippled that man so badly that he was never able to hold his wife again?

+ OUR CONTRADICTIVE BELIEFS +

We have gotten so confused as Christians that we have forgotten what is bad and what is good when we walk inside the walls of a church.

Disease is bad. Nobody likes to be sick. All week long a person may go to the doctor, fighting a physical problem with their body, but when they walk into church on Sunday morning, they suddenly accept their ailment and sometimes even thank God for it. Christians can be more schizophrenic than those in mental hospitals!

Jesus thanked the Father for revealing truth to children, rather than us older, "wiser", more learned, adults (Luke 10:21). This means that kids actually know things that adults have lost sight of. In light of this, ask a child if disease and death are horrible things if you are beginning to lose sight of what is good and what is bad in the world. Without fail, they will always tell you that they are bad. A child sees things as they are. They haven't been infected by faithless reasoning like many adults have.

Disease leads to death. Premature death leaves families broken and incomplete. Storms kill people, destroy homes, set nations back fifteen years, and make countless thousands of children as orphans. It doesn't take much discernment to see that these things are not good.

If God is good all the time like we profess, then He doesn't, even can't, deal out bad things to His children. Some people believe it is God's will for them to be sick, or that He gave them a disease like cancer, but God doesn't give people cancer. He doesn't have it to give! In heaven there is no cancer, so even if He wanted to give it to you, He wouldn't be able to obtain any! There aren't any cancer rooms in heaven where the Father goes and grabs a little sample and sends it down to a son or daughter on Earth in order to refine their character or teach them spiritual lessons. You, being a human that was born into sin, wouldn't do that to your child. No good father on Earth would ever even dream of doing such a thing. How much more good is God than us?

We aren't even convinced in the church that God is as good as the people we know. *If* we could start with this fundamental truth, we would find ourselves building our house on the Rock. Sadly though, the majority of the church has not discovered the bliss of this reality. Once we have this foundational aspect in place, we can begin to receive the revelation that God tremendously surpasses the goodness of those around us that have loved us well. Our crediting to Him things that are less than loving and good ceases, because we realize that our friends and parents would never wish anything less upon us except what is good. We start to understand that if they wouldn't do such a thing, neither would God.

If God did the things that much of the church says He does, He would be up for child abuse in the court of heaven. Yet the majority of the church continues to teach in this way.

Everything He does is good…good at face value. People say, "Well, God works in mysterious ways" when they are faced with something in life that doesn't seem to reveal God's goodness at face value.

God *does* work in mysterious ways, but not in bad mysterious ways, GOOD mysterious ways! Leave the working of bad mysterious ways to the enemy. Let the Hindus and Muslims say that of their gods, but don't say it of the Father.

It is amazing how much believers will unknowingly argue against the fact that God is good. You can ask them point blank if God is good, and they will say yes. But then if you ask them who is responsible for a loved one's death in their family, or who gave their aunt that disease, or why that child was killed on the highway, they will likely have some kind of doctrine that ascribes God as the responsible party. Not only will they openly blame God, but they will defend their view ardently.

It isn't that much of the church doesn't believe that God is good, but that much of the church has never taken the time to think about the logical conclusions that their professions lead to. If God is good, that implies a whole lot of things that they don't believe in, like raising the dead, healing the sick, and casting out demons (Matthew 10:8). Truly believing that God is good leads a person to the conclusion that He doesn't want His children sick and dying, and that the enemy is responsible instead of God. Therefore a person holding this understanding is immediately drafted into the Army of the Lord. This army does not fight against people, but the enemy's manifestations on Earth mentioned in verses like Matthew 10:8; sickness, death, and demonic oppression.

+ EXAGGERATING HIS GOODNESS +

The closer a person comes to Jesus the more they become aware how of how good He is. In simultaneous occurrence, the person also becomes aware of how little they know about the goodness of God. It becomes clear to this person that there is more to learn pertaining to His goodness than we could ever grapple or experience. His goodness could never be exaggerated, for it is endless. We will continue to discover new aspects of His goodness for not just a few hundred thousand years in heaven, but for billions and billions of centuries. The revelation of His goodness will never be exhausted, and can never be overstated.

Once I was spending time alone with the Lord and He told me, "I am good. I am *so* good that I am heretically good." I laughed at the humor of the Lord in that statement. He was making a clear point that for many in the Body of Christ, God's goodness only extends so far. To them, we can only go so far in communicating God's goodness, and going further than that is stretching it, exaggerating, verging on being heretical.

Most of the church sees God's goodness mysteriously limited by His judgment, wrath, and punishment. We put on a guise and say "God is good" while believing in the back of our mind that there are conditions upon His goodness and grace. Even our idea of justice has been tainted, not fully submitted first and foremost to the reality of the goodness of God, resulting in a God that does unspeakable things to horrible people for justice's sake.

But He is faithfully good. There is no shadow of turning in Him (James 1). Faith is impossible without having faith in something that is consistently good. Faith comes from Him being *faith*ful, or consistent. He is consistent in being good, that is why we can always put our faith in Him. Our God is consistent, predictable, and even faithful in His goodness. You can always bank on God to be good and to will what is good, all the time. But if you have a belief system that puts conditions and limitations upon God's goodness, you will never have true faith that will bring the Kingdom to Earth.

+ HOW TO READ THE BIBLE +

Everything that He does is good, because He is good. The only kind of theology that is holistically true and most accurate is one built upon the foundation of God's goodness. This goodness is revealed through the life of Jesus Christ. We must read the Bible through these lenses. If we are reading the Bible in a way that doesn't reinforce that God is a loving, caring, compassionate Father, then we are reading the Bible wrongly. More importantly, if our understanding of any scripture in the Bible, Old Testament or New, contradicts what Jesus portrayed to us through His life on Earth, it is misled. As Bill Johnson says, Jesus Christ is perfect theology. Jesus revealed *who* the Father is, despite what we think other portions of scripture showed Him to be. Jesus is the theological trump card.

Lets face it; a person can get anything they want out of the scriptures. People have used the Bible to legitimize genocide, drug use, the formation of cults, and just about any other evil thing that is conceived in the fallen heart of man. Once a person is convinced that *God* approves of what they believe, they are virtually unstoppable, functioning in the same spirit as the Pharisees. Just as a person can reinforce a misled belief about sin through scripture, men can also use scripture to reinforce their misled beliefs about God. This is where it gets especially dangerous.

For example, a person can either believe that God avenges His servants that were killed (Rev. 6:9-11), or that He forgives those who kill His servants (Luke 23:34). Both passages give different implications to the nature of God, but the example we have in Christ is always love, grace, and life. Another example; you can either believe that God is a cannibal that eats His enemies (Rev. 19:17-18), or that God loves His enemies (Matthew 5:43-48, Luke 23:34). There are countless contradictory examples like these in the Bible, but rest assured, for every verse in the Bible that seems to reveal God as a killer, harsh judge, condemning king, or cruel master that disposes of his children's lives as he pleases, there are many more statements or examples given through Jesus that speak contrary to what those verses seem to say. Actually, contrary to our assumptions, there are many more verses in the Bible that communicate God's goodness than God's wrath and damnation. It just takes eyes to see and ears to hear in order to have their obvious presence recognized.

The point is that if a person wants, they are able to believe that God isn't good and reinforce it through misread verses in the Bible. A first glance, scripture seems to clearly affirm this. If a person desires to, they are able to drag verse after verse out of the Bible that discredits and diminishes His goodness to a degree that is digestible and comprehendible to the fallen human mind. Frankly, it isn't hard to do. It takes little wisdom, revelation, or intelligence to read the Bible in a way that inadvertently condemns God for things that He did not do. And as long as we assume control over how good He really is through the misreading of scriptures, we don't have to change our own hearts. We are called to be like Him, and if He is unrelentingly good, it implies that we have to actually change. Overall, it is easier to just have an angry, condemning God.

So, the choice is yours. You can seek out a matter and act like a king in the Kingdom (Proverbs 25:2), in which the glory of God will be naturally attracted to you, or you can unquestioningly eat what you are fed, thus producing whatever comes out the other end; waste.

In order to read the Bible correctly, we have to let God's character define the scriptures as opposed to letting the scriptures define God's character. Jesus revealed the character of God to us. Everything we read in the Bible needs to be seen through the "lenses" of Jesus. The Holy Spirit, who teaches us all things, reveals Jesus to us as we read scripture, and Jesus reveals to us the true identity and nature of the Father.

We may not always have the answers for why God did what He did, but when faced with uncertainty or mystery we cannot jump to the conclusion that God is responsible for something that was evil. That is the only *impossible* option. As C.S. Lewis said,

"Two things one must not do are to believe on the strength of scripture, or any other evidence that God is in any way evil, and to wipe off the slate any passage that seems to show that He is. Behind the passage be sure there lurks some great truth which you don't understand. If one does come to understand it, one sees that it is good and just and gracious in ways we never dreamed of. Till then it must be left on one side."[3]

+ THE TRUMP CARD +

So what is the answer? Where do we draw the line with what the Father would do, and what He would not do? Additionally, who are we to decide if something the Father does is fundamentally good or bad when we are so limited in understanding and He is sovereign and all knowing?

Jesus is the answer; the theological trump card. He is how we determine what the Father did and what the Father didn't do. He is our measuring stick for understanding the Father's goodness. He is how we interpret the rest of scripture. He is the model of how to live our own lives. Regardless of what Paul, Moses, David, or anyone else wrote in the Bible, if it doesn't line up with who Jesus revealed the Father to be, it is mistaken. Christ is "the image of the invisible God" (Colossians 1:15), fully replicating the character of the Father.

Jesus didn't just come to Earth to die for our sins. Dying for our sins wasn't His only goal to accomplish while walking the earth in flesh. *He came to reveal the Father.* Jesus is the ultimate, most accurate representation of the Father. Jesus said,

"You diligently study the Scriptures because you think that by them you possess eternal life. These are the Scriptures that testify about me, yet you refuse to come to me to have life." John 5:39-40

---

[3] Excerpt from "Letters of C.S. Lewis"

As is true today, people in Jesus' day were deifying the scriptures. Jesus corrected them and revealed that life was found in Him, and if the scriptures were not leading the readers to Him, they were useless. It is wild, but the Old Testament was about Christ, every word.

"And beginning with Moses and all the Prophets, he explained to them what was said in all the Scriptures concerning himself." Luke 24:27

In Matthew 5 Jesus clearly declares that what He says is superior to the scriptures. Repeatedly He says, "You have heard it was said..." (referring directly to the scriptures), then adds "But I say unto you..." and follows that statement with a greater truth than what the people had gained from scripture. Jesus *fulfilled* scripture; He had the right to add more truth to it because He *is* the Truth. The implication the reality captured in Matthew 5 is dramatic and weighty; it means that if something in scripture seems to contradict what Jesus taught or exemplified in His life, then we must choose the example Jesus set forth rather than the understanding we have of what scripture says. Time and time again I have witnessed that the thing that most trips up people from receiving the full revelation of the goodness of God is their inability to choose what Jesus exemplified and taught over their understanding of scripture. Jesus is still the stumbling block. Jesus causes all men to either choose Him or continue to worship their idols. Sadly, one of those idols can be scripture. Men can exult the truth in scripture, or the Truth Himself. Honor both the word and the Word, but hold high the Word over everything else. St. Augustine said, "Christ is not valued at all unless He is valued above all."

Jesus advocated us reading scripture one-way: through the "lenses" of Himself. You cannot read the Old Testament apart from letting them testify in some way of Jesus. This is a bold statement, but if you read Job or anything else in the Bible in a way that doesn't lead you to Christ, stop reading it. Anything not Christ-centered makes something else the center. The spirit of the anti-Christ loves to put anything in the spotlight apart from Jesus, even scripture. Don't fall for it. Truth is not firstly an idea or a book, but a Person.

This is why if there is something in the scriptures that doesn't line up with who Jesus was when He was on Earth (non-violent, loving, non-judgmental, free from wrath), or what He taught (love your enemies, forgive those that mistreat you), it needs to be put in submission to the greater Revelation; Christ. Prioritize how you read scripture. Put Christ and who He revealed the Father to be at the top. It's all true, but not all truth is created equal. This is why Christ spoke of Himself and said that,

"No one has ever seen God, but God the One and Only, who is at the Father's side, has made Him known." John 1:18

Though the writers of the Bible had seen some of who God was and incorporated that into the scriptures, Jesus made it clear that they understood very little about the God they wrote about. He distinguished Himself as the only true representation of God and in addition, He communicated that He was the *only one* that had seen and understood God's nature, because He was at the Father's side, watching Him, interacting with Him, and knowing Him. It is a bold statement, but Jesus is the *only* one that has made God known as He is. As C.S. Lewis said, "It is Christ Himself, not the Bible, who is the true Word of

God. The Bible, read in the right spirit and with the guidance of good teachers, will bring us to Him."[4]

Lets face it...Jesus is the only one that really knew God's character in fullness, for He was the only one that hung out with Him for limitless amounts of time. If Jesus said something of the Father, surely it was true, and any other paradigm of God that opposes the view that Jesus brought must bow its knee and surrender. In fact, *the* message that John and the disciples witnessed through being with Jesus on Earth was that there is no evil in the Father; that He is only good.

"This is the message we have heard from him and declare to you: God is light; in him there is no darkness at all." 1 John 1:5

John is making a distinguishing, remarkable point. He is telling his readers that he spent considerable time with Jesus, and after the years of learning from Him and watching Him, John had deducted that the essence of the overall message of what Jesus was trying to communicate to mankind was that *God is good* and was incapable of evil or darkness. The reason John is saying this is because *men didn't believe that.* His readers had read the scriptures and thought that God was capable of doing anything, evil or good, even kill babies at points. John clarifies to his readers that despite what they think they have known or understood of God, that *Jesus* made it clear that it is impossible that God would have any darkness in Him. John tells us that *this* is THE message, or gospel.

The word gospel means "good news". The good news that John is communicating to his readers in 1 John 1:5 isn't just that Jesus came to die for our sin, but that

---

[4] Excerpt from "Letters of C.S. Lewis"

God was/is wholly different than we have assumed; completely good with no shadow of turning in Him. That is good news; that God won't give you sickness to refine your character or kill you if you sin. The good news is that God loves you much more than you ever thought possible. The good news, or gospel of Jesus Christ, is that God is good. This means He is incapable of doing things you wouldn't do to your kids, at the very least.

+ THE SON OF GOD +

Jesus is the Son of God. This is a widely understood, even obvious, theological point in Christianity. Have you ever thought about why? In practical terms, why is it so important that Jesus is the Son of The Father? This is why; if Jesus is the Son of God, then He represents who God is, and our view of the Father must drastically change till He is as good as Jesus was while on Earth. Jesus being the Son of God is an imperative because it correctly adjusts our view of the Father. Islam believes everything about Jesus that Christians do, *except* for the fact that He is the Son of God. The theological result is an angry god that commands his followers to annihilate infidels. I want to suggest to the reader that without the revelation of the Father that we received from Christ, *because He is the Son of God*, we would have the same view of the Father that Muslims have of their god. Judaism is not unlike Islam in that their conclusive view of the Father is an angry, distant god that functions through the nature of the Law rather than grace, all because they do not receive Christ as *the* Messiah and Son of God. We have a God that is clarified through the Christ, a uniquely imperative point.

Ever wondered what exactly was taking place on that mountain when Jesus and His boys sauntered up on its peaks?

Lets set the scene. Jesus brought to the mountaintop some of the key players that would one-day help lead the church (Peter, James, and John), as well as write portions of the Bible. He knew these three desperately needed the revelation that was about to be given to them if they were to wisely facilitate the move of God in Acts. They were about to get a theological overhaul.

Elijah and Moses show up. The reason these two specific characters from the past showed up was because they most accurately represented "The Law and the Prophets". Moses was the mediator of the Mosaic Law, and Elijah walked in the signs and wonders that are so emblematic of the prophetic ministry. Between these two, the Old Testament is represented because it was, "The Law and the Prophets". Everything that Peter, James, and John knew about God from their scriptures was standing in front of them, represented by Moses and Elijah.

Jesus is transfigured, demonstrating that He is no mere man. It was in *this* context that the Father spoke from Heaven and said, "This is my son. Listen to Him!"

The Father communicates two major points to these onlookers. First, Jesus is the Son of God. This implies that Jesus and the Father have the same genetic makeup; goodness and love. When the Father told Peter, James, and John that Jesus was His son, He was saying that Christ was born of His nature, a perfect representation of His character.

Secondly, the Father speaks audibly from Heaven to make a drastic point; Jesus carries greater revelation than the Old Testament, or anything else for that matter. With the two scriptural characters present that most accurately represented the Law and the Prophets, the Father tells the future leaders of the church *to listen to Jesus*. Having to spell it out for these three bystanders, the Father makes it clear that there is a need to prioritize biblical revelation. The Father communicates that to understand who He is, they needed to listen to Jesus first and foremost. The Father doesn't mention the two great leaders of the Old Testament, but virtually overlooks them as He gives all glory to Jesus.

Jesus is the answer to all of the questions in our heart and mind about the goodness of God. Look to Him, and the smoke clears. Look to Him and the veil is lifted.

+ GOD'S JUDGMENT AND WRATH +

God's wrath and judgment is commonly misunderstood in the Church. God does not punish or deal out His wrath to any person, believer or not. Jesus died so that we would be free of sin, which keeps the enemy from being able to have entrance to our life and inflict *his* wrath upon us. It was *never* the judgements of God that were stealing, killing, and destroying (John 10:10), but the enemy. Jesus came to clarify that point. If we can't stomach *that*, we may as well omit Christ from our theology thus leaving us with Judaism.

God is not angry with mankind when he is in sin. He is broken for him. He is not resisting mankind and turning His face from them, He loves them, to the fullest. He is not destroying sinners, He is raising up lovers that know how to impart His life and love to the lost. In fact, it could be easily argued that neither the Father nor the Son are judging humanity in the way that religion convinced us He is. The below verse reveals the Father's endeavor pertaining to judgement:

Moreover, the Father judges no one, but has entrusted all judgment to the Son..." John 5:22

Did you catch that? The Father does not judge anyone. He has given that responsibility to Jesus. Thus let us look at what Jesus does with that responsibility. Jesus is speaking in the following two verses.

"I judge no man." John 8:15

"As for the person who hears my words but does not keep them, I do not judge him. For I did not come to judge the world, but to save it." John 12:47

Gloriously, Jesus refuses to judge the world either. He wonderfully misplaces the responsibility given to Him by His Dad, and both simply skirt the issue. See, God is smart; He knows that there is no need to judge the world because there are already enough repercussions inherent in sin to sufficiently balance the scales of justice. You aren't punished for your sins but by them.

God isn't judging the world; He is saving it. And everyday His desire builds to extend that saving grace to those caught in sin and evil. His anger is not building; His power to free those caught in bondage is.

But don't misunderstand me, God's wrath and judgment are still alive and well today, and still very much at work in the world presently, just not in the way we traditionally think. God's wrath and judgment are being exerted *against that which harms His children, not towards His children.* Believer or not, all are children of God, made in His image.

He *is* a God of Justice, but only in ways that benefit us. He uses His wrath, anger, judgment, and sense of justice to destroy what tries to destroy us and to hurt us, but it is never aimed at men. What father would not bring justice to a situation where his son or daughter was being harmed? What husband would not burn with anger, wrath, and vengeance against someone that was attempting to harm, rape, and murder his bride? God's anger is very much alive today; *it just isn't aimed at you.* The enemy is the focus of God's rage, and God will exert this anger upon him until the total demise of his kingdom and existence.

Jesus, as He publicly quoted from Isaiah 61 in Luke 4, highlighting what His heart, calling, and motives in ministry were, also revealed something about God's punishment and vengeance. Have you ever noticed that Jesus quoted the start of Isaiah 61, but He conveniently stopped right at the part where the chapter mentions God's vengeance?

"The Spirit of the Lord GOD is upon me, Because the LORD has anointed me To bring good news to the afflicted; He has sent me to bind up the brokenhearted, To proclaim liberty to captives And freedom to prisoners; To proclaim the favorable year of the LORD." Luke 4:18

*"The Spirit of the Lord GOD is upon me, Because the LORD has anointed me To bring good news to the afflicted; He has sent me to bind up the brokenhearted, To proclaim liberty to captives And freedom to prisoners; To proclaim the favorable year of the LORD, **and the day of vengeance of our God...**"* Isaiah 61

A period has never been used so boldly. Jesus quoted only a portion of Isaiah 61:2 not because He didn't believe in God's vengeance, wrath, and punishment, but because if He had quoted this portion of the verse to the people listening, they would have thought of God the same way that they always had; angry, vengeful, eager to end their little lives for their sin. Jesus knew that God only destroys that which harms His children, but the people listening would have interpreted Jesus' words as God exerting wrath towards *them* rather than their enemies. In other words, if Christ had quoted the latter portion of the verse, the traditional mindset that He had come to change in the institutionalized people of the day would have been reinforced once again. Instead, He just left that part of scripture out. He closed the book and sat down, and all the eyes of the people were fixed on him. Why were they all staring at Him? Probably because they wondered why He stopped reading when He did. He made quite a statement about the wrath of God by closing the book and sitting down. He simply left God's vengeance out.

Have you ever notice that Jesus never manifested the wrath of God while He was on Earth? He never struck anyone by a lightening bolt because of their sin. In fact, He never had the need to slay anyone! Instead, when His disciples wanted to call down fire upon a village He rebuked them! Then told His disciples that He wasn't like the enemy; He did not come to destroy men's lives, but to save them. (Luke 9:54-56 NASB). He didn't stone the adulterous woman for her overt sin, which confounds those with old wineskin thinking. Sometimes we think that God being holy means that He must destroy sin in order to stay holy. Jesus was completely and totally holy, but wasn't threatened by sin. In fact, He hung out with the unholy crowd.

+ WRATH TOWARDS THE ACTS OF THE ENEMY +

Once, I had a face-to-face encounter with the devil himself. He stood before me and began to explain to me why he chose to fall rather than serve God. He was incredibly articulate, intelligent, and persuasive. I found myself mesmerized by his words. Unbelievably, a short way into his speech, his reasoning actually began to make sense because he was so influential and subtly evil. Suddenly, I realized that no matter what he was saying, he was the devil, and I needed to end this talk. I held a sword in my hand. At full speed, I charged him and swung my sword at his jugular as hard as my strength enabled me. My goal was for his head to roll. The sword buried itself into the devil's neck, but stopped short of cutting all the way through. Years later I asked the Lord why I wasn't able to kill the devil, for greater is He that is within me than he that is in the world. The Lord's reply surprised me. He told me that He was the one that stopped the blade from slicing all the way through. I couldn't imagine why God would do that. Later I learned that He doesn't function through the use of death, and will not, has not, and will never condone its use, even when dealing with the most evil being in existence. His ways are higher than ours. Even the Bible does not record that God kills or destroys the enemy, but rather that He throws him into a bottomless pit where the enemy will not be able to steal, kill, and destroy any longer. In fact, there is an instance in Mark 5 where Jesus actually *had mercy* on a legion of demons that are possessing a man. Chew on that one for awhile!

There are verses in the Bible that talk about the "wrath of God" resting upon people, but that statement isn't saying that God's wrath is being directed upon people. It is a matter of semantics. Just as the "knowledge of God" doesn't refer to the knowledge that God has, but rather the knowledge we have of God, the "wrath of God" doesn't refer to God's wrath towards His children, but the wrath His children have towards Him. When humans are in sin and rebellion, they become offended with God, and anger begins to stew in their hearts. This is the "wrath of

God"; not that He feels wrathful towards us, but that man without Christ is wrathful towards God.

+ GOD THE KILLER? +

God is the same yesterday, today, and forever (Heb. 13:8). Many of us in the body of Christ have matured to the place of understanding that if God healed people in the past, then He is healing people today because He does not change. At the same time, this wonderful verse could also imply something else if we believe that God used death to accomplish His purposes in the past; if God killed people in the past, then He would be killing people today, for He does not change. Moreover, He will be killing people for eternity in heaven, because the verse says, "…and forever." That doesn't sit right with anyone, does it? Being knocked off in heaven by the Guy that invited you there? That is like being kicked out of your own wedding reception party by the wedding planner himself.

Either God killed in the past, kills today, and will kill forever, or He doesn't and never did. I would suggest that because the Lord says in Revelations 21:4 that there will be no death in heaven and that God isn't destroying people in paradise, He never did because He is the same yesterday, today and forever.

"He will wipe every tear from their eyes. There will be no more death or mourning or crying or pain…"

Despite what our understanding of scripture tells us, whether pertaining to Old Testament verses or New, God does not kill. Ending life is outside of the character of God. It contradicts God's nature to kill.

"The devil comes only to steal, kill, and destroy. I have come that they may have abundant life." John 10:10

The enemy kills, but God will not stoop to the enemy's way of doing things in order to bring about His will on Earth. Even if there is a considerable amount of sin and evil present in that being's existence, God will still not resort to ending life. If you are challenged by this truth, think of it this way; if anyone deserves to die, it is the devil, but the Lord does not even kill the devil himself. He is not brought to death, but thrown into a lake of fire (Rev. 20:10).

At first glance this looks like a lack of God's justice. But think again. Killing the devil and giving him a quick and painless end is far less just than paying him back with eternal torment for the destruction he rained upon human beings for thousands of years. This is a more just method than death, and does not violate God's nature.

For me, when I began to entertain the validity of this truth about God's lack of ability to kill, the first thing that kept me from giving agreement to it was the many verses in the Bible that talk of God killing whole cities, armies, even babies. I will be upfront in saying that I don't have the answers to all of the situations in the Bible where it looks like God did something out of anger and wrath. I see only in part. But God has given us some answers to a few of the tough situations in the Bible. Throughout this book you will find some of these answers. I pray they give you life, as I know they will lead you closer to Jesus.

+ THE HEBREW MINDSET +

All scriptures are inspired by God to lead us closer into relationship with Him. Something to keep in mind as we read the scriptures is that they were written through the filter of a Hebraic mindset and paradigm.

One of the most interesting aspects of the Hebrew way of thinking is how they viewed delegated authority. In biblical days, when a king would send his messenger to another person, it was understood in Hebrew culture that the messenger was not only the representative of the King, but was viewed as carrying the very authority of the King himself. In fact, the messenger would sometimes act out the message to the receiver of the message in the same way that the King communicated it to the messenger. If the King was angry when he gave the message, the messenger would storm into the room and verbally explode in the same manner that the King did. If the King was happy and peaceful when he gave the message, the messenger would act in the same way to those receiving the message. In the mind of a Hebrew, the representative of the King and the King were not two exclusive authorities, but seen as one, because the representative needed to be obeyed as though it was the King himself.

This can be recognized in the accounts of the Centurion's faith in the Gospels. The account in Matthew 8 says that the Centurion came to Jesus to ask Him to heal the servant, but the account in Luke 7 says that the Centurion sent others to give his message to Jesus.

"When Jesus had entered Capernaum, a centurion came to him, asking for help." Matthew 8:6

"The centurion heard of Jesus and sent some elders of the Jews to him, asking him to come and heal his servant." Luke 7:3

Did the Centurion go to see Jesus, or did he send a messenger? Is this an error in the scriptures?

Not at all. In fact, it simply reveals the way that a Hebrew viewed delegated authority in that day. The messengers sent by the Centurion were in fact sent, but the account in Matthew 8 implied the Hebraic view of authority onto the situation instead of explaining that the Centurion didn't go himself, but sent his authority with others.

Hebrews viewed God and His angels in the same way. If God sent an angel, sometimes it is referred to in scripture as the Angel of the Lord, and sometimes it is simply referred to as The Lord. There was no line drawn between the angel and God, because the angel was carrying out God's bidding, acting in His authority, and thus *was*, in essence, The Lord. This view was an assumed cultural norm in those days, and the scriptures are written in light of it.

The problematic aspect of this is that at one time, satan and his angels *were* servants of God. They were Angels of the Lord. But long ago they chose to rebel against God and serve their own evil desires. The problem with the Hebraic view is that it didn't fully acknowledge that satan rebelled against God. Instead of recognizing that satan was in total opposition to God and an enemy to God, the Hebrews believed that the enemy was still a tool in the hand of God. Because of their distorted view of God's sovereignty (that many have today), they believed that everything that happened must be God's doing. They concluded that God would make use of satan when He had something distasteful to deal out to humanity like judgments, punishments, wrath, and death. They figured that when Satan did something, it was ultimately God's doing anyways because God was sovereign over all. In reality, the enemy was no longer a messenger of God's will, nor a friend of God, but the Hebraic mindset still encompassed satan's acts as God's.

This is imperative to understand, the ultimate trump card, if we are to grasp some of the things in the Bible that seem to contradict one another and discredit the goodness of God. There are times in the Bible when God is credited with doing things that the enemy did, simply because the Hebraic mindset lumped the two together.

Why do you think David, Abraham, Moses, and Solomon didn't even mention the devil in any of their writings, though they wrote the majority of the Old Testament? The Hebraic view of satan inadvertently wrote the devil out of the Bible. As C.S. Cowles said in his fantastic literary work titled, "Who Is God",

"Old Testament scholars help us by pointing out that attributing violent and destructive acts to God can be partly explained by the fact that the ancient Israelites had no concept of Satan until after the Babylonian exile. As a consequence of their strict monotheism, they attributed all things- life and death, sickness and health, blessings and cursing- to the intentional will and direct action of the Sovereign Lord."

Not convinced? A blatant example *in scripture* of the Hebrew belief about satan can be found in the account of David numbering Israel. David's numbering of Israel caused 70,000 people to die. There are two accounts in the Bible of the exact same story. Notice in the first story, it is the Lord that is attributed with inciting David to number Israel;

*"Again the anger of the **LORD** burned against Israel, and he incited David against them, saying, 'Go and take a census of Israel and Judah.'"* 2 Samuel 24:1

Here is the second account of the same situation involving David;

*"**Satan** rose up against Israel and incited David to take a census of Israel. So David said to Joab and the commanders of the troops, 'Go and count the Israelites from Beersheba to Dan. Then report back to me so that I may know how many there are.'"* 1 Chronicles 21:1,2

Same story, but one version tells us that it was the Lord that had David number Israel, and other says that satan incited David to number Israel. When we understand the way that a Hebrew viewed a King's messenger and the function of satan, we can easily deduct that it was in fact satan that incited David to number Israel, and that God had nothing to do with it. The Hebraic paradigm meshed the act of the enemy with an act of God. In this situation, this mindset projected the anger of the devil upon God, making God out to look like He was furious, ready to balance the scales of justice with His wrath. Fortunately, this isn't the case.

The devil is brought up in the Old Testament very few times compared to in the New Testament. Though very few writers of the Old Testament mention the devil, every writer in the New Testament does. To the Hebrew mind, because satan was seen as a servant of God, there was no reason to bring him up. This changed in the New Testament because Christ came and enlightened humanity of the reality of the devil. In fact, one of Jesus' aims in ministry was to awaken people to the reality that there was an enemy that was bent on their destruction. Jesus said that the very reason He came to Earth was to destroy the works of the devil (1 John 3:18), because man wasn't even aware of the works of the devil. Jesus spoke of the devil more times than the entire Old Testament ever mentions him. Why? Because in order to have a good God, you have to have someone to blame the bad stuff on, and Jesus came to reveal a good God.

+ A MISUNDERSTANDING OF SOVEREIGNTY +

When dealing with the suffering in the world, one of the biggest hindrances to truth is a misunderstanding of God's sovereignty. Sovereignty means to have supreme reign and authority.

God's sovereignty is misunderstood in two ways. First, one can make the error that God isn't sovereign. Most Christians don't fall into that obvious blunder. The second misunderstanding comes from believing that God is sovereign in a way that leads the person to believe that everything that happens is God's will.[5] This is an incorrect view of God and life, and will actually undermine your ability to believe that He is good in the long run.

We witness God's sovereignty being misunderstood every time we hear someone say, "We prayed for the sick to get better, but they didn't recover so it must not be God's will to heal them." Confused, the Christian deducts from this experience that is it not always God's will to heal. They reason that if it were always God's will to heal, then the sick would have been healed when they prayed because God is sovereign. Another example of not fully understanding God's sovereignty is revealed when we say that God's judgment has fallen on this or that city because a storm or tsunami destroys it.

---

[5] The Armenian theological stance is just as incorrect as the Calvinistic. Both end up attributing evil to God, thus are thoroughly incorrect. Saying God passively allows bad things to happen is the same as saying He causes them. As Martin Luther Jr. said, "He who passively accepts evil is as much involved in it as he who helps to perpetuate it. He who accepts evil without protesting against it is really co-operating with it."

The difference between the God of Christians and the gods of Hindus and Muslims is that our God is predictable in His goodness while their god is not. For a Muslim or Hindu, when something happens in their life, good or bad, they believe it was god's will. They have such a sovereign view of their gods that anything can happen and they will blindly trust that it was their god's will. No matter how many people died, were harmed, or suffered, they conclude that it was good because it was the god's will, and their god "would know best". People throw out their brains, not acknowledging that things like death, sickness, and storms are bad. They simply accept their existence in quiet submission to their god's will. They think that because god is sovereign, everything that happens takes place because god wanted it to, so it must be good in some mysterious way that they don't have the insight to see. They take up a position of "humility", and resign themselves to their lack of influence over their circumstances.

Doesn't this sound like the stance taken by the majority of the Church? Yet the difference between our God and the gods of Hinduism or Islam is that ours is held to a standard of goodness while theirs can do whatever they want. While Muslim and Hindu gods are unpredictable in their actions, our God only does good things. He is predictably good. If He isn't predictable in that He will always do good things then He is the same as any other god. If we do not let our understanding of His goodness shape our understanding of His sovereignty, we suddenly look just like the Hindus and Muslims, or any other religion that is on the earth.

The answer to the sovereignty dilemma is not solved through blindly accepting horrible things as though God is making them happen, or by saying that God isn't sovereign at all. Both are faults. The answer is found at the start of time, in the Garden of Eden.

God created the earth. He owns it. The Bible says, "The Earth is the Lord's, and the fullness thereof" (Psalm 24:1). When He created the earth, God created man and set him upon Earth to govern it, manage it, and to have dominion over it. Just as an owner of a business hires managers to manage, govern, and make decisions that will benefit the business and thus the owner, God desired to give us the honor of caring for His creation, trusting us with what He owns.

Man was given a choice that he could do anything but eat the forbidden fruit. When man ate the fruit, he willfully disobeyed God and sinned. In doing so he forfeited his authority to govern, manage, and dominate the earth to the enemy.

When we sinned, sin was released into the world, as well as sickness, because sickness' origin is sin. God did not allow sin and sickness to enter the world. *We* allowed sin and sickness into the world, even invited it. God did not hand the management of the earth over to the enemy, we did. God did not allow horrible things into the world, we did. By badly stewarding the authority that He gave us all manifestations of sin were brought into the world; murder, sickness, destructive weather patterns, premature death, rape, slavery, etc.

This is why the enemy could offer Jesus the cities of the world if Jesus had just bowed down and worshipped him. He offered Jesus the cities of the world because they were actually under his "management" (Luke 4:5-7). But Jesus knew that soon He would die on the cross and buy back the right for man to have all dominion and authority, so He resisted the enemy's offer. Jesus knew that once He died and rose again, any person that received Him would have authority to take back the dominion the enemy had been given in the garden.

God's sovereignty is not at question; He owns the earth. The issue is about management. We gave the right to manage over to the enemy when we sinned in the garden. Yet, because God is gracious and loving, He made a way for us to again have dominion and authority through Jesus' death.

Fantastic, isn't it? When you start to allow your view of God to be shaped first and foremost by His goodness, you can see that all throughout history man has made a mess and God mercifully helps us clean it up. Here are a few examples; God creates the earth and gives it to us, but we give it away, so He sends Jesus to buy it back for us. He makes a covenant with us that clearly states how we can stay in relationship with Him (Old Covenant), but we turned to serve other gods, so He sends Jesus to instigate a new covenant that is even more gracious than the first, wherein we are made clean simply by accepting Jesus. But instead of accepting Jesus, we kill Him, so He raises Jesus from the dead. Over and over we made a mess of His love and blessings, and every time God graciously responded from heaven with another revolutionary plan to draw us near to Him. Can you hear the Father's cry to draw us into relationship with Him through all of His efforts in history?

+ THE OUR FATHER +

God is sovereign in that He is *the* King with all authority, but He is not controlling every event that takes place on Earth. If He was, He is to blame for child prostitution, abortion, human trafficking, and the many other evil things that happen every day in the world.

Some Christians are taken back at the thought of God not being in control of everything that happens on

Earth today. They believe that in order for God to be sovereign, He must be in control of every event that takes place on Earth. But sovereignty has to do with power and authority, not control.

There is a difference between control and authority. For example, a police officer directing traffic in the middle of an intersection has all authority, but people can still choose to speed. Authority doesn't guarantee control, but power. Control on the other hand, eliminates choice from of all that are involved. God does not work through control, but freedom. In fact, the enemy is the one that works through control. If God controlled every event on Earth as some Christian's believe, He would have robots that were incapable of love rather than sons and daughters that voluntarily offer their love to Him. Love is only able to be love when choice is involved. If God controlled everything, we would be rid of the evil in this world, but we also wouldn't be able to voluntarily choose to love Him. In eliminating evil through removing free will, the possibility for genuine love is also erased. Thus, God grants man free will for the sake of love. Many times man doesn't use his free will well, resulting in hell breaking out on Earth.

The cold-hard truth is that God's will has yet to be manifested on Earth in its fullness. This is why Jesus prayed, "Thy Kingdom come, *thy will be done, on Earth as it is in heaven.*" If the Father's will was always taking place on Earth, why did Jesus pray this simple prayer? In heaven there is no disease. Wars do not exist in heaven. Storms that kill thousands, abortion, or genocide are all nonexistent in heaven because God's will is being fully manifested there. Jesus prayed for God's will to be done on Earth because it *wasn't* being done on Earth; that's why He prayed for it.

Inherent in Jesus' prayer is the stunning reality that not everything that happens on this Earth is God's will. Does the fact that things happen on Earth that God does not will mean He is not sovereign? No. What it *does* mean is that He has given us all the authority we need to change the earth into a place that reflects heaven's likeness. It means that we have yet to fulfill the job He has given us as ambassadors of heaven. The lack is never on God's end.

+ GOD'S WILL IS A MATTER OF CLARITY +

God's will is not a mysteriously unclear aspect of Christianity. The Bible says that God has made His will plainly clear to us.

"And He made known to us the mystery of His will according to His good pleasure, which He purposed in Christ..." Eph. 1:9

Jesus revealed the will of God through His life and actions while on Earth. God's will is no longer a mystery. Though this be true, a person can still hear the statement "If it is God's will..." ring out in the hallways of churches during conversations after church, or worse, from the pulpit itself. This occurrence reveals to us how little the majority of the Church knows God, as well as the book they read. It also shows some of us how little our "higher education" has helped us actually become fruitful ministers. Lastly, it reveals the lack of understanding we have about who Jesus is; the exact representation of God (Heb. 1). If we ever question what is God's will and what is not, we simply need to look at the life of Jesus for our answer.

Unlike Muslims that say, "If it be God's will" in almost every sentence they speak, Christians should know what God's will is about general issues in life. It should be plain to them, not an unfathomable revelation that is too high and weighty to grasp. Our God invites us into relationship, not a spiritual kidnapping where He blindfolds us so that we can't see where He is taking us. Eph. 1:9 shows us that He actually *enjoyed* revealing His will to us. It brought Him pleasure to include us in on His plans and motives. That is the nature of a true relationship. God reveals His heart to us so that we can be grounded in what He wants to do. A person's heart dictates their desires.

In other words, God's will is borne out of who He is; Good. Those that know God will know His will. Those that know tradition, the ways of man, and a form of godliness will always be unclear on God's will. You will recognize "them" because they will be frequently praying to know the will of God about issues that are plainly stated in scripture. They will be like the man of James 1, tossed about by uncertainty, floating in a vagueness of life.

A good indicator that a person isn't totally convinced that God is good is revealed when they second guess if it is God's will to heal, to save, to give mercy, to bless, to protect, and to raise the dead. Faith is impossible unless the will of God is known, and the knowledge of the will of God comes from a revelation of His complete and total goodness. If you question that it is God's will to always do the things mentioned a few sentences above, your deficiently is simple; You do not yet understand His goodness.

God's will is derived from *who* He is. Get to know Him and you will know His will, or simply look at the life of Jesus.

+ You Get What You Believe For +

A stunning reality about God's goodness is revealed to us in Luke 19:12-27, showing us that the subject of God's goodness is an absolute imperative to understand in the walk of a believer.

Jesus tells a story about how to steward that which God gives to us. Jesus tells us that a man of nobility gave to three men different amounts of money, trusting them to use it wisely as he is away. To put in modern day terms, he gives ten dollars to the first man. To the second man, he gives five dollars. To the last man, he gives one dollar. The man that is given ten doubles the amount through wise stewardship, and in return is given ten cities to watch over. The man with five dollars has a similar conclusion; he is given five cities because he doubled his money.

Most of us have heard this story, but the portion that needs to be highlighted presently is found towards the end of the story, when the man that was given one dollar speaks:

"Then another servant came and said, 'Sir, here is your mina (or dollar); I have kept it laid away in a piece of cloth. I was afraid of you, because you are a hard (severe, harsh, austere) man. You take out what you did not put in and reap what you did not sow.' "His master replied, 'I will judge you by your own words, you wicked servant! You knew, did you, that I am a hard man, taking out what I did not put in, and reaping what I did not sow? Why then didn't you put my money on deposit, so that when I came back, I could have collected it with interest?' Then he said to those standing by, 'Take his mina (dollar) away from him and give it to the one who has ten minas (dollars).'" (v20-24)

Notice that each man was judged in accordance with how they viewed God. Some men anticipated a Master that was fair and kind, thus took risks with what they were given because they knew they wouldn't be punished if they failed. Their risk revealed their beliefs, and their beliefs determined their actions. The man with one talent assumed the Master was harsh, and that belief influenced how he stewarded what he was given. Instead of faith, he moved in fear and didn't take a risk with what he had been given. Because fear never brings about any measure of harvest, the man with one talent had nothing to show for what he had been given when the Master returned.

We are judged in accordance with how we view God. *God will give us exactly what we anticipate about Him.* If you believe He is an evil taskmaster, then He will appear in that fashion to you. Please understand, I am not saying that you can change who God is. He is good, undoubtedly, and unable to be changed or to change. But if a person has such unbelief to treat God as though He is anything less than overwhelmingly good, then that is what they will receive. He is so good that He will give us exactly what we believe for.

If you believe God's wrath will engulf you if you do anything wrong, wrath will. It won't be the Lord's wrath, but wrath will consume you. Thinking of the Lord in such a manner opens a person up to a spirit of fear, and that spirit becomes an open door for the enemy to attack them as he pleases. In thinking that God would ever harm you, you are discrediting His nature, calling Him evil, and have unconsciously positioned yourself in opposition to Him. The enemy has every right to attack you when you think in this way. If you think that He is a harsh taskmaster, you will live through fear rather than faith, and you will not produce anything of worth for Him while on Earth. You will find that your life was not stewarded well, and that you hid your life away and never took a risk.

But, if you see Him as He is, He will be revealed as such. If you see Him as good, you will realize that He would rather have His kids step out in risk and possibly fail than to have His kids hide away in fear because of what He would do to them if they stumble. Risk is the manifestation of faith, and faith is always grounded in an understanding of His goodness. The man with one talent had no faith, because he possessed no understanding of God's true nature.

Lastly, it must be said that while what we believe about God makes a stark impact upon how we live our lives, and while there is an aspect of getting what we believe for, we must also remember that when we totally miss it and accuse God of evil and being everything He is not, He doesn't give up on us. His grace is never-ending. It is not our ability to do *anything* that gets us what we need, but His ability. It will dramatically increase the fruit of your life to believe He is good, but when we stumble to credit Him the goodness He is due, He is patient with us. We get what we believe for, but the good news is that we also get much more than we ever believed for through grace.

+ BEING AN ACCURATE REPRESENTATION +

Not only is it a good idea to assume that God an incredibly good Master that is patient and slow to anger, but it is good idea to represent God to others in the same manner. Moses failed to do this and actually lost out on something that he had worked more than forty years to see come to fruition.

In Numbers 20, God told Moses to speak to a rock and it would become the source of water for over a million people. The people had been complaining to Moses once again, telling him that they would rather have stayed in Egyptian bondage than to die of thirst in the desert.

Instead of speaking to the rock like God had said, Moses rebuked the people, then angrily struck the rock with his staff twice. Water poured forth from the rock despite Moses incapability to follow simple directions, and hundreds of thousands of people drank their fill. But immediately afterwards, God let Moses know that he wouldn't be finding his way into the Promised Land because of that little stunt.

At first this seems to be quite a reprimand for hitting a rock with a rod rather than speaking to it. But it wasn't particularly the use of the staff that was the problem, but how Moses represented God to the people in his use of the rod. *God wasn't angry, but Moses' actions communicated to the people that He was.*

It is an immense mistake to communicate to God's people that He is angry when He is not. Did you know that many ministers and pastors in this present day will be barred from seeing the fullness of their destiny because they are misrepresenting God as an angry, wrathful god? Instead of seeing healings, signs and wonders, restoration in families, and abundant finances breaking out amidst their people they have bored congregations that lack life. Why? Because the gospel they are preaching isn't *good*.

As a sidenote, God didn't punishing Moses for his mistake, just as God won't punish ministers for preaching a gospel that has mix. Instead it is that the Promised Land can only be found by those with a good report and a gracious heart. If you want to walk in your destiny, believe that God is good.

If you are a leader in the body of Christ, take heed. You are representing God Himself, so be assured that you are preaching the *Good News* of a good God. If not, you *will* loose direction and find yourself parched, walking around in the desert instead of drinking deep of milk and honey.

As you read, some may ask, "But what about God's discipline? It doesn't always *feel* good, but does that mean that it is bad?" Good question.

Scripture is clear that the Lord disciplines those that He loves. Anyone that is a parent is very aware that discipline is much needed in order to not just keep yourself sane, but in order that your child learns self-control, how to love themselves and others, and how to steward their life in a way that gives glory to God. To not discipline our children would be unloving. Let it be understood that while God's discipline may not feel good, it is nonetheless one of most beautiful, delightful ways that God loves us. Without it, we would be drastically lost.

Discipline is a way of leading another person so that they are ensured to have a happy life once they are walking on their own. It involves the necessary instructions, guidance, and occasional correction that helps provide someone the direction they need in order to succeed. In the Bible, the word "discipline" literally means *to train*. Thus, is no wonder why the word "disciple" is so closely related to the word "discipline". The two words are alike in word and application, for a disciple is disciplined or *trained* by a teacher more experienced and wise then themselves.

But the word, "discipline" is often seen in a negative light because typically the instructions given by a teacher are regulated through punishment if unfulfilled. Thus, discipline and punishment have melded together in the minds of most people to become one reality.

But discipline and punishment are two separate, totally unrelated concepts. Discipline has nothing to do with punishment. Jesus didn't ever punish His disciples. He may have sternly corrected or rebuked them, but never punished them for their mistakes, even when one of them hacked the ear off another man. While discipline's aim is *to train* in the hopes of leading someone into a good life, punishment's aim is to give someone what they deserve for their actions. Punishment is derived from the nature of the law; you pay the penalty for your actions.

In fact, punishment has nothing to do with discipline, but fear. Love, God Himself, drives out fear and punishment. God is so adamantly opposed to punishment and fear that He actually casts them out of a human soul when He is near (1 John 4:18). Therefore, it is a dramatic mistake to confuse discipline and punishment. Yet that is exactly what we do when dealing with verses in the Bible, particularly Hebrews 12:5-6:

> *"My son, do not make light of the Lord's discipline, and do not lose heart when he rebukes you, because the Lord disciplines those he loves and he punishes everyone he accepts as a son."*

The word "punishes" in this verse is interchangeable with "scourge" or "chasten", as some translations exemplify. It is the same word used in the Bible to describe the whipping that Jesus was given before He was nailed to the cross, as well as the beatings that Jesus told His people they would experience because of persecution (Matthew 10:17). This is no spanking from dad, but a full-blown thrashing that leaves you bloody and near death.

It is understandable why people would see discipline and punishment as closely related because of the use of the two words in this section of scripture. But in case you don't know already, this portion of Hebrews is a direct quote from Proverbs 3:11-12. The odd thing is that the original portion of scripture in Proverbs doesn't say what the quote in Hebrews says at all. In fact, it reveals a good God, one that delights in His children.

*"My son, do not make light of the Lord's discipline, and do not lose heart when he rebukes you, because the Lord disciplines those he loves **as a father the son he delights in.**"*

Did you notice the last part in that verse? Where did the punishment, scourging, and chastisement of Hebrews 12:6 go? How did a bloody thrashing of punishment replace the delight God has for us that is clearly communicated in Proverbs 3:12?

Most likely, the problem probably originates from when the Hebrew texts were translated into Greek to later become the Septuagint. The result is a *misquote* of an Old Testament verse by the writer of Hebrews. Despite what English translation of the Bible that you read, you can look for yourself and plainly see the discrepancies between the verses in Proverbs 3:11-12, and the quote of the scriptures in Hebrews 12:5-6.

Remember, 1 John 4:18 clarifies our understanding of punishment by telling us that, "There is no fear in love. But perfect love drives out fear, because fear has to do with punishment." The two opposing forces of the universe are plainly set forth here; fear that comes from punishment, and love. God is love, choosing not to work through fear that comes from the belief that there is retribution for sin when in relationship with God. Clearly, 1 John 4:18 tells us that God does not punish, but loves.

So, take your pick; You can believe that God wants to show His love to you by beating you like Jesus was before He was sent to the cross, or you can believe that Daddy wants to show His love to you by delighting in you. Your choice; He will be revealed to you who you believe Him to be. I learned a long time ago that the knowledge of God's delight for me governs my moral life much better than the fear of punishment does.

As the Body of Christ, we must stop twisting this verse in Hebrews in order to reinforce a misled belief. God did not, in the name of love through discipline, give you a disease or "allow" this or that negative situation to afflict you. He is not out to punish you through perverse means, all under the guise of "love". He likes you more than that.

+ THE JONAH SPIRIT +

Jonah was abhorred by the sin that the city of Nineveh was constantly committing. God spoke to him to tell them to repent, that they may be spared. After dragging his feet, Jonah finally went and spoke as the Lord commanded him to do. The city repented, and Jonah's response was peculiar; he was extremely disappointed!

"But Jonah was greatly displeased and became angry. He prayed to the LORD, "O LORD, is this not what I said when I was still at home? That is why I was so quick to flee to Tarshish. I knew that you are a gracious and compassionate God, slow to anger and abounding in love, a God who relents from sending calamity. Now, O LORD, take away my life, for it is better for me to die than to live."

It is not an exaggeration to say that Jonah wanted to *commit suicide* because he was so disappointed that the Lord gave grace to sinners. Instead of rejoicing with the fact that the Lord spared sinner's lives, he was upset.

What would cause a man to *be upset* when he witnesses the goodness and grace of God in the lives of others? Why was Jonah so inconceivably angry about the lost not being destroyed? I would suggest that it is because Jonah wanted to see the people pay for the sins they had committed. I would suggest that Jonah was in a spirit that caused him to be impressed and offended by other's sin, which caused him to desire their destruction. He wanted to see the city burn. Jonah wanted to see "sin destroyed" and "the justice of God" manifested.

Interestingly enough, the way the Lord wanted to deal with the sin and bring justice was wholly through grace; repentance. No sacrifice was made, no price was paid; the Lord simply forgave the people of Nineveh. Repentance can only take place in the context of the revelation of grace, because repentance presupposes that the wrong will be forgiven without any payment in return for the sin. Repentance is the most blatant form of the knowledge of grace. This is why John the Baptist and Jesus preached repentance; because the Law came through Moses, but grace and truth came through the Christ (John 1:17).

When Jonah heard the Lord say that unless Nineveh repented it would be destroyed, he didn't hear that God wanted to give grace to the people of Nineveh and save their lives. We always interpret the voice of God through our filter of what we understand of His nature. Really what God was telling Jonah was that He loved Nineveh, and if the city didn't repent, the enemy would have the legal right to destroy it, because sin gives entrance to the enemy. God even knew the specific day when the destruction would come upon the city if they didn't repent. Because of His concern for the people, He sent His prophet to proclaim repentance so that their lives could be spared. When they repented, they took themselves out of the enemy's legal right to afflict them, thus destruction didn't come upon them.

But instead of hearing God's heart of love for the people of Nineveh when He spoke to Jonah, he heard God saying that He was upset, tired and offended with the sins of the people, and if they didn't get their act together, He was going to wipe them off the face of the earth with His purifying fire and wrath. This is the understanding we typically have of the Father in the Old Testament, isn't it? A God that is holy, that we assume can be dirtied by our stumblings, infected by our imperfection, abhorred by our sin, thus has to deal with it violently?

I have news for you; God is holy, but the sin you walk in everyday, the stumblings you commit and will commit until the day you die don't threaten God. He is bigger than our sin. He wasn't and isn't threatened by the sin of New Orleans or Haiti, and doesn't have the need to clean it up by destroying them in order to feel better about Himself. He is clean, *He is holy*, no matter what we do. In fact, instead of our sin infecting His holiness when we get near to Him, His holiness overcomes our dirtiness when we get close to Him. He wants us to come to Him dirty, because He is a God that is able to clean us up if we come wanting to be clean (repentance). Your sin doesn't threaten God's holiness.

We must be careful not to take on a view of God, like Jonah, that draws our heart into a place where we subtly rejoice when destruction falls upon an evil city or person. We must be careful to remember that God is not a God that works through punishment, but only love that casts out fear. When we begin to understand this concept about God, instead of praying for circumstances to get hard enough in a person's life so that they give up and turn to God, we pray the grace and blessings of God over them, remembering that it is the Lord's kindness that draws us to repentance, not the threat of punishment.

1 Corinthians 11:28-34 presents quite a challenge to those that desire to understand God's goodness in all aspects of life. Here is the scripture.

"A man ought to examine himself before he eats of the bread and drinks of the cup. For anyone who eats and drinks without recognizing the body of the Lord eats and drinks judgment on himself. That is why many among you are weak and sick, and a number of you have fallen asleep. But if we judged ourselves, we would not come under judgment. When we are judged by the Lord, we are being disciplined so that we will not be condemned with the world. So then, my brothers, when you come together to eat, wait for each other. If anyone is hungry, he should eat at home, so that when you meet together it may not result in judgment."

Without insight and revelation, this scripture seems to give us ample proof that God will kill us if we do not take communion in an honorable way. I would suggest that the conclusion Paul desired his readers to come to is very different. But in order to understand these verses as Paul wanted us to, we have to lay some groundwork.

First off, we must remember that satan is called the accuser of the brethren (Rev. 12:10). Second, there is now no condemnation for those that are in Christ Jesus (Romans 8:1). Third, discipline means "to train" in the Bible (coming from the word "disciple"), and is not related in any way to punishment. Forth, when people sin, they give the enemy an open door to afflict them. Since the devil has no authority, he has to get agreement with Earth in order to do anything. Sin is that agreement; his open door to afflict men (to steal, kill, destroy). If you can agree with the above statements, the rest will be easy to stomach.

Here is what is going on; translators took two different words in the Greek and translated both of them into the English word "judgment". Sadly, what Paul is trying to communicate to his readers is totally lost through our English translations.

In verse 29, the first time the word "judgment" is used, it is the Greek word "krima" which means judgment in the sense of condemnation, the decision in which one passes on the fault of others, and even damnation. We know God is incapable of condemning us according to Romans 8:1, so this verse reveals it to be the enemy that is coming in to condemn men that have opened themselves to sin through a dishonoring use of communion. People were doing some weird and revolting stuff back in Paul's day when it came to communion.

The second time "judge" is used in verse 29, the word "Diakrino", it means to make a distinction, or to separate, or decide. It is applicable to keeping ourselves accountable before God, closely watching the state of our hearts, and choosing to be separate from sin. Its meaning is akin to what verse 28 communicates about a man examining himself. It is checking your heart, motives, and thoughts with what God wants. Verse 31 uses the same word as is used the second time in verse 29, Diakrino. It uses a form of that word again in 31, krino, again, meaning to separate, make a distinction, or to decide. Remember, Krino is very different from krima. In 32 it uses krino again. Lastly, the word "condemnation" in 32 is akin to krima, in that it means one is worthy of punishment. Below is the scripture with the meanings of the Greek words that have been translated as "judgment".

"But a man must examine (test, inspect) *himself, and in so doing he is to eat of the bread and drink of the cup. For he who eats and drinks, eats and drinks judgment* (condemnation, damnation, from the enemy) *to himself if he does not judge*

(rightly separate, decide, or make a distinction) *the body rightly. For this reason many among you are weak and sick, and a number sleep. But if we judged* (rightly separate, decide, or make a distinction) *ourselves rightly, we would not be judged* (rightly separate, decide, or make a distinction, in this case by God). *But when we are judged* (when the Lord rightly separates, decides, or make a distinction), *we are disciplined* (trained) *by the Lord so that we will not be condemned* (punishment, damnation, which satan will do, not God) *along with the world. So then, my brethren, when you come together to eat, wait for one another. If anyone is hungry, let him eat at home, so that you will not come together for judgment* (condemnation, damnation)."

Ultimately, this scripture is not saying that God will kill you if you take communion wrongly. That couldn't be further than the truth if you look at the Greek. The Greek makes it clear that the condemnation is not coming from God, and that the only kind of "judgment" that He is making towards us is one of convicting us of issues we need to deal with, in order that we don't open ourselves us to demonic attack. He is all about protecting, giving life, and gentleness, not killing us.

Paul is encouraging the people to deal with their own issues so that the enemy doesn't have the right to afflict them. Paul is NOT saying that when God has to help us deal with our issues that He does so through punishment, condemnation, or death. It says He trains us. Discipline is not punishment. Punishment has to do with fear (1 John 4:18), and love casts out fear, so it is not of God, because God is love. The Bible also says that it is His kindness that leads us to repentance (Romans 2:4).

Paul doesn't want the people to get taken out by the enemy through taking communion in a dishonoring way. It is not, in any way, saying that God punishes us, condemns us, or damns us, or it would have used the Greek word "krima" at the end of verse 31, but it does not.

No man has a fully matured revelation of the knowledge and nature of God, including the men that translated the Bible. This isn't to dishonor any translator or translation, for nobody sees clearly and without any dimness. Thus, reading many different translations of the Bible helps affirm in our hearts the truths God has spoken to us in prayer, and helps us navigate past the pitfalls of other's theological errors that they unknowingly translated into the Bible. If we read only one version of the Bible, we are blindly receiving someone else's theology. As St Augustine of Hippo said, "a variety of translations is profitable for the finding out of the sense of the Scriptures".

+ WHO IS HELD RESPONSIBLE +

If we have a belief about the Father that cannot be clearly demonstrated through the life of Jesus, we need to adjust our view of God. Jesus was and is the exact representation of the Father.

Without Jesus, we would not know what the Father looks like. John 1:18 says it like this,

"No one has ever seen God, but God the One and Only, who is at the Father's side, has made him known."

Nobody had seen the Father as He was, nobody had understood the Father's nature, nobody had accurately comprehended, identified, recognized, or known the Father, until Jesus came and made Him known. If you can't substantiate the way you view the Father with who Jesus was when He was on Earth, your view needs to change. Jesus came to show us exactly what the Father is like. Jesus always healed everyone that came to Him, and raised every dead person that He is recorded to have encountered. He never turned one person away.

God loves New Orleans, Indonesia, Haiti, and anywhere else that has been destroyed by natural disasters. Jesus never met a storm that He liked. In fact, He even *rebuked* the weather, demonstrating that it wasn't acting in accordance to His will. It is not the Father that is causing the hurricanes, Earthquakes, and the floods that kill thousands of people every year. Ask a child if a storm is good or bad when the news on television flashes a picture of a destroyed neighborhood with firemen pulling dead bodies out of a collapsed house. The child will tell you the truth that may have strayed far from your heart. We are kidding ourselves to believe that it is an act of God.

In every disaster situation, God desired to give mercy despite the sin in the land. To God, mercy triumphs judgment every time, because He is good (James 2:13). The *devil* desired to wipe everyone out in the above mentioned cities and lands before they had a chance to repent and come to Jesus. In stark contrast, Daddy desires that none perish (2 Peter 3:9). God is not responsible for these messes; the enemy is. The enemy is given entrance through sin to legally afflict men, for he has no authority unless the sons of God, who were given dominion originally, surrender it to him through sin. God never has anything to do with killing or destruction. Don't mistake the enemy's legal right to steal, kill, and destroy because of men's agreement with hell (sin) for an act of God that "purifies" the land from sin and sinners. There is no such thing as the latter, only the former.

Our theology must begin to match our confession of, "God is good". Why, if God caused the Haitian Earthquake to happen, would a believer go about helping the situation improve and thus work in contradiction to His will? The same illogical, unsound thought process is used when a person believes that it is God's will for them to be ill. If God gave you that sickness or physical problem, why do you go to a doctor to get rid of it? Likewise, if you believe God brought about this Earthquake, why would you want to work against God by helping to improve Haiti's situation? Why would you feel grief, compassion, and love for Haiti if you think that God did it? If God did caused the earthquake, you should rejoice with each story of destruction, disease, and death that you hear about because then, and only then, would you be in-line with "God's will".

But you don't rejoice with the testimonies of death and loss. Instead, you feel the sadness and weight of the situation. You feel the awe of destruction. Why? Because your heart knows better than your theology. Even when diseased teaching and heresies blind the mind, your heart is not as easily duped.

Pharisaical thinking brings us to the conclusion that God is responsible for things that He hasn't done. But God is not, and was not, angry with Haiti. He loves Haiti. He was in the relief work and the millions of dollars being given. He is in the cup of cold water. He is in the supernatural healings that took place and are taking place, working in direct opposition to what the earthquake caused.

When we attribute death, storms, and sickness to God, we are saying that God is doing evil things. As crazy as it sounds, that is blasphemy! Blasphemy aside, imagine how much that breaks the heart of our perfectly loving, heavenly Daddy! He even sent His own son to die for us, and we turn around and blame Him for the very things that He sent His Son to die for and give us authority over!

We don't have to attribute death, storms, and sickness to God if we don't remove the devil from our theology. But if we do, as most of the Western Church has done, we have nobody except God to hold responsible for the horrible, disgusting things that happen on Earth. A person that does this may have a façade of believing God is good, but inside they will not be so sure. You cannot hold a contradiction in your hands firmly. You need to have a devil in your belief system, but one that is less impressive than God. Either people don't have a devil at all, or they have too big of one. Neither leads you to faith.

+ Job Descriptions +

If we do not know what is a work of the devil and what is a work of God, we will live in a state of confusion that will never produce real faith that is able to bring forth miracles out of impossible circumstances. On the other hand, when we become totally convinced that certain issues are *always* inspired by the enemy, a righteous anger fuels us to become agents of change in the world. We begin to set our faces like flint against the enemy, and the result is that we prevail.

You want to know how to be able to tell what things God does and what things the devil does when you are watching the evening news? Jesus and the devil both have job descriptions. Jesus gave them to us in John 10:10 saying,

"The devil comes only to steal, kill, and destroy. I have come that they might have abundant life."

That makes it simple enough, yet the majority of the church still doesn't get it. Lets simplify it even further, with some "theology for dummies":

Steal, kill, destroy = devil.

Life = Jesus.

For those that have a hard time remembering, here is a little tip straight from the names we have given the two opposing sides: **Good = God, evil = devil.**

If you don't like how simple this is, go argue about it with Jesus, because He said it. That is how you can determine what is from God, and what enters your life that is from the devil. Remember, it was not God who destroyed Job's life, it was the enemy. God just restored everything when the devil was done. Then there is the book of Revelation. Jesus broke seals that loosed things from the heavenly realms that helped men make a choice to serve God or the devil because the time was short. If He didn't do that, many would perish because they wouldn't know of the urgency of that hour. When men choose to serve Death rather than the Father of Life, God cannot drag them into heaven because He will never override free will. Their choice to serve the enemy leads them to death and hell. God never sends anyone to hell. Man puts himself there. Remember, God made hell for *the devil and his angels*, not for men (Matthew 25:41).

If you lost someone you love, you need to know that God did not take them from you, the enemy did! Why? Because He is good. He gives abundant life. Death is from the enemy. Instead of being offended with God, aim your anger at the enemy and start to get even! If you lost a loved one, go pray for the dead to be raised so that someone else doesn't go through the loss you went through. Stop being a victim and start to victimize the devil. You have every right to torment him. Do so through getting people saved (stealing his possessions), getting the sick healed (severely messing up his plans), and raising the dead (embarrassing him in front of all of hell).

+ THE UNFORGIVABLE SIN +

Much of this chapter has to do with things that God has done being attributed to the devil, and things the devil is doing attributed to God. Oddly enough, that was the one sin Jesus was incredibly concerned about. It is called the blasphemy of the Holy Spirit, and first mentioned by Isaiah in Isaiah 5:20. According to Jesus, one of the most serious things we could do is blaspheme the Holy Spirit by attributing His works to the devil. He said that it the only sin that was unforgivable (Matthew 12:31). It is when we call evil good and good evil.

There is something serious taking place in a person's life when they see what is good as evil. People who see that which is good as evil, people that attribute that which is God to satan, hold to this observation tighter than anything in their lives. They clench it with their fist so tightly that their knuckles turn white. No amount of talking to them will change their mind. They are willing to cut off relationships for it, willing to divide churches over it, willing to crucify other's lives over it. It is very important to them. I wonder what it will be like for that person the day they stand before God and His angels. Will they see God as He is, or will they think they see satan, disguising himself as an angel of light? To this person, God can show up in simplicity and splendor, yet they discard Him, sure that satan was who appeared to them, not God.

But how could a completely compassionate, loving, and gracious God not forgive someone for a specific sin? If He is incapable of total forgiveness, then He is not completely compassionate, loving, and gracious.

If there is a loophole to His love, then it was never really unconditional love to begin with.

Here is the answer. The prerequisite to forgiveness is to acknowledging that what was done was wrong. The people that commit this unforgivable sin aren't wondering in the least bit if what they are doing is wrong, let alone then taking the leap of humility to ask for forgiveness. Because these people hold to their belief about something being evil with such tenacity, they never allow themselves to be forgiven. This is why Jesus said it was the unforgivable sin. *It isn't that God won't forgive them, it is that they won't allow themselves to be forgiven.* We know that God forgives any sin, even rape and murder. But God cannot force man to ask for forgiveness for something that man does not acknowledge as wrong.

This is why attributing the things of the Spirit to the devil is very dangerous. You begin to sit in on judgment of God Himself, and because you have judged God, you will not go to Him to ask for forgiveness. You begin to be so sure of yourself in your judgment that the possibility of your asking for forgiveness becomes an impossibility. God would forgive a person for blaspheming the Holy Spirit, but the people who commit this sin do not want to be forgiven. As a result, forgiveness becomes an impossibility.

The Pharisees, the most studied in religious matters of the day, completely missed God when He came to the earth. They mistook Him for a normal man, or even worse, a tool of beelzebub. They didn't just reject His words, they took it into their own hands to kill this Man, because He contradicted their belief system so violently. And yet, He was God.

I have a hunch that things aren't as they seem, and that if Jesus showed up today (which is more than plausible), many of us would not recognize Him. Let us see that which is of God, be from God, and that which is from the enemy, from the enemy. God, give us eyes to see and ears to hear.

And like Stephen, those that get a hold of the revelation of Jesus, offend those around them that are still stuck in the old way of thinking about God. A person that is more ingrained in the traditions of man rather than the Spirit of God will see that which is of heaven from hell. If you are full of God, they will disagree with you, abhor you, and will even throw stones at you, because their drive is to rid the world of that which is not of God. If they only knew who God was and what He does, then they would throw their stones in the right direction.

+ WHOLE NATIONS SAVED IN A DAY +

King David had one drive, one aim, one primary desire; to understand and acknowledge God as good. The calling of David's heart was to spend time with the Lord so that he would begin to see God as He was;

"One thing alone I ask from the Eternal, one thing do I desire, a vision of the Eternal's goodness in the temple at the morning hour." Psalm 27:4 (Moffatt)

As David would lift up praise to God, his vision would clear and he would begin to see God as He was; beautiful, breathtaking, and utterly good. *This* is how we see whole nations saved in a day. When we begin to be convinced of the Lord's goodness and beauty, we are then and only then able to effectively communicate who He is to a lost world. The world thinks that God is angry, judgmental, and condemning. When we reveal to them that He is a gentle, gracious, beautiful, attractive, fun God, there is no convincing needed. The world hasn't wanted Jesus because we haven't accurately shown them who He is! When the veil is taken off a person's eyes, the veil that tells people that He is anything less than their hearts deepest desire, they instinctively run to Him. Who would reject raw Pleasure, the fullness of Joy, and the source of Happiness?

+ THE VERY ESSENCE OF THE GOSPEL +

Did you know that even the English word, "God" is identical to the Anglo-Saxon word, "Good"? God's literal name is actually just, "Good". You can start saying, "Praise Good" when something happens that causes you to rejoice! You will be as aligned with Heaven as you could ever be. "Good" is a very accurate name for our God. In addition, the word "gospel" means "good message" or "good news". We are to preach to all nations the overwhelming goodness of God, which *is* the Gospel. In fact, *the* message that John and the disciples witnessed through being with Jesus on Earth was that there is no evil in the Father; that He is only good.

"This is the message we have heard from him and declare to you: God is light; in him there is no darkness at all." 1 John 1:5

The Gospel, or good news, is that the Father is actually a very happy, wonderful person. The very essence of the message that we are to declare to the world is that our God is completely and totally *good*, a God that will never leave you in want, but totally fulfilled. This is the reason He is the desire of the nations.

+ TRADING A FAÇADE FOR THE REAL +

Most Christians think that they believe that God is good. Do you? You likely answered "yes" to that question, but how can you be sure? In Matthew 10:8 Jesus said,

"Heal the sick, cleanse the leper, raise the dead, and cast out devils."

Remember, faith is the result of believing God is good. There is no verse that helps us better evaluate if we are walking in faith or not as this one. Since faith is rooted in knowing God is good, and Matthew 10:8 takes faith to manifest on Earth, this verse reveals to us if we really believe God is good or not. If we are attempting, simply just trying, to walk out these supernatural realities in our lives then we can be assured that we *really* do believe He is good and don't just *think* we believe it. If these things aren't present in our lives, then there is likely a deficiency in our understanding of His goodness. Our actions reveal the true state of our heart. Demonstration exposes belief.

If you believe God is good, you will not deny yourself any good thing. God desires to give you righteousness, intimacy with Jesus, miracle working power, divine protection, love, prosperity, freedom, joy, peace, healing, restoration, and authority over hell. God's will is not undefined, foggy, or complicated to those that really believe that God is good, revealed in the life of Christ.

The primary way a person can get a revelation that God is good is simply by spending time with Him. He Himself will tell you, and when He tells you this secret of the ages, it will never leave your spirit. The more you sit on His lap, drink of His love, look into His eyes of fire, and behold His beauty, the more the revelation of His goodness will pierce deeper and deeper into the depths of your heart. It will start to burn in your bones like an unquenchable fire, and nothing will put it out.

+ PART 2 +
RAISING THE DEAD

"Now if Christ is preached, that He has been raised from the dead, how do some among you say that there is no resurrection of the dead? But if there is no resurrection of the dead, not even Christ has been raised; and if Christ has not been raised, then our preaching is vain, your faith also is vain. Moreover we are even found to be false witnesses of God, because we testified against God that He raised Christ, whom He did not raise, if in fact the dead are not raised. For if the dead are not raised, not even Christ has been raised; and if Christ has not been raised, your faith is worthless; you are still in your sins."

1 Corinthians 15:12-17

There are many different genres of study encompassed within the vast expanse of Christ. Theology is the study of God. Eschatology is the study of the end times. Pneumatology is the study of the Holy Spirit. Just as is true in anything within Christendom, dead raising has a biblical logic behind it that can be studied and understood. Maybe we could call it Lifeology. This paradigm of thinking pertaining to dead raising is the endeavor of this chapter, helping you understand what the Bible has to say about this wonderful miracle of life.

Dead raising is more about abundant life than it is about overcoming death. Christ overcame death for us on the cross, that we may rest in His finished work and simply receive the benefits of His labor and sacrifice.

If we understand the normalcy that the Bible sets forth pertaining to dead raising, we stop thinking that resurrection power is something that only a select few can walk in. Dead raising power is for all. And when we understand that God does not instigate death, we become sure that we are praying in accordance to His will when we pray for the dead to be raised. Faith is the result.

+THE ELEMENTARY SCHOOL OF CHRISTIANITY +

The first time my eyes of understanding were opened to the beginning of chapter 6 of Hebrews, I was flabbergasted. The writer of Hebrews has just gotten done exhorting us in chapter 5 to walk in maturity by weaning ourselves off of lesser revelatory truths (milk), and move to the greater truths of Christianity (meat). The writer tells us that his readers should have already become teachers, but that they were still sucking on their pacifiers and filling their diapers.

In Hebrews 6, the writer enlightens us as to what are the *elementary teachings* of Christianity. The word "elementary" means the most basic principles of a subject. The writer lists the *most basic principles* of Christianity, exhorting us to master these things and more on to greater, more weighty realities. Lets see if we have graduated from elementary school of Christianity. Here is the list:

> *"Therefore let us leave the elementary teachings about Christ and go on to maturity, not laying again the foundation of repentance from acts that lead to death, and of faith in God, instruction about baptisms, the laying on of hands, **the resurrection of the dead**, and eternal judgment."* [6]

The Bible tells us that *elementary* teachings of Christianity are understanding righteousness, having faith, the baptism of water *and* the baptism of Holy Spirit, impartation and healing the sick, being aware of the reality of hell, and *dead raising*.

Yes, you read it right. The writer of Hebrews, which many suppose to be Paul, believed that raising the dead was an elementary teaching of Christianity. This is beautiful and shocking at the same time.

---

[6]Most of the above basics are written off in part because they are viewed as a denominational characteristic rather than a biblical necessity. But this doesn't follow a biblical pattern; you can't label Apostle Paul as a Pentecostal because he spoke in tongues (1 Cor. 14:14-18), nor Jesus a Baptist because He valued the scriptures and baptized people in the Jordan.

The only problem with this is that if a person walks into 98% of the churches in the West and starts talking about any one of these topics mentioned at the opening of Hebrews 6, it will mostly likely not be received well by the congregation. Sadly, according to this verse, most of the Church hasn't begun to receive spiritual milk, let alone the meat of the Word (Hebrews 5:13). If we aren't even drinking the *milk*, we can surmise that many of us are still be in the womb. And if that is the case, we have to wonder how many of us have even been born (again) yet! I write that with a playful smile on my face.

Thankfully, there are holy tribes of people in the globe that have not compromised the commission that is set before us. These warriors of love are seeking God for the fullness of the Kingdom to be manifested before their very eyes.

Once after reading Hebrews 6, I asked the Lord, "Dead raising seems to be viewed by most people in the church as the pinnacle of spiritual maturity pertaining to the miraculous. If You consider dead raising to be elementary, then what *is not* elementary? If we are to do 'greater things' and dead raising is the considered 'milk', then what can be considered meat? What are the greater things?"

His answer was simple, yet profound. He said, "Knowing me."

As I have stated previously in this book, we will forever discover more and more about this God of goodness as we continue in relationship with Him. He views the aspects mentioned in Hebrews 6 as *elementary teachings*, and as we master them, we will come into the greater depths of Christianity; to know Him. We discover much about Him as we walk in the demonstration of His power.

There are numerous arguments and doctrines that have been created by the enemy to keep man from walking in his commissioning and destiny pertaining to divine healing. In holy retaliation, many books have been written to biblically dismantle and destroy these erroneous and illogical doctrines and falsities. To repetitively cover these same issues is not the focus on this book, therefore if a "catching up" is needed, please refer to the "Recommended Reading" page at the end of the book. A previous book we wrote, "Stories of the Supernatural", is story after story of times when my wife and I witnessed miracles firsthand. It may help build your faith pertaining to the miraculous.

In the meantime, it is assumed that the reader grasps some of the factual imperatives necessary for possessing faith. A few examples of these imperatives are that it is always being God's will to heal, and that Jesus died for both sin *and* sickness. Without foundational truths in place such as these, the rest of this chapter will be one big offense, or at best, thoroughly confusing.

Merely seeing people healed is much less than what God would have for His people. We don't want to stop at the "Nazareth" level (Mark 6:5). We need a higher vision when pertaining to demonstrating the miraculous as we fulfill the call of God to love Him.

At this present time, God is preparing His body for the "more". For those that believe, healings and miracles are becoming common, and surprise is no longer an element in their occurrence. As Paul said in Act 26:8,

"Why should any of you consider it incredible that God raises the dead?"

God is taking the occurrence of miracles to such an incredible degree that if we do not ground ourselves in thankfulness and gratitude towards the Lord when we witness a miracle we could begin to simply shrug when we witness them because they are so usual. There are "hotspots" in the globe where this rate of frequency of miracles is already taking place.

As the Body of Christ, we need to strap in and hold on, because God is *moving*. He is about to break our understanding of what we think He will do because He is going so far beyond our grid for the miraculous.

Miracles are becoming more and more bizarre to those that do not understand that God likes to show off in any way He pleases. If people see miracles as anything less than a sign that points to a Greater Reality, they will become greatly offended. People will be levitating, flying, raising the dead, being transported, and funding ministry with winning lottery tickets because God gives them the correct numbers through accurate words of knowledge.

Instead of teaching about aspects of power that have been extensively covered in the past (healings, signs, wonders) this chapter is about abundant life. Namely, raising the dead.

+ Your Destiny Is Decided: Dead Raiser +

Most people need a bit of exhortation to come to a place where they can even begin to believe that dead raising is something that we should do as Christians. I have found that when people witness what the scriptures plainly state about a topic, they typically surrender their will to God's and let go of their excuses. If you are not convinced that God desires you to raise the dead, this section may help exhort you otherwise.

As is previously mentioned, the writer of Hebrews mentions *dead raising* as an elementary teaching in

Hebrews 6. The first time that registered mentally I almost fell out of the seat I was sitting in. I wondered how the most astounding miracle when dealing with the human body was *elementary*.

The writer of Hebrews viewed dead raising as an elementary principle in the life of faith because he assumed that most of the church would actually *obey* Jesus when He commanded us to raise the dead in Matthew 10:8.

"Heal the sick, raise the dead, cleanse those that have leprosy, drive out demons. Freely you have received, freely give."

Sometimes I don't believe something someone says until I see it in my own Bible. If you need to, get out your Bible and *look* at that verse in your own Bible. You need to see that it is right there, plain as day.

Now that we know that my Bible says the same thing that yours does, highlight the verse. Read it over and over. Remind yourself that Jesus isn't a liar, and He really does intend for you to lay your hands on people that are completely dead in order to raise them to life. Reorder your life according this verse. Whatever it takes in order that you obey Jesus' commands in this verse, do it. Don't worry about being controversial, just be obedient. Jesus said that if we love Him, we will obey Him.

The Bible isn't full of suggestions, but commands. Many make excuses to side step the above command, but excuses do not change the fact that we are still commanded to raise the dead. What the Word sets forth is non-negotiable. If Jesus commanded us to raise the dead, it should not be viewed as odd, off-kilter, or even radical. It should be viewed as normal. It should be an encouragement, because anything He commands us to do,

He gives us the grace to fulfill. He has already enabled you to raise the dead, simply by telling you to do it.

Therefore, you have a destiny to raise the dead. If you didn't, God wouldn't have told you to do it! The Spirit within you is the answer to the grief and pain in the world caused by disease and death. Nothing is more powerful than the Power wrapped up in your skin. You are a dwelling place of God, a temple of habitation for the Most High. Greater is He who is within you than he who is without you. Surely your hands have power of the most extreme nature, able to overcome lifelessness and death.

Healing the sick, casting out evil spirits, and raising the dead is not for a select few who have "a gift" for the working of miracles. Jesus gave the commandment to anyone that followed Christ, which means YOU!

Think of someone in your city that is well known and imagine that one day you get word that they died suddenly. Suppose that hundreds of people are grieving, viewing the body, and readying themselves for the funeral. Imagine yourself gaining entrance to the body, laying hands, and declaring life over the deceased. Breath enters their lungs, and as their chest begins to slowly move up and down with the rhythm of inhaling and exhaling, they stand up, raised from the dead. You present the person to the funeral home director, who cannot speak because he is struck with awe. You obtain the death certificate, now rendered useless legally but beautifully useful for testimony. Instead of telling anyone about this person's death, you wait. As the funeral ceremony begins, you walk the person up to the front stage so that everyone that is dressed in black can witness the manifest power of God. Some weep, some cry out in praise. The families and friends of the one that had died spontaneously pour out from the meeting place and into the street. Songs of praise and joy begin to rise as this company of people begins to literally parade this person around town so that everyone can see that they were once dead, but now alive. People driving by in their cars begin to pull over and ask what the crowd is celebrating. When the answer is simply, "Jesus", and the story is related about how He raised the dead, the drivers and bystanders begin to give their life to the Lord on the spot. The newspapers get word of this, and churches begin to pack out. A city is changed, and families filled with joy and thanksgiving.

This is your destiny, and it could happen to you.

+ Loop Holes +

I have heard people use all kinds of loophole arguments in order that they feel justified in writing off what Jesus clearly commands us to do in Matthew 10:8.

For example, a friend of mine named Mike Wallace told me of a time when someone presented to him one of these arguments. Mike was ministering in a church, and had been speaking on Matthew 10:8. Once he finished, a man approached Mike that had been sitting in the crowd. This man had PhDs in ministry training and theology, and made that known to Mike. He told Mike that Mike needed to read that section of scripture in context. Mike quietly listened. The man went on to describe what Mike already knew; that Jesus was speaking to the twelve disciples when He gave the command to raise the dead. He ended his intellectual spiel with the conclusion that because Jesus gave this command to His disciples and not directly to the future Body of Christ, we were subtly omitted from this commandment. He added that we are not only omitted from this command, but that we should be deterred from praying to raise the dead, lest we be led astray or harmed by the enemy because of the sin of presumption.

First off, how did we ever get so off track that *anything* good in the Word of God is off limits to us, especially when the Lamb was slain for the very purpose of securing good things for us? Surely Jesus' sacrifice was enough to obtain us everything and anything. *Surely He was and is worth that much.*

Mike calmly opened his Bible and led the man to the Great Commission in Matthew 28, where he read him one verse:

*"Therefore go and make disciples of all nations, baptizing them in the name of the Father and of the Son and of the Holy Spirit and **teaching them to obey everything I have commanded you."*** v19-20

In this verse Jesus was speaking to His disciples, sending them out one last time. He told them to teach everyone they discipled to do the things that He commanded them (the twelve) to do. This includes raising the dead. Praise God, there are no loopholes!

Despite this man's many years in study of the Bible and his many credentials, he had missed what is plainly stated in this verse. Dumbfounded, the man walked away speechless. By the cunningness of the Holy Spirit, Mike devastated this man's argument in one moment with one verse, just as Jesus outsmarted the Pharisees time and time again.

+ RAISING THE MASSES +

Resurrection power is a necessity not only because Jesus told us to do it, but because there will come a day when many people will die on Earth. In that hour, unless God's people are grounded in an unwavering faith and love, they will find themselves completely overwhelmed and overran. The Body of Christ needs to be ready to not just raise a few people from the dead, but masses of people! There isn't time to waver about raising the dead. Look at the following verses;

> *"I looked, and there before me…was Death, and Hades was following close behind him. They were given power over a **fourth** of the earth to kill by sword, famine and plague, and by the wild beasts of the earth."* Revelation 6:8

> *"A **third** of mankind was killed by the three plagues of fire, smoke and sulfur that came out of their mouths."* Revelation 9:18

Do the math. There are approximately 7 billion people on Earth at this time. By using that number in the following equation, the end sum is conservative in nature since the population on Earth is only going to grow from now until the more intense seasons of the end times begin.

A forth of 7 billion is 1.75 billion people. Now, lets work the other verse into the equation. A third of five hundred billion, two hundred and fifty million (what was left after Revelation 6:18) is 1.75 billion again.

The total sum of people that will die near instantly from just *two incidents* in the end times is *3.5 billion people*. That number is proportionate to having a Holocaust every two weeks. Bodies will be everywhere.

Death is going to be something that we are going to face head-on as the Body of Christ. Don't be frightened; it will not be the people of God that will experience these circumstances. Instead, God's people will have the same joyous commission that they have always had; "Raise the dead". In the midst of the darkest hour for those that choose not to follow The Way, the Body of Christ will be thriving in unprecedented power and love, incomparable to anytime in history. The Bride will walk in the fullness of what her Lover paid for.

Many people in the church today have taken on a view pertaining to dead raising that undermines the power that is presently available to anyone that will believe; the Martha paradigm.

When Lazarus died in John 11, Martha came to Jesus and told Him that if He had been present when Lazarus was sick, he wouldn't have died. This was the best profession of faith that Martha had at the time. In response to her statement, Jesus says, "Your brother will rise again", plainly telling Martha that He was about to raise Lazarus from the dead. Martha responds saying, "I know he will rise again in the resurrection at the last day."

When Jesus spoke, Martha didn't hear a plainly stated declaration of power, but a mysterious remark of sympathy that didn't seem help her in her present situation because its fulfillment was far off in the future. She didn't hear Jesus in the "now", but thought that He was referring to the resurrection of the dead that will happen at second coming of Christ. Martha's "faith" was exposed to be hope. Her ability to believe God could resurrect her brother was limited to the future, when the Answer to her problem stood before her! Jesus slanted her interpretation of future events by letting her know that the resurrection wasn't just a future event, but a Person. Even then, she didn't get it.

Faith is now, while hope is based on a belief in the future. While hope is a total necessity for the Christian life, *hope substituted for faith results in unbelief*. When God is standing right in front of us ready to work a miracle and we think He wants to do it later, we are found without faith.

Many situations in our lives, or teachings in the Bible, are viewed in this manner, thinking that God will only raise the dead and do greater works *in the future*. This is how we have traditionally read 1 Corinthians 15:12-17. My hope is that changes. If we read this portion of scripture believing that it is only about those that will be raised when Jesus returns to the earth, we are doing exactly what Martha did. Martha didn't have the faith that was needed to understand His word in the now. But she did have the hope to believe that Lazarus would be raised up at the end of time. She had knowledge of theology, but not faith. 1 Corinthians 15 was written not just to acknowledge that the dead will be raised when Jesus returns, but that Jesus raises the dead *now*. He wants to raise the dead *now* if we will be people who have faith and believe that He wants to *now*, literally, not just spiritually. He wants to raise the dead literally. If He didn't, He wouldn't have raised Lazarus. He would have simply agreed with Martha and walked away. Thank God that He is the God of the now, not just the distant future.

+ HOLY GHOST INSURANCE +

In becoming a person that is has set their heart on bringing life wherever you go, a dead raiser, you become one of the safest people in world. If you die, all the people around you that have heard you talk about resurrection power will not hesitate to pray to raise you up!

I know of a missionary that constantly preached the whole Gospel, including the abundant life that Christ offers us in this present life, not just the life to come. He had raised many people from the dead. One day while riding in his truck with his daughter, the enemy attacked him and took his life. He died on the spot. Because his daughter had listened to him talk about resurrection power for twenty years, she had no problem with reaching over and commanding life into her father's dead body. After sometime he came back to life, raised from the dead by his daughters prayers.

As we are faithful to believe the entire Gospel, including the commission to raise the dead, we inadvertently train up an unseen army around us. This army is our friends, our family, our church body, those we minister to, and anyone else that hears our radical conviction that Jesus bought us abundant life on the cross. When we find ourselves in a place of need, even death, these people will spring up in faith and will raise us up. You want real life insurance? Start to immerse yourself in overwhelming life that is found in Christ's sacrifice on the cross. The life that Jesus carries snuffs out the power of death like a flood snuffs out a candle.

"Most men judge the credibility of what they hear
according to the measure of their own experience, and
what is beyond the power of the hearer they insult with
the suspicion of falsehood, as outside of the truth."
-St. Gregory, 329-390 AD

Dead raisings are becoming a commonality, and as
time moves forward, you will only hear of their
increase. Without a doubt, resurrection is an incredibly
impressive miracle. Unlike other miraculous workings of
God, dead raising is a phenomenon that combines many
facets of God's manifest power; healing, creative power,
and the breath of God's life. Healing needs to come to
organs that are diseased that possibly invited death in the
first place. Creative, miracle-working power is needed to
recreate damaged or altogether missing organs and body
parts. And just as Adam experienced, the breath of God,
or the Spirit of Life, needs to be blown into a dead body
in order for it to be fit for the person's spirit to be clothed
by it again. Without one of these three aspects in
functionality, a person is unable to be raised from the
dead. Thus, dead raising is an incredible event.

But God is taking that which is incredible and
making it common. This chapter is about the fact that
God is raising the dead today, and has been since man
ushered in the presence of death upon the earth. God has
always been in the business of bringing life, and history
exemplifies this fact.

Most Christians have heard of the accounts in other countries such as Africa, Mexico, and Asia of the dead being raised.

A few of the present day miracle workers that have either raised the dead themselves or trained others to do so are David Hogan and Heidi Baker. These two are mentioned because of the noticeable amount of people raised in their ministries. David Hogan and the pastors that he oversees in Mexico have had around 500 people raised from the dead. These Mexican pastors expect the dead to be raised when they pray, thus it is common for them. David went to these mountain people when they were unreached, consequently they never had to unlearn bad theology because nobody ever taught them incorrectly from the start. David started them off right, so since they have been saved they understood that they were commissioned to raise the dead, thus, they have.

Heidi Baker, a wonderful woman of God's love and power, oversees many pastors across Africa. Nobody knows the exact number of people that have been raised by these pastors because they don't want any limelight for what God has done, but it is believed that around 100 people have been raised.

We have all heard of the dead being raised in third world nations, but what about America? The question, "Why isn't God raising people from the dead in America" is a question based on a false premise. The assumed belief hiding behind that question is that God *isn't* raising the dead in America. Remember, a question with a false premise never produces an accurate answer. First you have to ask, "Is God raising the dead in America?"

Yes, God *is* raising the dead in America today! Many churches have reported of this miracle taking place in their congregations, and as my wife and I speak in different places on the subject of resurrection power, people regularly tell us of circumstances where they were raised from the dead or prayed for someone and raised them from the dead. Even doctors that can give no more medical help to a dead patient are whispering quiet prayers over bodies and seeing the dead raised. Some of these situations are so undisputed that they have even been covered by the evening news, with the doctor explicitly giving all credit to God for the outcome.

The Dead Raising Team, spread across the United States and in other countries around the globe, has had a handful of people raised from the dead, but I am sure that by the time this book hits the printing press there will be many more people brought out of death and into life. The DRT has raised the dead to life in restaurants, hospitals, on the beach, and in the womb. North America is not being left out of God's plans and supernatural desires.

While it is encouraging to hear of the moving of God in our day, it is heartening, even surprising, to hear of God raising the dead on a *regular* basis in the past. What follows is our inheritance, and we will only go higher. What was their ceiling is our floor.

+ DEAD RAISINGS IN HISTORY +

Historical accounts of what God has done are priceless, for they not only tell us of the inheritance *we* have in the miraculous, but they also give us a marker on the horizon to head towards. God's history gives us our bearings in a world of confusion. The workings of God in the past reveals to us the permission we have from Heaven to move into the desires of our hearts. You cannot help but raise the dead because too many people have done it before you. The breakthrough has already been attained!

Most of the following accounts are well-documented miracles, recorded primarily by Catholic sources, and while not included in scripture, are thoroughly credible. Numerous historians and scholars worldwide acknowledge many of the following stories as authentic and credible.

Other accounts below are less clear in their details, and documented by only a few sources. This does not discredit these accounts except in the mind of a skeptic, for the credibility of a miracle does not ultimately rest upon the credibility of the one recounting the story, but if the god in question is capable of such a feat. Our God is.

This section will be especially brief in comparison to the overwhelming abundance of testimonies of the Lord raising the dead in the past. There are *thousands* of accounts in the archives of history that attest to the dead being raised, and not enough room here to cover them all. Much like John said of Christ's miracles, there are so many accounts of the dead being raised that their recounting would fill many books. Because many of the accounts of the dead being raised are alike in their storyline (someone died, was prayed for, then came back to life), included below are the stories that are in some way unique and set apart from other resurrection stories.

In addition it should be added that the eight accounts in scripture of the dead being raised, as well as the "many" that were raised by God when Jesus died on the cross, are not included in this section. It is assumed that the reader is already aware of these magnificent Biblical accounts.

Martin of Tours (316-397) raised at least three people from the dead in his lifetime. The first was in Ligugé, where one of Martin's companions came down with an intense fever and died. Martin was away, and when he returned on the third day, found his friend dead and ready for burial. Grieved, he sent his disciples out of the room and locked the door. Martin laid down on the body of his friend as Elisha had and began to pray. After two hours of consistent prayer, the limbs of the dead man began to stir. Suddenly, the man's eyes opened half way, and he began to blink at the brightness of the light coming through the window, raised from the dead.

The second account of manifest abundant life in Martin's days happened as Martin was walking across the property of a high-ranking dignitary named Lupicinus. Martin heard cries coming from a house nearby, and upon inspection, found a group of people grieving the loss of a slave that had hung himself. Martin stretched himself out on the body as he had done before, and the slave was brought back to life. Martin raised the man to his feet in front of the grieving crowd, to their obvious awe.

The third documented dead raising of Martin happened after he became a bishop. On a journey to a large town, a huge crowd of pagans approached Martin. There were so many people that it was described as "covering the whole plain". Once he was in their midst, a woman broke through the crowd and shoved a dead baby into the arms of Martin. She said, "You are God's friend, we know. Give me back my son! He is my only son!" With everyone watching, Martin knelt down with the baby in his arms. He prayed quietly over the child, as the silent and motionless crowd waited as if suddenly frozen in place. As soon as Martin finished praying, he stood with the child alive in his arms. He handed the child to his mother, and moments later, the entire crowd of pagans became Christians.

St. Benedict (480-547) was returning to his monastery one day when he was met by a farmer on the road. The farmer said, "Give me back my son! Give me back my son!" Confused, Benedict said, "But I have not taken your son from you, have I?" The farmer spoke more plainly and said, "He is dead. Come! Bring him back to life!" After some coercing, Benedict followed the father to the body of his son, prayed, and instantly the boy was brought back to life. In many of these stories we see children being brought back to life. That doesn't mean that God isn't motivated to raise those that are further along in years, it is that we aren't as motivated. Through many of these stories you witness *desperate* people. They are desperate because the person they lost was young, and they take on a violence of spirit that is undefeatable. If we take on this same violence of spirit with the elderly, we will see the same kind of breakthrough. God is consistent in His desire to raise the dead. We need to emulate Him, regardless of how people are.

Another time, Benedict was praying in his room when satan came to him and told him that he was going to take the life of one of his monks. Benedict headed for a room in the monastery where he knew the monks were constructing a new wall. When Benedict arrived, he found one of the monks crushed by the wall they had been putting up. Now dead, the monk's body was so damaged that they could not pick it up by hand, but rather had to place it on large blanket in order to carry it out of the room. Benedict had the body placed in his room, where he told everyone to leave, and knelt down to pray. Within an hour, Benedict sent the young man back to work, not only raised from the dead, but totally healed, with no broken bones.

Around the same era of Benedict, a man named Libertinis is believed to have raised the dead through the use of "residue anointing" that is demonstrated in Acts 19:11-12. Libertinis apparently would keep on his person a *sandal* from a man of God that he respected, Honoratus. Once, Libertinis was riding on his horse to Ravenna when a woman carrying a dead baby grabbed the bridle of the horse and said, "You shall not pass until you have brought my son back to life."

Talk about a demand. God loves this stuff. He loves it when we get demanding about things, because in doing so we are demonstrating our trust towards Him; that we know He will not get angry with us if we get adamant about something. Libertinis was frightened by the woman's demand, which was virtually a threat. But God sees the intention of the heart, and knew the desperation of a mother towards her children. God loves it when we love our kids in the way that He loves us; violently. Nothing was going to take this baby from this mother, not even death itself. Libertinis, on the other hand, tried to turn the woman out of his way. He was trying to run from her, struggling between fear and compassion. Finally, after enough "persuasion" from the woman, Libertinis dismounted, got on his knees, prayed, and raised his hands to heaven. He then took out the sandal that once belonged to Honoratus, and laid it on the body of the child. Instantly, because of the anointing still resting upon the sandal, the child was brought to life.

I know how desperate I am by how much I care if I disturb someone else in my pursuit of God. Don't let men of God get away without blessing you. It is ok to chase them down, be desperate, and disturb their world with your problems. Miracles happen when you do. God has put them where they are so that they can help people in tough situations, and true men of God will always try their best to help desperate people in desperate situations.

Anthony of Padua (1195-1231) had a number of resurrection miracles take place during his lifetime, but the following account is by far the most anomalous and glorious of them all.

Anthony was serving at a monastery in Padua, which was a 12 days walk from the city that his family lived in, Lisbon, Spain. One day in Lisbon, a man was murdered and Anthony's father was framed for the crime. The trial was scheduled to be held only a few days after the crime took place, and because of the time it would take for someone to travel to Anthony's monastery to deliver the news of the accusation, it would be impossible for Anthony to be present during the hearing. Nonetheless, during prayer God made Anthony aware of the situation, and after gaining permission to leave the monastery, Anthony began the long journey to Lisbon on foot. Even by horseback there was no possible way that Anthony could make it to Lisbon in time to catch the trial, but he went anyways, rationalizing that maybe he could be of some help after the bogus verdict of guilt had been issued to his father.

As soon as Anthony left the outskirts of his city, he found himself walking through the doors of the courthouse and into the room where the trial was taking place in Lisbon. He had been transported from one city to the other. All present knew there was no way Anthony could have known about his father's situation, as well as gotten to the hearing with such speed, thus his arrival alone spoke overtly of God's divine work in the situation. All fell silent as Anthony made his way to the judge in the front of the room.

Anthony declared that his father was innocent, and in reply, the judges asked for proof to such a claim. Full of the boldness that comes upon a person when they are in the anointing for faith, Anthony replied, "The murdered man shall bear witness as to the truth of my testimony." He then led the people, including the judges, to the grave of the man that had been murdered.

When they arrived, Anthony asked that the grave be opened and the body uncovered. He then commanded the dead man to speak to the crowd and tell the people of his father's innocence. Just as Anthony commanded, the dead man *sat up and spoke*, telling all that were present that

Anthony's father was innocent. Astonished, and still in need of bringing punishment upon whoever committed this crime, the judges asked who *was* guilty, because Anthony's father was obviously blameless. Anthony replied, "I come to declare the innocent, not to denounce the guilty."

And the accounts go on and on. Dead children were given back to their parents wholly restored, the elderly were given more years after passing away, even animals that were cooked and eaten were raised to life. Below is a brief list of manifest resurrection power;

+ GOD USED THE DEAD TO RAISE THE DEAD +

God is so eager to raise the dead, *He even used the dead to raise the dead* in the Bible (2 Kings 13:20-21). If God can use the dead to raise the dead, then surely He can use you to raise the dead! No matter how worn out, beat up, and lacking in faith you are, you still have the spirit of Jesus living inside of you, and surely you are in better shape than a dead body! God is going to use you in mighty ways. The following stories will infuse you with faith and hope, because if a lifeless, buried body can raise the dead, then surely you can!

Many resurrection miracles that were recorded by Catholics ironically took place at the graves of saints. Catholics will say that is because the person in need went to their grave and prayed, and the saint made the request known to God, thus resulting in a miracle. We now know that we do not need any mediator besides Christ, who we all have dwelling inside of us by His Spirit, and that we have a direct line to the Father. The reason that so many miracles took place at the graves of saints that had died is because of the residue anointing, an actual quantifiable substance in the spirit, that rested upon their physical bodies. A few examples of this from scripture are when the woman with the blood problem in Mark 5:21-34 was healed after touching Jesus' garment, the dead man that sprung to life when thrown into Elisha's grave in 2 Kings 13:20-21, the belief that Peter's shadow in Acts 5 would heal the sick, and the handkerchiefs and aprons that were brought to Paul in Acts 19. All these cases point to the reality of residue anointing, not the intercessory ability that some people have over another. God hears anyone and everyone that prays.

+ ACCIDENTAL RESURRECTIONS +

God is a God of grace. He is so excited about giving life that He will use faithless, unmotivated prayers to work His will. He loves to bring the dead to life.

Another example of God's excitement is as follows. Once a few years ago, a Catholic man died in a hospital in California. A relative knew that this man would want someone to pray for him after he died, so this woman went in where the man's body was and prayed the, "Our Father" prayer. She didn't have any faith, didn't believe in dead raisings, and wasn't even praying out of a motive of God being glorified, but rather out of relational duty. Nonetheless, this man that had been dead for two days sat up, raised from the dead. You can imagine the relative's surprise! She "accidentally" raised the dead. I wonder if anyone had to raise *her* to life after having a heart attack from the shock of this man being raised to life. Be careful what you ask for, because you will get it! There is power in your prayers, even when you don't really believe what you are praying for. Isn't that a relief?

God isn't waiting for perfect faith in order to work in this world. He is constantly and eagerly searching for ways to infiltrate the world with His love and life. He is not withholding His spirit, but hanging over the balcony of heaven, looking down upon Earth, searching for any person that will give Him any kind of entrance, even by accident. God wants to restore the world! He isn't ok with His children living in a low-income area of the universe. He is eager to redeem the earth and make it a place of complete, flourishing life.

Some have died in sin, even in blatant opposition to God, and He has raised them from the dead and saved them nonetheless. This offends our mind, but it is the nature of God. God is a God of grace. He doesn't have a point which when crossed, makes a person out of the reach of His love.

One such example was when a chief witchdoctor got deathly ill in Mexico. The witchdoctor had cursed his son with a curse of death because his son had given his life to Jesus. Big mistake. The curse came back to the witchdoctor and rested upon him, and within a few days he was inches from death. The son, whose mind was now renewed, knew that God wanted to heal his father, despite his father's sin. He asked his pastor, David Hogan, to come pray with him for his father. David did so. As they were about to pray for the witchdoctor, he began cursing David, his son, and the God that they followed. Like the suggestion given by Job's fickle wife, the witchdoctor cursed God, then *died* on the spot. Broken hearted, the son stayed by his father's side, despite the overt sin that his father had walked in his whole life, even up until the moment he breathed his last. The son believed that God still wanted to save his father, because that was the nature of God. He prayed through the entire night and into the next day. Suddenly, a day and a half after his father stopped breathing, the witchdoctor came back to life. He awoke in tears of repentance, saying that he met a man in the spirit realm that told him three words, "I love you". The witchdoctor knew the Man was God, and fell at His feet in worship. He awoke not only raised from the dead, but *saved*, despite his evil lifestyle and the state in which he died. Nobody is too far-gone for God to save them for the nature of God is grace, love, and salvation. Let that throw a wench in your theology!

Heidi Baker also tells a story of a woman that died who was particularly disliked by those in her village because she was so unkind to those around her. As the woman's body was being carried to the gravesite, the Lord spoke to an onlooker, telling the young man to pray to raise the woman from the dead. The young man disliked this woman so much that he told the Lord "No". The Lord asked the young man again, and again the young man reminded the Lord how evil and unkind the old woman had been to everyone in her life. Nonetheless, the Lord did not relent in His desire to bring this sinner back to life. The young man regrettably walked over to the simple wooden casket and laid his hands on it. Instantly, the woman sprang to life.

I am convinced that more than we could ever desire for things like dead raisings and revival, God desires them much more for us. He needs no convincing. I am convinced that we do not need to pray for God to send revival in order to motivate Him, but to motivate *us*. I believe that He already wants to bring revival, even that He already has. But in order for us *experience revival*, we have to step into what He has already done and get free from our old thinking. Suddenly, we aren't asking for revival, we become it.

It is the same with dead raising. God is much more eager to bring the dead back to life than you and I are. In fact, God will raise the dead with those that *don't want the dead to come back to life*, if they will only have a grid for such a miracle. The young man didn't have any problem with believing that God wanted to raise up the woman, or that He could do it. In fact, in his resisting to pray, he oddly exemplified rock solid faith that God *would* raise that woman from the dead if he prayed. It is a hilarious story, and the lessons run deep. If someone that *doesn't want* to raise the dead can affectively raise the dead, it will surely take place when someone prays that *does want* it to happen, someone such as yourself. Just believe.

"The thief comes only to steal and kill and destroy; I came that they may have life, and have it abundantly."
-John 10:10

*R*esurrection power produces a gamut of questions for anyone that takes but a moment to digest what *dead raising* actually means. One pertinent line of questions is *"What do we do once a person is raised back to life? How long will they live? What if they die again? Do we just keep raising them back to life over and over?"* This string of questions, while borderline humorous to imagine, turns out to be quite relevant. The practical aspect is of course in need of answering, but the practical facet leads us to a greater and deeper reality sown throughout scripture that we have somehow simply missed. What has eluded the majority of us will be plainly revealed in this chapter. Christ called it *abundant life*. And no, I am not referring to the life we experience once we die, leave this earth, and go to heaven. I am referring to the kind of life you can have right here on the face of the earth, in your body woven of flesh and blood.

+ THE HEART OF GOD +

If it is in any way unclear after reading the past six chapters how God feels about death and life then you may need to get new glasses. Nonetheless, it bears repeating. In order to tackle abundant life, we have to firstly confront how God feels about death. I have found that when I don't lay this scriptural foundation when I teach at conferences or DRT trainings, people get lost in their traditional and contradictory beliefs about God.

Remember, these verses, while extremely helpful, are second to the blatant example of the life of Christ that plainly demonstrated to us the heart of God pertaining to life and death, regardless of what was written of the Father in the Old Testament. Christ always raised the dead. He always brought life. He never killed anyone. And He is the exact representation of God (Hebrews 1:3), the most accurate example of who the Father is. If that ultimate authority doesn't convince you, hopefully these verses will. Most people are unclear who brings death. For example, most people believe that God flooded the earth and killed an evil generation, but Jesus said something different in the book of John:

"The thief comes only to steal and kill and destroy; I came that they may have life, and have it abundantly." John 10:10

According to Christ, the enemy's modes of operation are stealing, killing, and destroying. Jesus' mode of operation is to give life. In one sentence Jesus clears up the age old question of who brings death and who gives life, then takes it to a whole new level by saying that God wants his children to have abundant life, not just life. We *"may"* have it, in that it is being offered, but not guaranteed unless we reach out and take it.

In case Jesus didn't make it clear enough, the writer of Hebrews clarifies that death is not in heaven with God, ready to be sent at His command in case someone gets out of line and dirties themselves with sin, too far gone and out of reach of grace:

*"Since the children have flesh and blood, he too shared in their humanity so that by his death he might destroy **him who holds the power of death--that is, the devil...**"* Hebrews 2:14

Who holds the power of death? The devil. It is pretty clear. You can never step outside God's reaches of grace. He won't punish you for your sin by taking your life. He doesn't take life. He doesn't give death to anyone; He doesn't have it to give!

You can never wear God down with your sin to such a degree that He gives up on you. You can't run far enough away that His love won't hunt you down and arrest your heart with gentleness once again. Wrath from God isn't the result of your sin; Grace is.

But I must clarify; when we allow sin into our lives, we also allow the wages of sin: death. Is it God mitigating this sentence of condemnation? Never! It is the accuser of the brethren that uses the law against us to reveal the guilt of sin. The enemy holds the power of death and he only has legal right to afflict a person with it when the person has opened the door to death through sin. To God, death is an enemy, as Paul states in 1 Corinthians 15:26,

*"The last **enemy** to be destroyed is death."*

Is death a friend to God? An ally of God during humanity's many eras of significant sin throughout history and in the future? Or is God complete at odds with death, working against it in every way possible, even by sending His one and only son to be sacrificed on our behalf, that we may be cleansed of all sin that gives the enemy the legal right through the law to put us to death? Even when presented with perfect moments to demonstrate this supposed partnership with death when circumstances are great enough, Christ still stood in direct opposition to using death for punishment for sin or to accomplish His will. In the below verse, Jesus was just rejected by an entire Samaritan village, a people group not valued by the Jews.   On top of being a people that historically hadn't melded well with God's people, they had *rejected* Christ. Step back and think about that. If there is any sin that is of the utmost severity, it would be what this village just did. Rape, murder, genocide pail in comparison to *rejecting Christ Himself.* Not a good situation. If there was any situation in which to demonstrate the wrath, judgement, or punishment of God because of sin, this was the perfect scenario. James and John recognize the sin that the village just stepped into, and because they don't understand who God is and what He will and won't do, rationalize that the only "just" treatment for such a sin is to torch the place. Seriously! This is actually what they recommended to Jesus what they should do! Be assured that there were women and children in that village.

"....they went and entered a village of the Samaritans to make arrangements for Him. But they did not receive Him, because He was traveling toward Jerusalem. When His disciples James and John saw this, they said, "Lord, do You want us to command fire to come down from heaven and consume them?" John 9:52-53

I imagine Jesus slapping his hand to his forehead in disbelief of how thick-headed His disciples were, even after spending so much time with him. They still didn't get it. They still didn't understand that Jesus was a greater and more accurate picture of who the Father was than all of the teachings they had got at church or read in their holy scriptures. They still determined what the Father would do by what they had been told He had done rather than by who Christ was, though He was standing right in front of them. Thus, He has to speak plainly to them and tell them *not* to destroy the village with the power of their tongues;

But He turned and rebuked them, and said, "You do not know what kind of spirit you are of; for the Son of Man did not come to destroy men's lives, but to save them." Luke 9:54-56

Isn't Jesus fantastic? Isn't He so different than what we expected of God? He brought a whole new revelation to humanity of the nature of God. He was the embodiment of love and grace. There are multitudes of verses in the Bible that show that God is pro-life, but we will end with Matthew 10:8;

"Heal the sick, raise the dead, cleanse the lepers, cast out demons. Freely you received, freely give."

Why does Christ command us to raise the dead? *Because you aren't supposed to die!* This chapter will explore such a claim, so gird up and hold on. If you don't like biblically based, non-traditional, Christ centered teachings, then back out now.

✛ START AT THE BEGINNING ✛

In order to grasp what God desires for us to understand about abundant life, we have to rewind and start with understanding what happened in the Garden of Eden.

Adam and Eve were created in an atmosphere free of sin and death. "The wages of sin is death", and nobody had sinned yet, thus there was no death present. They were free from *end*, their bodies were never to give out, and there was no amount of years that was too great for them to live on the earth.

That is, until they ate of the fruit. The sin of eating of the fruit opened the door to the reality of death, and the moment that Eve sank her teeth into what she plucked from the tree, she became mortal. A moment before she was immortal, in that she was not going to ever experience death. Death was an impossibility, but now it was an impossibility to live. When before it was an impossibility to die, now the presence of sin had changed everything.

It needs to be highlighted that even at the start of time God did not usher death into the scenario. We did. God created humanity in a state free from death. Death was never on His agenda from the start, and never will be. He didn't send death into the world as a result of or punishment for Adam's and Eve's sin. He had, and has, no need to punish us; the repercussions of our sin already does that more than sufficiently.

As Eve entertained the idea of eating of the fruit, God told her what would happen if she did. God's warning clarifies that the choice in Eden was never primarily about obedience and disobedience or even sin or righteousness. God cuts to the chase and reveals the real essence of what would happen if they ate and the ultimate choice men have on earth:

"If you eat of the fruit, you will surely die." Genesis 2:17

The choice for mankind has *always* been to live or to die. We chose death. Today, what do you choose? Do you embrace death as your means to entrance to heaven, or do you set yourself against death as an enemy, resisting its every attempt to convince you that it is normal to die, that everyone must die one day, that death is a thing we must come to accept, and even that death is a friend to those in suffering?

God wanted men to live, and warned Eve of the immediate consequences of her actions. He wasn't allowing death to afflict her if she ate; He was trying to deter her from severing the abundant life that was already resting on her.

Let it be clear that God did not let, allow, or invite death into the world. *We* allowed death into the world through our sin. Our sin opened wide the door for death to come rushing onto the scene and begin sowing mortality into the essence of the sons of men. The enemy had no authority, so he sought it from those that had been given dominion over creation; man. In the eating of the fruit we surrendered our deathlessness and our dominion.

Interestingly enough, men continued to have very long lifespans, with Methuselah taking the title of longest living man in the Bible (969 years). This is because the residue of life that was in Eden was still resting on men to a degree, just as the anointing rested on the bones of the prophet and was able to raise a man from the dead years later (2 Kings 13:21). The further away from Eden that we get on a timeline, the less years men lived. This, and not because God limited the years of men's lives, is why the years of men dwindled down to double digits, as they are commonly today. Later in this chapter we will discuss how God never limited the years of men as we have traditionally thought, because of a misreading of Genesis 6:3.

+ THE SECOND ADAM +

Thankfully, after we screwed everything up God still had a plan. In order to remove the power of sin, He sent His son to die on our behalf. Don't mistake me; the Father didn't kill Jesus. Jesus laid His life down and gave His life on our behalf, that through His death we could receive righteousness. God wasn't demanding for someone to die in order to cover the sins of men; the enemy was. The enemy had legal right to steal, kill, and destroy men, so Jesus came and was stolen from, killed, and destroyed on our behalf. After the cross, Christ busted out of the grip of death, came to life, and made abundant life available to anyone that receives His sacrifice.

And this is the point; before the fall men were free from death because there was no sin. Jesus came that by his death and resurrection we could be set from from sin, so what does that mean for us?

Ready yourself. It means that *you can live forever*. The wages of sin is death, but you have been freed from sin's wages because of Christ. Thus, you are free from death. You never have to die.

Sound nuts? Well, read the coming verses. Jesus spoke quite regularly of this "abundant life", in fact so much so that it is very hard not to believe unless you want to purposely ignore much of what Jesus mentions.

+ MORE THAN A TICKET TO HEAVEN +

The reason we have missed what the following verses are communicating about immortality is because we have been taught and assumed that they simply refer to *going to heaven* rather than *not dying*. How foolish it would be to believe that what Christ's sacrifice secured for us has a limitation. Be assured that Christ's death did *everything* you will ever need. You cannot overstate the gift of His death, nor the results of what it did for you.

Thus, in order to understand that many of the things Christ spoke about when dealing with life had to do with living forever rather than dying and going to heaven, we have to look at John 11. This passage clearly displays the difference between the two paradigms.

We are picking up in the story of Lazarus' resurrection at the point where Martha approaches Jesus and tells Him that if He had been around, her brother wouldn't have died. She then asks Jesus to raise her brother from the dead. Jesus plainly tells her that He will raise Lazarus from the dead, to which Martha responds, revealing that she misunderstood Jesus' assurance as a doctrinal pat-on-the-back. Then Jesus clarifies His statement. He reveals to Martha something *much more amazing* than the fact that He is about to raise her brother from the dead. Isn't it like Jesus to be asked for something and give much more than what was asked of Him? She asked for a miracle (which she later receives), but is given a revelation that is more weighty than glory He is about to release on her brother's dead body.

"I am the resurrection and the life. The one who believes in me will live, even though they die, and whoever lives by believing in me will never die. Do you believe this?" John 11:25-26

Did you catch it? Jesus first acknowledges that belief that every Christian has; that if you receive Jesus, when you die you will go to heaven.

"The one who believes in me will live, even though they die..."

Its good news! But there is even greater news! Jesus steps it up a notch from what is widely believed and opens to Martha a whole new world;

"... and whoever lives by believing in me will never die."

Never die. He didn't say "die and go to heaven", He said "never die". He had just acknowledged the belief we all have of dying and going to heaven, then He blatantly spells out the greater reality of life free from death.

This is what Paul was referring to in 2 Timothy 1:9-10,

*"...This grace was given us in Christ Jesus before the beginning of time, but it has now been revealed through the appearing of our Savior, Christ Jesus, **who has destroyed death and has brought life and immortality to light through the gospel.**"*

Jesus didn't just destroy death on the cross; He obtained life and *immortality* for those that believe upon Him and rest in His presence. Paul refers to such life as "grace". Before the cross, nobody had brought this abundant life to light nor had the ability to reveal it. Christ alone did so, and it is to us a grace of unimaginable proportions. And as a side note, if we believe Christ destroyed death, why do we it destroy us?

Some may try to use 1 Timothy 6:16 to disregard what this verse and all other verses mentioned in this chapter are communicating; immortality through Christ. 1 Timothy 6:16 says that, "...[God] alone possesses immortality...". This simply reinforces the obvious point that immortality comes from Christ alone, not from men. Just as only God is righteous but imparts it to us through Christ, so it is with immortality.

There are numerous times Jesus mentioned this reality of abundant life. John 8:51 and John 6:47-51 are other examples;

*"Truly, truly, I say to you, if anyone keeps My word he **will never see death.**"* John 8:51

Jesus is pretty clear that if you believe the words He speaks and walk them out, you will never experience death.

"Very truly I tell you, the one who believes has eternal life. I am the bread of life. Your ancestors ate the manna in the wilderness, yet they died. But here is the bread that comes down

*from heaven, which anyone may eat and **not die**. I am the living bread that came down from heaven. Whoever eats this bread will **live forever**. This bread is my flesh, which I will give for the life of the world."*

Again, Jesus doesn't say "die and go to heaven", He says "live forever". If Jesus was referring to eternity in heaven rather than immortality, why would he use the example of a natural death when referring to the people's ancestors? He uses an example of a natural death, not a spiritual death, and then tells the people that they may experience something different from their ancestors if they receive and eat of Him. Without a doubt, Christ is attempting to lead His listeners into a higher vision for their lives. They can have much, much more than just dying at 95 years old and going to heaven. They can skirt death and never die. They can be immortal. It is glorious.

Don't get me wrong: It isn't wrong to believe that you will have eternal life in heaven. God is so gracious that for those that don't receive the message of immortality through Christ, He still has a backup plan to bless His kids. He never punishes us for our lack of faith, but gives us the next best thing that our faith can receive. *But* if we want more, He is gladly offering it. Here is another verse that invites us into abundant life,

"The world and its desires pass away, but the man who does the will of God lives forever." 1 John 2:17

If you look up the word "lives" in the above verse in greek, you will find that it means a plethora of wonderful things. A few of them are: to remain, to abide, not to depart, to continue to be present, to be held and kept continually, not to perish, to last or endure, to live, and to survive. My favorite is "to be held and kept continually". Isn't it beautiful? And you can have this wonderful gift of abundant life!

"And I give them eternal life, and they shall never perish; neither shall anyone snatch them out of My hand. My Father, who has given them to Me, is greater than all; and no one is able to snatch them out of My Father's hand." John 10:28-29

We shall never perish! The enemy cannot snatch our lives away, for our lives rest in the hands of Christ, fully kept safe and secure, for the Father is greater than all and the life He gives is greater than death could ever be. This. Is. Good. News.

"But whoever drinks the water I give them will never thirst. Indeed, the water I give them will become in them a spring of water welling up to eternal life." John 4:14

Am I saying that Christ *isn't* talking about securing an eternal seat in heaven for us? Never! I am communicating that He did that and *more,* and that He is not *not* referring to immortality in this verse. It is an invitation of faith; You can stop at the place of believing that Christ only secured you an eternal place above, or you can go on to a greater place of faith that He also secured you an eternal place *on earth.* What have you?

Ask yourself. Why would we have to die if Christ did for us? Why would He tell us to raise the dead if they were destined to just die again in a few years?

"...he suffered death, so that by the grace of God he might taste death for everyone." Hebrews 2:9

This is part of the beauty of the Gospel: He tasted death so you didn't have to. In the Garden, the choice was to live, or to die. The choice is still the same. Through

Christ you may choose to live, and live in abundance. Abundance means more than enough; to overflow and spill over because there is too much to be contained.

David exhorts us to remember the *all* the benefits of receiving Christ in Psalm 103;

*"Praise the LORD, my soul, and forget not all his benefits — who forgives all your sins and heals all your diseases, who redeems your life from the pit and crowns you with love and compassion, who satisfies your desires with good things so that **your youth is renewed** like the eagle's."*

David tells us that a elementary understanding of Christ's sacrifice lies in knowing that He died for your sins and saved you from hell, but that He also died for your sickness! He then goes on to present the logical conclusion to God healing every disease we could ever experience; your *youth* being made new. We have to remember that it is vain to think that God only heals our bodies and does not give us everlasting life, otherwise what is the point of being healed? The most pertinent reason to be healed of a disease is so that it doesn't end in death. In fact, the job of disease is to give entrance to a spirit of death. Remember, everything was always about two forces battling for mankind: Life and death. God heals His kids because He wants them to live. If He ended with healing and not life that is renewed with youth, then you have a gap in logic.

God feels so strongly about us understanding His desire for us to live on the earth in dominion that He even told us through Paul to *seek* immortality.

*"To those who by persistence in doing good **seek** glory, honor and **immortality**, he will give eternal life."* Romans 2:7

What does this mean? It means that you will live without death *if* you believe for it. *If* you want it and seek it out. *If* you set your faith upon it and receive it through believing that Jesus is giving it to you. *Seek* immortality. Look for it around every corner. Pray it over other people. Speak about it to others. Get labeled as a new-age, off-based, unbiblically-based heretic for Jesus. Who cares: You will outlive your accusers anyways!

How have you missed this in your Bible? How did I read this verse with such limitations for so many years? These verses are just sitting on the pages of a book that we have had and read for thousands of years, yet somehow we missed them! Here is another verse that applies to abundant life;

"...you will not abandon me to the realm of the dead, nor will you let your faithful one see decay. You make known to me the path of life; you will fill me with joy in your presence, with eternal pleasures at your right hand." Psalm 16:10-11

Jesus is the path of life. In Him is life (John 1). If you are full of faith for immortality and will live in Him your body will not see decay. This doesn't refer just to not dying, but the decay a body experiences over the normal lifespan of a human. He can renew your youth (Psalm 103:5). He can cause your body to stay free from decay and age. He will not abandon you to death. He will not forsake you to disease. Why would He? According to the Bible, Christ tasted death so that you didn't have to. The death we deserved was experienced by Christ on our behalf so that *our mortal bodies* could be instilled with supernatural life. Paul said it like this;

"We always carry around in our body the death of Jesus, so that the life of Jesus may also be revealed in our body. For we who are alive are always being given over to death for Jesus' sake,

so that his life may also be revealed in our mortal body." 2 Corinthians 4:10-11

You are destined for abundant life. Yet sadly, most people don't just accept death but they agreed with it and even invite it into their lives. People do this for many reasons, but in this next section we will explore some of the verses in the Bible that people use to reinforce the misled exultation of death.

+ A CHURCH THAT WANTS TO DIE +

If we believe that the only way to heaven is through the preverbal "door" that death provides, then we won't view death as an *enemy* (1 Corinthians 15:28) but something that leads us to our true home. This is partly true, but less than what the Lord suffered for and bought for us on the cross. Why should we not receive all that the Lamb was slain for?

After hearing this teaching on abundant life a friend of ours said it like this;

"Death is not the doorway to Heaven. Most people mistakenly believe that we go to heaven when we die. This is not true. You entered Heaven when Jesus died. Your death is not the doorway to heaven. His death is your doorway to Heaven. It was your co-crucifixion with Him that has now seated you in heavenly places."

Death is not your only way into heaven, and surely not God's suggested method of getting there. If death was the only way into heaven, then what of Elijah and Enoch? Even Christ entered heaven while being *alive*, not dead. If fact, scripture says that during the the three days when Christ *was* dead, He went to *hell* for a soul winning crusade (Eph. 4:8-10, 1 Peter 3:18-20).

Most of the scriptures that Christians use to reinforce their belief that death is not an enemy are read out of context. There is no biblical support to believe that death is something to be embraced and that we are to live a life focused on going to heaven rather than bringing heaven to earth, as Christ prayed. One verse people use to communicate that they should die is Philippians 1:21.

"For to me, to live is Christ and to die is gain."

True, Paul. Very true. If you live, that is God. If you die, that is gain. In other words, dying is good, but Christ is better. Paul is telling us that if we die, all hope is not lost because God has secured for us a spiritual life in heaven that is eternal, and that heaven is a wonderful place. But he clarifies that if we are to go on living, *that* is Christ. What do you want more? The good or the best? The "good" has always lured the masses away from what is best. I would recommend holding out for everything Christ bought for you; life. Paul is basically making the same statement that Jesus made in John 11:25,26; Living long comes from Christ. Dying and going to heaven is fine and good, but living forever is one better.

Oddly enough, giving into thinking about going to heaven rather than heaven coming to earth results in someone *wanting to die.* It should not surprise us that science and law would simply refer to that desire as suicidal. It may sound odd, but the church has in various degrees given itself to *a spirit of suicide.* What else would you call it when people want to die? Whatever the logic, or however people come to that conclusion, matters not. It is scientifically verified to be *whacked.* It is high time we unmask the spirit of suicide prevalent in the church. No more passively accepting what you get dealt. Fight death. Fight it with everything in you and claim, as the psalmist did in Psalm 118, *"I will live and not die!"*

Paul goes on in verse 22 to clarify that he is *not* endorsing the belief that we should yearn to go to heaven rather than witness heaven invade earth.

*"If I am to go on living in the body, this will mean fruitful labor for me. Yet what shall I choose?... but it is **more necessary** for you that I remain in the body. Convinced of this, I know that I will remain, and I will continue with all of you for your progress and joy in the faith..."*

When everything in Paul's life was surveyed, he determined that it was *a necessity* that he go on living on earth. Why? There are souls to be won, reward to be gained, glory to be secured for God, and bliss to be discovered in the Presence of God.

I am not denying that going to heaven will be wonderful. I am suggesting that you can be with Christ *now* and do not need to wait to experience heaven. Scripture tells us that we are already seated in heavenly places! If you are so determined to go to heaven, close your eyes and go there, but don't give yourself over the enemy by inviting death into your life.

Even *Christ* prayed not that we would be taken out of the world!

"I do not ask You to take them out of the world, but to keep them from the evil one." John 17:15

Christ purposefully prayed that *we wouldn't be taken out of the world*. Instead, He prayed that we would be protected from the enemy, who brings death.

Jesus didn't have a paradigm of a dreamer. He wasn't one that day-dreamed about his going home in heavenly places but instead we witness Him healing the sick, raising the dead, casting out demons, and cleansing the lepers. What was He doing? He was *bringing heaven to earth* rather than dreaming about going there someday. His primary focus that gave Him hope wasn't that he would one day return to heaven, but what He saw taking place on earth. We are to focus on heaven in order to replicate it on earth, not to use the thought of going to heaven as our backup plan for hope. If we are lacking hope, we haven't stewarded the revelation of what He *already did for us*. The authenticity of your hope should be suspect anytime it is dependent upon something God is going to do rather than what He already did. If your hope is dependent upon something you think God will do or will happen to you *rather than what He has already done*, you should step back and ground yourself in thankfulness.

Even in one of Christ's most well known prayers, He prayed in this manner.

"...Your Kingdom come on earth as it is in heaven." Matthew 6:10

You are called, first and foremost, to bring heaven to earth and demonstrate the will of God *on earth*, not leave the earth and go to heaven. Jesus never prayed for us to leave the earth, but to manifest heaven upon it!

Let any spirit of suicide be unmasked in your thinking. Start to *want* to live and not die. Line yourself up with scripture, with the prayers of Christ, and with your destiny.

+ THE EXTENDING OF LIFE +

There are few verses in the Old Testament that people use to fortify their belief that death is inevitable and something we should just surrender to. This belief comes to the surface few times in life, but will always raise its head when someone is praying for resurrection.

If you want faith to raise the dead, you must have this stuff sorted out in your heart and mind.

For some reason, though the word "limit" isn't even in the verse, people believe that God limited the years of men's lives in Genesis 6:3 to 120 years. I have news for you; God never limits life. He never will and never did. He is the giver of life and nothing else. Here is the verse:

"Then the LORD said, "My Spirit will not contend with humans forever, for they are mortal; their days will be a hundred and twenty years."

First off, lets clarify that this verse does not use the word "limit" in any translation, nor in the hebrew. We have assumed that is what the verse is saying, but in fact it is saying the exact opposite.

To understand this verse we have to grasp the context in which this statement was given. God makes this statement prior to even the first covenant. In other words, at this time there was nothing man could do to make propitiation for his sin. At all times he was vulnerable to death because of his sin. In fact, the moment men were born the enemy had the legal right to destroy them. Hence, the Father steps in and *extends* their lives to *at least* 120 years. Instead of this verse being about limiting life, it is a statement of extending life. It is an action completely drenched in grace.

When the Lord says that His spirit will not contend with men forever He was referring to the fact that men were no longer a place where the Spirit could inhabit. Humans were created to be temples for the Spirit of God, but men didn't have Christ in that day, thus they were unclean habitations for the Spirit of God. Christ changed that, and we see the outpouring of the Spirit of God in Acts 2 as proof. Thus, just as the Spirit couldn't inhabit men and contend with them forever, now the Spirit can. We are immortal because of Christ, with the Spirit of Life living inside of us, safeguarded from death.

Some people aren't convinced God wasn't limiting life. They bring up Psalm 90, where it says that the years of our lives are 70 years, 80 if we are stronger. But that was *Old Covenant.* Do you actually think that Christ's death and resurrection obtained you so little? This new and glorious covenant that we live in magnificently surpasses the limits set upon the old.

Perhaps you are still not convinced that Genesis 6:3 is a statement extending life rather than limiting it. That is fine. But you have some explaining to do then. If that verse is saying that God limited the lives of men to 120 years, then why did men live much, much longer than that after this statement was made? Even more, if that verse is saying that men's lives would be limited to 120 years, that means that *nobody* in our day would be able to live past 120 years old.

But that is exactly what happened in 1995. In 1995 Jeanne Clement, a woman living in France, was thoroughly documented for having turned 120 years old. In fact, she even lived two years past the supposed "limiting" of life in Genesis 6:3, with the total time she lived being 122 years.

If Genesis is undoubtedly about the limiting of men's lives, how does one explain the many exceptions of it? They can't. One must change the way they view that verse.

Men were still living in the afterglow of Eden long after Adam and Eve were thrown out. It was powerful stuff they had lived in, and Methuselah walked in it so thoroughly that he lived to be 969 years old. And that was before the far more glorious and powerful covenant we live in now! We have been taught that the years of men's lives dwindled over time because God limited men's lives but in fact it was that they were simply stepping further and further away from Eden and the anointing of life therein. On a timeline, the further men got from Eden, the less years they lived. That is, unless the Second Adam.

+ THE MISSING PIECE +

You may be wondering by now, "If abundant life is something that we can possess through Christ, why haven't more people gone on to live forever?" My response would be in a question as well, "How many people do you know that are believing for it?"

You receive what you believe. I would suggest that more people haven't lived longer lives through the power of God because they didn't have a grid for it. In fact, more Christians have more of a grid for the idea of immortality *outside* Jesus and scripture than within them. If you go tell a Christian that you are going to live forever, they will probably assume you are a New Age or buddhist rather than a follower of Christ. That is because most Christians are totally unaware of what scripture presents to us pertaining to abundant life. It is the lack of knowledge that causes God's people to die (Hosea 4:6), but if people get a vision for abundant life they will begin to live long.

In addition, Proverbs 18:21, which we covered thoroughly in a previous chapter, has this to say about life and death;

"The tongue has the power of life and death, and those who indulge in it will eat its fruit." (Amplified)

The former portion of this verse we covered in depth already, but the repercussions of the latter portion of the verse are just as significant. Solomon tells us that however we use our tongue will determine what happens to our own lives. If we speak life, we will live. If we speak death, we will die. You feed yourself on what you indulge in.

Maybe it isn't clear to you yet how subtle what Solomon is communicating is. He isn't just confronting our improper use of speaking death to others, but how you speak of your *own* life. For example, do you ever say something like, "When I die..."? You prophesied death to your life, declaring that you would one day die. Have you ever let the words "Before I die...." escape from your mouth? Why? Here are a few more examples, "Life is too short for...." or "Their time was up". Some phrases we have about death are the right idea, but stated about dying rather than living. For example, "When I go to heaven"or "When God takes me home" or "When its my time to go" or even "I hope I get to meet my grandchildren before I die." All these phrases reveal our complete lack of contending against death's assault on our lives. Tragically, we even give assistance to death's assignment with the professions we speak.

People are still dying because they are still speaking death over their own lives. Why do they do this? Because they are believing for death, inviting death, and embracing death. You will speak out what you believe. From the heart, men speak.

Another reason why more people aren't living *long* lives, as is their destiny and paid for by Jesus' blood, is explained in two verses:

"My people are destroyed for lack of knowledge..." Hosea 4:6

"Where there is no vision (revelation), *the people perish."* Proverbs 29:18

Ask yourself, how many ministers are preaching this message of immortality? I would say the number is very small. The result is that most people are not aware of what Jesus has taught and bought. They do not possess the *knowledge* that Jesus died so they don't have to, thus they never believe for it. Most people aren't even aware this is a possibility. Without this *revelation*, people perish. Pretty simple. Faith comes by hearing, and hearing by the Word of God. Read and believe what Jesus said. The implication is that you can life forever.

+ THOSE THAT HAVE OVERCOME DEATH +

It would be a fallacy to argue that *nobody* has tapped into abundant life. There are people living *today* that are hundreds of years old, coming and going from heaven to earth as they please, doing the will of God. Many are intercessors and purposely do not make their existence know to many.

Maharishi of Mt. Kailash is one such example, discovered by Sadhu Sundar Singh in 1912. Sundar, a missionary and minister of extraordinary proportions (so much so that he won the affection of C.S. Lewis), went out in search of the Maharishi and happened to find him. The Maharishi of Mt. Kailash said that he had been with St. Xavier (who lived 300 years prior to 1912), and had been baptized by him. The Maharishi still had a document that Xavier had given him whereon Xavier had written in greek a portion of the gospels. The Maharishi told Sundar that his assignment on earth was to intercede on behalf of *the world*. After visiting with the hermit three times, Sundar could not find him again and told others that he assumed the Maharishi had not died but been taken away by God to heaven like Enoch had been.

There are people on earth today that have learned how to overcome death like the Maharishi. There are people that have lived for hundreds of years because they have believed for it by believing in the abundant life Christ gives.

When asked if there are people on earth today that are older than 200 years old, a well known prophet responded with, "Yeah, they come and they go." They are here, among us. And you can do as they are; live.

+ THE FOUNTAIN OF LIFE +

All throughout history man has looked for ways to escape death. This desire is of God. The greatest of epics involve someone ascending past the limitations of flesh and soaring into the realms of immortality. The desire to live is at the core of every decision you make and has been the desire of every heart of every human being since the creation of man.

And this is the secret of the ages; There is, in fact, a Fountain of Life. Despite what the movies and fables say about it, it takes no map to find and isn't hidden away in a place where only a select few can sample of its Waters.

The Fountain of Life has a name; Jesus. Drink of His waters of life and you will live and not die. These waters that are not in lack or impossible to obtain, but are freely flowing from within your spirit like a river and in abundance.

The Body of Christ has not been taught on the issue of dead raising, so naturally what comes next after hearing about dead raising is a plethora of questions. What follows are answers to some of the questions we are asked most frequently, but first, a brief explanation about dead raising from the Bible.

God initially created man to be free from death and end, able to enjoy God and His creation forever. Yet, death, disease, and corruption were ushered into the world when man partook of sin. Though it was *man*, not God, that brought demise upon mankind and creation, God graciously had a plan to bail us out. The Father sent Christ to die for the sins of the world, and in doing so, defeated death, disease, and corruption in anyone that receives Him. We were ushered back to our first inheritance of abundant life through Christ's sacrifice on the cross. Most of us believe this, but the implications of our professions are more beautiful, shocking, and challenging than any of us initially thought.

Jesus died for sin and sickness, but also to defeat death. If Jesus died to overcome death, it would be contradictive of God to will that we die when Jesus already paid for it. Christ's death would be in vain if God willed that we die. Jesus tasted death for us so that we didn't have to.

In order for you to have faith in dead raising situations, you need to be sure of the will of God so that you know that you are praying in agreement with Heaven. Faith comes in such a place. Anyone that has studied the scriptures about God's will pertaining to divine healing comes to the understanding that it is always God's will to heal. It is no different with dead raising; it is always God's desire to raise the dead, regardless of age, reason for death, or how the family feels about bringing the person back. The will of God was demonstrated fully and exactly in the life of Christ; *every time* Christ came across the deceased, He raised them to life, thus the will of God is clear.

Hence, get praying, because you have a destiny to fulfill! If this view still seems foreign, read on. You will have a fuller picture of God's heart in dead raising as you continue to read this chapter.

"WHEN IS IT GOD'S WILL FOR A PERSON TO BE RAISED FROM THE DEAD, AND WHEN IS IT NOT? "

The above paragraph should have sufficiently answered this question, but if not, here are some additional insights of simplicity.

Jesus embodied the will of God. Every time scripture records Jesus coming in contact with a dead person, He raised them up. Be like Jesus and fulfill the Father's will; to bring life to the dead!

God told you to raise the dead. He wouldn't command you to do something that He didn't already will, so just agree with Him and start to pray to raise the dead. Also, don't be satisfied with just praying to raise the dead. Pray until you *raise the dead*, because He didn't tell us to try to raise the dead, but to raise the dead! Don't be hard on yourself when someone isn't raised, but continue in a posture of faith until someone is! This is about being faithful to our King, and delighting in doing what He says to do. Dead raising is a joy!

"How old is too old to raise someone?"

This was a question of mine years ago. Since it is a settled issue that God wills to raise the dead, is there an age limit to how old someone can be to qualify for dead raising? It seemed that if someone was 95 years old, we should just let them go because they had lived a long, full life, right? I found verses in the Old Testament that said we were to live for seventy to eighty years at least in this life. Though those verses gave me a high standard, Jesus gave us an even higher standard; Jesus said He came to give abundant life. He also raised people from the dead that had already been buried (Matthew 27:52, 53, John 11). Though the standard of the Old Testament and old covenant was high, Jesus' standard was even higher! He showed us that old age doesn't affect God's desire to raise the dead. It is beautiful! There is no age limit!

Again, the whole issue revolves around Jesus defeating sickness and death when He died on the cross. Don't reason in the natural, arbitrarily deciding if someone is too old to raise from the dead or not. If you are dealing with someone that was 100 years old and dies from heart failure, you are given permission by Heaven, even commissioned, to pray for their resurrection.

My great grandmother, a mighty woman of God, was 93 years old when she had massive heart failure. After the initial attack, Tad's heart was leaking in four places, her stomach was bleeding, and her lungs were not working properly. She was on a breathing machine, and more than one doctor told us to prepare for her death. She actually did die for a period of time, but the doctors succeeding in resuscitating her. After that, we were waiting for the doctors to walk down the hall at any moment and tell us the news. A week and a half went by with her in the hospital in this state.

People that knew Grandma had already began letting her go, but now they were virtually packing up their bags and heading to the funeral. I was very upset, and my wife and I decided that we would storm into her room to pray. We were in the ICU and needed to dress in hospital gowns in order that we didn't compromise her fragile state with germs. With our masks and gloves on, we began to pray. The Presence of the Lord showed up, we rested in it, and then we left. Prayer is Presence, and we could feel it thick in the room. Knowing that we had done what we needed to do, we walked out of her room and left the hospital. My grandpa solemnly waved goodbye to us as we drove away from the hospital, thinking that his mother would not last for more than a few more hours. Physically, she had been in a delicate place for a week and a half and at that point the thought of her recovery was far from anyone's mind.

Two days later, I walked into my great grandma's house and was surprised to see her in her room, conscious, alert, not laying down, but sitting up with a large smile on her face. I didn't greet her properly at all, but rather blurted out, "You are home?" in surprise. Nobody had even told me she was back at her house, let alone feeling any better! For some reason, Grandma had suddenly recovered and was sent home from the hospital.

At the time of this writing, great Grandma Tad is still alive. I have rarely encountered faith as her own. Every time we pray together, I can feel the sweet Presence of Jesus fill the room.

If we had believed that age affects the will of God pertaining to someone being healed or raised from the dead, we wouldn't have prayed in faith for Tad. If we hadn't prayed for Tad, I cannot be not sure we would have been able to enjoy her all this time, but because we knew that sickness was never God's way of taking someone from this Earth, we stood in faith. And it worked.

It may cause less grief and pain when an older person dies when compared to a child's death, but that doesn't negate the fact that *both* were still in contradiction to the will of God. It is easier emotionally to let go of an older person because they have lived a full life, but if someone has lived a full life or not should not be what motivates us to raise the dead or not. We are usually more motivated to want to raise a five-year-old child from the dead because they haven't experienced the joys of life, but if we pray out of our emotional rationalizing rather than the will of God, we will never raise the dead. Faith comes from knowing God's will, not emotions.

You must to know God's will in order to produce true faith. Do you unquestioningly know the will of God pertaining to dead raising? Without a sturdy conviction of God's will pertaining to dead raising, your emotions will toss you about like a wave on the sea, and you will not possess the violent faith it takes to raise the dead.

"IF IT IS GOD'S WILL TO RAISE THE DEAD, WHEN IS IT GOD'S WILL FOR THIS EARTHLY LIFE TO END?"

Some people reason that if we keep raising people from the dead they will never go to heaven, and will continue to get older and older. People have actually used this reasoning as grounds for why we should not raise the dead. Hilarious.

First off, I wouldn't mind living until I was 700 years old like the guys in the Bible did. You could get a lot of ministry done in 700 years. More ministry to God and people results in more rewards on the other side. No downside there. Granted, Christmas and birthdays would be quite a handful because of the near thousands of children and grandchildren that you would have to buy presents for, but you would seriously cash in on Father and Mother's day. Its ok, you can laugh. Don't get solemn about this stuff!

But seriously, the above point aside, the aim of dead raising is to step into the fullness of God's will for our lives. He desires that we live and not die, and He even gave us a back door through Christ dying for us so that we don't have to! Even pre-Christ, Enoch and Elijah experienced this, recounted in the Bible. They left the earth and entered into the realms of heaven without experiencing death.

"By faith Enoch was taken from this life, so that he did not experience death; he could not be found, because God had taken him away." Hebrews 11:5

"...and Elijah went up to heaven in a whirlwind." 2 Kings 2:11

The phenomenon of leaving the earth without dying is believed to have happened to many people in history, not just Elijah and Enoch, though there obviously isn't any tangible proof of this. How can there be proof when they person is taken from Earth! Christ Himself learned how to ascend into heaven without having to use the gate of death. He had died once, and that was enough!

God desires that we never have to have the experience of death, but rather, that we simply go from this life to the next. It is a lie that the only way to get to heaven is through the door of death. Death is not apart of your inheritance. People are able to live out the fullness of their destiny before God when the years of their lives are extended, and in turn, God receives even more glory. We are people that should long for heaven, as it is our true home, but desire even more to stay, accomplish God's will on Earth, and enjoy Him *now,* not just later. Remember, it is was Jesus that prayed that we wouldn't be taken out of the world, but instead, that the Father would protect us from the evil one (John 17:15).

"WHAT IF THEY DON'T WANT TO COME BACK?"

Countless times I have been told by people who prayed to raise the dead that they sensed that the person they were praying for didn't want to come back once they made it to heaven. The DRT is asked *regularly* how to deal with this type of situation. Though I understand people's desire to know why their prayers of faith didn't manifest and bring the person back to life, my answer to them is quite simple.

We know that most people would want to stay in heaven once they get there. That is obvious. No more pain, strife, demonic opposition, sickness, and death makes the decision a no-brainer. So if people wanting to stay in heaven played such a large role in determining the outcome of dead raising, how have so many people raised the dead throughout history and in the present day? Were the prayers of past saints, or the prayers of Jesus Himself, dragging people out of heaven kicking and screaming, or does a person having the ability to choose to stay in heaven not have as much weight in the spirit realm as we believe it does?

Besides being an unscriptural concept, believing that people may or may not want to come back to Earth after dying isn't an effective way to come into faith for raising the dead. Hebrews 11:6 tells us that it is impossible to please God except by *faith.* That means that the only way to please God is by faith. I would like to suggest that the whole focus of our lives revolves around pleasing God. The most basic and imperative aspect of your relationship with God is undermined if faith is not apart of the equation. This means that any belief that we have that does not lead us into faith is counter-productive at the least, but most likely, even leading us away from our destiny and harming other's ability to please God (have faith) in the process. This is why the issue of people believing that others have the choice to come back is so important; it causes people to stray away from the commissioning of Christ and settle for an unbiblical excuse.

In fact, of the stories I have heard about someone dying and going to heaven where they are given a choice to come back or not, most of the time the Lord is encouraging the person *not* to go into heaven, but go back to the earth to bring more of the Kingdom into that realm. Oddly, these same stories are the ones people bring up to invalidate our commissioning to raise the dead. I have to remind them that God that was trying to convince the person to go back to Earth, not God that was giving them a choice to go into heaven or not. In fact, I have heard of the Lord *blocking* the way into heaven so that the person would hear Him out as to why they needed to go back because they so impulsively wanted to dart inside.

The problem with believing that a person may or may not want to come back is that it becomes the trump card against the persevering prayer that many times is associated with dead raising. We cannot be a people that are easily swayed from what Jesus told us to do which is to raise the dead. I have realized that, sadly, many times people have more faith in the fact that they believed that a person didn't want to come back to Earth than that God told them to raise the dead.

Please understand, I realize that there are points where the Lord speaks to us and we stop praying for a resurrection. But even when that happens, we don't need to come up with answers to our questions as to why a person wasn't raised. We don't know why someone wasn't raised when we exerted every ounce of faith that we had. But in not answering the questions, in simply still believing that God wanted to raise that person from the dead though they weren't raised, we preserve our faith.

There are many unanswered questions that we live with as Christians. We need to know how and when to say, "I don't know." We need to be a people that can still have faith in the midst of many unanswered questions. We must be a people grounded, rooted, unable to be moved from our conviction of God's good will.

Once, a good friend of mine approached me and told me that her mother that was close to dying. Her mother was totally at peace with passing on, even wanted it to happen. She was old, and understandably, was ready to go. My friend felt that if she prayed to raise her mother from the dead she would be dishonoring her mom, but also wanted to follow Jesus' command in Matthew 10:8 to raise the dead. She was stuck.

I understood the bind that she was in, but I looked at her and with a smile on my face said, "Tell your mom that it is not all about her."

The point that I was making to my friend was that there is still a lot of work to be done on Earth for Jesus, and her mom had a role to play in Jesus getting the glory He deserves. There are souls to be won in this life, whether you are in high school or a retirement community. The world needs you, regardless of your age. People still need Jesus, and fields are white!

It is understandable that some people would just rather go onto heaven rather than be raised from the dead. This Earthly realm isn't exactly the easiest place to exist in. Regularly, the sick or dying will tell the family to not resuscitate them or pray in an attempt to raise them from the dead because they are ready to move on to heaven. Most of the time when they make this request they are old, tired, in pain, or even have given up on the hope of things getting any better in this life.

How our loved ones feel is understandable, but I'll tell you a secret...it can't change the aim of our prayers. Don't let what your loved one wants change what your *King* told you to do. If they have died, they won't know if you sneak in a resurrection prayer anyways! If they do find out, it will be because they are raised, and they won't complain to you then, because God won't do half of a miracle. God will raise them from the dead, but heal the problem that led to their death as well. The elderly would feel differently about being raised or resuscitated if they knew they were going to be raised back to life in health, without pain, and with a renewed vision and purpose on Earth. And that is exactly what God likes to do.

It isn't our job to decide if someone wants to come back or not. Our job is to have faith, then raise the dead. Jesus didn't say, "Heal the sick, cast out devils, cleanse the leper, and raise the dead, but only when they don't want to stay in heaven."

"JESUS DIDN'T RAISE EVERY PERSON FROM THE DEAD. WHAT ABOUT JOHN THE BAPTIST?"

This is a great point. If Jesus embodies the will of God, and He didn't raise John the Baptist from the dead, then we could deduct that it isn't always God's will to raise the dead. But is this the whole picture?

Jesus didn't heal everyone that was sick in His day, but He did heal every person that came to Him for healing. He even healed those that weren't able to come to Him when someone else came on their behalf.

We can deduce from this that God *does* will for all to be healed, but many times the healing won't take place till we come to Jesus, or someone else does on our behalf.

Many times in the Gospels, *someone* exerted some measure of faith and Jesus always met them in their request.

This principle is the same pertaining to dead raising. Anyone that came to Jesus that wanted their dead raised, He raised them. Anyone Jesus even came across that had been afflicted by death, Jesus raised them. Jesus demonstrated the will of the Father through His lifestyle.

Thus, when dealing with the death of John the Baptist, we have to wonder, "If someone, anyone, had asked Jesus to raise John from the dead, would He have?" The rest of Christ's life seems to confirm that He would have. Instead of believing that the Father arbitrarily willed John to stay in death when Jesus always demonstrated and taught the opposite, let's consider that the lack wasn't on God's end, but mans. If Jesus healed the sick of anyone that asked for it, even on other's behalf, all it would have taken for Jesus to raise John from the dead was for one of the disciples to simply ask Him to. The reality is that the disciples were likely not yet convinced that it was always the Father's will to give life, thus they didn't think to ask. And nobody else thought to ask either, for John was without family, thus no wife or children to be desperate on his behalf.

Additionally, we have to take into consideration *how* John died, and the permanency it can communicate to people that are not yet convinced that nothing is impossible for God. God attaching a head to a body isn't a challenge for Him, nor outside of what He allows Himself to do. Remember, we serve a God that created man by simply *breathing* into dust. He has such creative abilities that He can make flesh out of dust; a head detached from a body is no big deal for Him. Nonetheless, it could have been quite a faith destroyer for the people in John's day.

In closing, if someone had believed for John's resurrection, the Gospels paint a setting that suggests that

Jesus would have been more than happy to raise him to life. Only believe.

"ARE YOU SAYING THAT DEATH IS HOLISTICALLY BAD?"

The distinction between God and death is foggy in the eyes of the Church. We have had an interesting view of God, believing that on some level He works alongside death or uses it to work His will on Earth. We reveal these beliefs of our heart when we say things like, "God took them", or "God numbers our days and it was their time to go", or "God's judgment fell on that city". Furthermore, how we read certain situations in the Old Testament makes it exceedingly clear that we believe that God used death to accomplish His purposes; the flood, the plagues of Egypt, the genocide of whole people groups by the Israelites, and the list goes on and on. Regardless of what denomination we come from or what theological stance we take in reading the Bible, one belief that every Christian holds to some degree is that God uses death to accomplish His purposes, or at least has in the past.

When the Dead Raising Team first started, I rationalized that death wasn't holistically bad, but a gateway to our eternity with God. I focused on differentiating between premature death and death, making the point that premature death wasn't of God, but death could be if in the right context (no sickness involved, peaceful circumstances, etc). But that view was incomplete, unintentionally assaulting the character of God. This is why; scripture says that satan holds the power of death (Hebrews 2:14). If satan holds the power of death, that means that anytime someone dies, peacefully or not, with disease or not, God didn't initiate it, because you can't give what you don't have. If God didn't keep the spirit of death, it meant God didn't have death to give. It meant that the spirit of death was not hanging out with the Father in heaven like an assassin at the ready, geared up to be sent to anyone that needed a mafia-style end. It meant that God is unable to do anything but that which gives life. I had to come to the conclusion that death is not God's coworker.

Honestly, this was a hard pill to swallow. It meant that God never killed. Ever. Old Testament or New. If He doesn't now, and He is the same yesterday, today, and forever, it meant He never used death to accomplish His purposes. This flew in the face of everything I had ever been taught in Christianity. I had to go back to the example of Jesus, who was and is the exact representation of God (Heb. 1) in order to come to grips with that truth. Jesus is always the answer.

Scripture is clear that God is not the keeper of the spirit of death, satan is, thus God does not use death to bring forth His will.

"...him who holds the power of death—that is, the devil..." Hebrews 2:14

Paul tells us that Jesus does not work alongside death, but in opposition to it. In fact, Jesus came to destroy death, which man let into the world, not God.

"...since death came through a man..." 1 Corin. 15:21

Furthermore, Paul clearly states that death is an *enemy* to the King and His bride, not a friend.

"The last enemy to be destroyed is death." 1 Corin. 15:26

If God didn't bring death into the world, and if the Father sent Christ to destroy death, then it is clear that according to Christ and the writers of the New Testament that God does not partner with the devil by using death to accomplish His purposes.

God *is* unable to do certain things, but only things that work contrary to the goodness of His nature. Just as God is incapable of lying (Titus 1:2), He is incapable of using death to accomplish His purposes. Jesus is actually the source of life itself, through which all things live (John 1:3,4). He is not God with a split personality, using death to accomplish His will one moment, and being the source of life the next. God only functions through life, thus, He does not use death. Why would God command His people with "Thou shall not murder", then contradict Himself by violating that commandment Himself? Our God is not a hypocrite, is He?

Some rationalize that certain facets of God's nature, such as His justice and holiness, are infringed upon if God is viewed as holistically good and doesn't use death to accomplish His purposes. But man's justice looks different from God's justice. Man's justice looks like dealing out punishment to the one who committed the wrong, but God's justice looks like healing the one who was wronged. Jesus never went to harm the one that harmed, but heal the one that had been harmed. In other words, God's justice has more to do with restoration than it does punishment. Thus, we find that the Father is exactly like Christ, non-violent in nature, one that would rather be killed than kill.

Choosing to function through nonviolence is not about choosing to be weak, but choosing to be strong. It does not take courage or power to kill. It takes courage to love and sow kindness, despite the intimidation, the beatings, the threats, the murder. It takes the most superior forms of valor to not descend to their standard by raising a fist. It took the utmost courage, bravery, and honor to do as Christ did and be killed rather than kill. As Martin Luther King Jr. said, "To our most bitter opponents we say: 'We shall match your capacity to inflict suffering by our capacity to endure suffering. We shall meet your physical force with soul force. Do to us what you will, and we shall continue to love you. We cannot in all good conscience obey your unjust laws because noncooperation with evil is as much a moral obligation as is cooperation with good. Throw us in jail and we shall still love you. Bomb our homes and threaten our children, and we shall still love you. Send your hooded perpetrators of violence into our community at the midnight hour and beat us and leave us half dead, and we shall still love you. But be ye assured that we will wear you down by our capacity to suffer. One day we shall win freedom but not only for ourselves. We shall so appeal to your heart and conscience that we shall win you in the process and our victory will be a double victory.'"

Anytime in history that men have sought to see a situation changed by passive resistance or non-violent protest the situation has been dramatically changed in their favor, and usually affected whole nations in the process, if not the entire world. Mandela went from prison to president in a matter of weeks. Martin Luther King Jr. brought peace where there was unrest and hatred, and all without discharging one bullet. Gandhi managed to push Britain out of India and back to their native land by merely fasting and never using murder to further his plans. St. Telemachus is credited with stopping the gladiator games in Rome and eventually the world, simply by pleading with the gladiators themselves in the ring, holding to his nonviolent conviction even after they had sliced his belly wide open. No fists were raised, no blood was lusted after, no armies were assembled; yet power was present. Nonviolence does not imply powerlessness; Impossible situations bowed to these men of nonviolent resistance.

And conversely, anytime in history a man has taken up sword in an attempt to change a situation through violence, we generally look upon the past with shame, now admitting its error. Dietrich Bonhoeffer, a dedicated Christian and astute theologian that lived in Europe during the reign of the Nazis, miserably failed in his attempt to assassinate Hitler. God was obviously not in the attempted murder, or Bonhoeffer would have succeeded. Yet, if a person follows the teachings of Jesus, they will always be triumphant. Jesus' teachings of passive resistance are so powerful that regardless if you are a Christian or not (Gandhi as one example), they work. On the other hand, if you take on a jihad mentality against flesh and blood to any degree, it will not only fail but will create a situation that you, and future generations will one day look back upon with regret.

Don't get me wrong; I am the first one to cheer in a movie theater when the bad guy finally gets what was coming to him and dies. I am also very glad that Adolph Hitler is no longer alive. But I cannot deny that my disposition and inclination pertaining to what justice should look like is in stark contrast to what Jesus taught and demonstrated. Jesus gave us the most powerful ways to change circumstances: love and forgiveness. These two tools of Heaven's warfare shatter the web of spiritual darkness that is the force behind any real problem on Earth. Nonviolent resistance is not about backing down from the enemy, but charging directly into his camp.

The justice and holiness of God are very real and wonderful facets of His nature. He *is* holy and just. But instead of being mutually exclusive traits of God, God's holiness and justice are always in submission to the greatest reality and facet of God; His love. Every aspect of His nature, such as His holiness and justice, flow from the greater reality that He is good. When our view of God is firstly shaped by His holiness and justice rather than His goodness and love, we begin to sketch a misshaped picture of the Father in our heart. Yet in stark contrast, when we remember that God's holiness, justice, or anything else about Him, are natural *products* of His love, then we cannot distort His character to match our understanding of certain parts of His character, as in the case of His holiness and justice.

So in light of this, what then of the Canaanite genocide, the flood, or situations in the Bible like the plagues of Egypt? What of the words that God spoke to Moses, to "show them no mercy", and kill every last man, woman, and child? Did God sanction murder as holy (though He commanded the opposite in the Ten Commandments), but only under the correct situations? Was Moses the initial inventor of jihad, or holy war, not Mohammad as we have assumed?

Simply said, you can either choose the teachings of Jesus and who He revealed the Father to be, or you can believe what Moses believed and wrote down about God. Your choice. God was either killing all along and will be in heaven (Hebrews 13:8), or He never did.

Hopefully by now in your reading of this book, you have more of an arsenal against some of the ideas, even in scripture, that seem that God was the one responsible for mass killings, sending plagues, and the like. Because of the nature of God, the only *impossible* option of interpretation to those events is that God was the responsible one. There are only two options for finding the responsible party when dealing with evil; it is either satan or man that caused the death, killings, sickness, or destruction.

For example, what if the sin from men in the days of Noah created such an open door for the enemy that he had the ability to strike the entire Earth with a flood?

What if God warned mankind of the enemy's plans, but only one man was listening? What if God is concerned about sin, not just simply because it is *bad* but because it gives the enemy entrance to destroy us, and He cares for our well-being? What if the plagues of Egypt were not brought about by the Lord, but God was telling Moses what the enemy would do next, hoping that repentance would occur through the warning so that satan couldn't walk out his plans? Tweaks with our theology doesn't it? We need to start approaching the scriptures, especially the Old Testament, realizing that *sin gives entrance to the enemy* and God always wanted to preserve life, regardless of how scripture seems to read. If we get unsure about how to handle the scriptures, we look back to the example of Jesus in order to steady our head and gain back our bearings. Always go back to Jesus, His character, His words, and His actions while on Earth. He is our clearest example of the Father. Some may not like this, but Christ is actually a clearer example of who the Father is than what scripture can give us, because Jesus is God, scripture is not. We must let the nature of God determine scripture, rather than letting scripture determine the nature of God. In addition, Jesus is not defined by our understanding of God; God is defined by Jesus. The only way to the Father is through Christ, and reversing that reality disposes of the entire point of Christ coming to Earth and walking amidst humanity.

So, is death holistically bad? Well, remember that God created man free from death. We were not created to die. It was the fall that began to limit the life that man was able to drink of eternally. When Christ died, He ushered man back into his first, uncorrupted state. This is experienced through faith in Jesus. There are people on the face of the earth that have accessed this truth and have lived for hundreds of years, literally.

You do not need to die. Ever. Believe and it shall be. Abundant life is life without end. There are literally *loads* of verses in the Bible that state that we have *eternal* life through Christ. Faith takes those verses out of our traditional understanding that they are referring to merely our existence in heaven, and opens the availability for them to apply to our natural life on Earth. Jesus said in John 11:26 that "...whoever lives and believes in Me will never die." In John 6:47 He said, "He who believes in me has everlasting life." Let me clarify; He did not say that we would die and go to heaven, He said we would never die. In fact, He affirmed that fact in verse 50: "This is the bread that comes down from heaven, so that man may eat of it and not die."

Remember, Enoch and Elijah ended their life without burial or death. They were men that left this Earth in a state of life.

It is up to you how long you want to live on Earth. God says you can go on as long as you want. He wants to teach you how to access realms of heaven so that you can come and go as you please, and one day, stay.

So, instead of asking if death is bad, we should be asking if we should take up the blessing of *eternal life* that Christ bought for us with His precious blood. The answer is yes! What a testimony to our families, non-believers, and the world!

"BUT I WANT TO GO TO HEAVEN!"

Me too! To live is Christ, and to die is gain. Granted, we are headed to a much better place but Jesus encouraged us that we can *bring heaven to earth.* There is work to be done on Earth for Jesus, and more importantly, we can experience the bliss of the gospel right now rather than having to wait for heaven to get it! If we live our lives looking forward to what we will have in the future rather than enjoying what *we have already been given* we miss out on our present life, never satisfied and forgetting the cross.

Right after Paul writes the above passage in Philippians 1:21, he communicates if he had to choose between staying on Earth and reaping glory for God or going to heaven, that it is a *necessity* that he stay on Earth. Paul's motivation was the same motivation that caused Jesus to leave Heaven and come to a dying planet to hang out with a bunch of messed up, dirty, inglorious people. He could have stayed in a perfect place, but He decided to come and sleep in a feed trough for animals.

Our aim on Earth is to bring Him more worship and glory through being satisfied by the His pleasure of His love. When we are living in the bliss of what God has already accomplished through Christ, our desire to leave this Earth is replaced with a desire to spend more time with Jesus *on Earth* in the realms of His goodness and glory. We stop waiting for Heaven and start experiencing it in *this life*.

But if you don't understand what Christ did for you so that you can have Him *now* and you still want to go to heaven, then go get martyred! Don't take on a spirit of suicide masked as holiness, but live in a way that stirs hell up against you, and lay your life down for those that persecute you. The martyrs in the Bible did not have their lives taken from them, but willingly laid their lives down, as did Christ (John 10:17-18, 19:11). Nobody can take your life from you unless you decide to lay it down.

Jesus guaranteed us persecution, and while this doesn't always mean death, it can in some countries! If you want to go to heaven, live radically for Jesus and you have a good chance at seeing Him soon! Preach the full gospel of Jesus in Mecca during Ramadan and you will probably be given a one-way ticket to the Throne room. Glory!

Some people bring up martyrdom as an example of a person's death that God approves of. God doesn't send people to their death in order that they glorify Him, man does. God isn't responsible for man's decisions to kill Christians, but He does honor, even reward, those that stay faithful through such a trial. Christians sometimes confuse God's ability to draw beautiful things out of horrible situations as God causing horrible situations in order to glorify Himself. The difference between the two is vast. He isn't the divine troublemaker; He is the divine Housekeeper...a Father that is incredibly skilled at cleaning up His children's messes.

Dead raising and martyrdom are not mutually exclusive. They work hand in hand. Though I strongly believe in dead raising, I would be honored to be counted worthy to be martyred for my faith.

As the last days count down and the curtains of time draw to a close, we will hear of martyrs that will die by the sword of extremists, then raised back to life by those that believe in resurrection power. These martyrs get rewarded twice; the honor and reward of martyrdom, but also the reward that comes from continuing on in doing ministry on Earth. For them, is the best of both worlds, literally!

"WHEN DO WE PRAY FOR RESURRECTION, AND WHEN DO WE STOP PRAYING?"

This question is different from the above questions in that it is not a question pertaining to the will of God, but the state of the person who is praying for resurrection. The person that asks this question already knows God wants to raise the dead, but is trying to learn how to walk that out practically.

For example, we have had families contact the Dead Raising Team in absolute desperation and sadness, months after the person has died. The body is buried or cremated by this point, and the family wants us to pray for resurrection.

God is able to raise anyone, regardless of how long they have been dead. Being dead for fifty years is not too long for God to raise a person. They can have been buried for years, for God raised up "many" people that had been dead and buried (Matthew 27:52-53). Elijah's bones raised a man to life when his dead body was thrown into Elijah's grave. If that doesn't challenge your view on how far God will go to raise the dead (using the dead to raise the dead), I don't know what will.

We support people that desire to pray in faith in this manner, even though it may seem odd. Why? Because nothing is impossible with God, and we are not going to tell someone that is hoping for a miracle God can't do what they are praying for.

At the same time, we must pray from a place of victory and faith. Pray as long as you have faith for it. Once you move past that place, you may start to pray yourself into unbelief, even offense. If you find yourself arguing with God, you may want to give it a break. When we find ourselves pleading or arguing with God, we are most likely not in a place of faith. We may even have taken offense with God subtly. We must remember that He is already on our side, and wants to bring life to the person, even if they aren't being raised. When we get to a place of frustration rather than faith, we need to take a break from praying and receive God's love afresh in order that we are grounded back into God's heart for us. Once we do that, offense leaves and faith is renewed.

The paradox of faith is knowing what God wants in a situation, though the situation may not change when you pray. You can give up and change your mind on what God wants because the situation isn't budging, or you can stand in faith regardless of the circumstances. The real issue is continuing to believe God is good even when bad things persist.

Families are sometimes eager to pray for their loved one's resurrection after they have been cremated or buried. There is nothing wrong with this. In fact, it is the radical will of God. At the same time, the family needs to govern their emotions and know when it isn't healthy to continue to pray for resurrection. For example, my mother still has my father's ashes, and though I know that God wants me to have a father, I do not pray over my father's ashes for his resurrection. Why? Because there is a sneaking suspicion in my heart that it would be unhealthy for me to do so. I have painfully embraced a paradox, and in doing so, continue to stand in faith. From here on out, I have funneled my pain into an anger that I direct towards the devil, in hopes that through the fire God has given me pertaining to dead raising, others can be spared of the pain that I have experienced.

When a family begins to feel that for their own health they need to cease in praying for resurrection, at *that* point the family should shift into thankfulness and gratitude towards the Lord, even praise, for the fact that their loved one is in heaven. If the deceased wasn't suspected to have known Jesus, we rest in the truth that the Lord is a fair and exceedingly gracious Judge, and that He will be graciously fair to their loved one.

If you aren't a friend or family member of the one that has died, you may also wonder how long you should pray for resurrection. Some ministries pray and fast until the person is in the grave, which could be days, while some ministries pray for an hour or less. The Dead Raising Team doesn't have a set amount of time that we pray when attempting to raise the dead. At times we have fasted and prayed for four days straight, while other times we only get an hour with the body to pray. Dead raising isn't so much about a formula to follow as much as it is exerting and releasing the Holy Spirit. If we feel ourselves beginning to lag, we take a break and let our faith and bodies recoup. Dead raising isn't a activity of striving, but one of rest, passion, peace, and joy.

"IS IT STILL GOD'S WILL TO RAISE THEM IF THEY WEREN'T A CHRISTIAN?"

God desires that none shall perish (2 Peter 3:9). You can apply this verse to salvation in that God desires that everyone be saved, but it can also be applied to dead raising. God desires that all experience life, whether it be our natural lives, or our heaven lives in eternity. He desires that all come to know His love.

Why would we ever suppose that God wouldn't be even more broken about an unbeliever dying before it was their time than a follower of Christ? Just as Heaven rejoices when one sinner repents, so Heaven is brokenhearted about one sinner that dies without receiving God's gift of love in Jesus.

I have heard many stories of people that died without knowing Jesus, had an encounter while they were dead, and were raised back to life. When they were resurrected, they were either already saved, or wanted to know how they could be saved.

Nobody is too far-gone for God to save them. If God can raise and save a witch doctor that cursed God moments before he died, surely He likes to raise unbelievers.

"HOW CAN YOU SAY THAT GOD DIDN'T TAKE MY LOVED ONE, BUT THAT THE ENEMY DID?"

My dad died in his early fifties of a heart attack. When it happened I just assumed that God was the one that had taken my father. I thought this largely because of my view of God's sovereignty at the time. Oddly enough, it comforted me to think that God was the one that was responsible. Somehow it made me feel that everything that happened in life was a part of a divine plan that would work out for my good in the end, even if I didn't understand at the present time.

Yet, synonymous with the Lord being the one that took my father was the fact that my mother was now a widow. My children would never have a grandpa. My sister and brother would miss out on the guidance, love, and security that comes from having a father, as would I. These facts made me search deeper into the Bible, and I began to find answers to my questions and pain.

I remember sitting down with my mother four years after my father had died and telling her that I was no longer sure that it was God that took my father's life. You would think this would be good news, but she started crying. Such a shift in thinking when you are finally grasping something that is already beyond your comprehension is disturbing and fearful. It is not easy to alter your understanding of circumstances when you weren't taught correctly from the start. It took my mother and I *years* to unlearn the teachings we had been previously taught, but we finally came to a place where we could fully embrace the goodness of God without holding contradictive beliefs at the same time.

In no way do I mean to be insensitive to anyone's pain and loss by stating the truth. I personally know the fragile state of one's emotional being after losing a family member, and if you have lost a loved one, I am so sorry.

What I am communicating in this section is not meant to heartlessly dismantle your fragile world, but to heal your heart towards God and make you strong again. There may be an initial breaking of your old paradigm, but the overall picture will become more clear and palatable as faith enters the equation. Faith brings healing to not only the physical body, but also mentally and emotionally when integrated into our theology rightly. Theology that isn't damaging will always involve faith.

So, how can I say that God didn't take your loved one, but that the enemy did? Well, I *didn't* say it; God did. Jesus was clear in John 10:10 that the enemy is the one taking people's lives;

"The theft comes to steal, kill, and destroy. I have come that they may have life, and have it in abundance."

It may be hard to stomach at first, but God did not take your loved one. The enemy did. Jesus quickly bounced back from John the Baptist's death not because He ignored it or stuffed its actuality into the recesses of His heart, but because He had a paradigm of God that helped Him deal with it in an effective way. His paradigm did not cause Him to ascribe the Father the responsibility for John 's death. Because He understood that the Father wasn't responsible, He not only continued on, but was fueled with more passion to destroy the enemy. You will discover this same expansion of the fire of God in your life if you blame the enemy rather than the Father for things that steal, kill, and destroy in your life.

Something you will discover as you pray for the dead to be raised and the sick to be healed is that *your* healing will be found in you bringing others their healing. The pain of loss that you feel is best medicated through doing the work of the Kingdom. Through other's having their loved ones restored to them you will find healing for your pain of losing a loved one. Loss and attack upon our life should force us further into serving the King rather than paralyzing us with grief.

"But hasn't God numbered our days?"

Some people believe that God numbers our days, and that when we die it was simply our set time to go, as though He has the number of our days mapped out, and nothing can extend our life past that sovereignly appropriated amount of days.

It is true that God *has* numbered our days, but that statement doesn't refer to a limit of life that God has placed upon each of us, but rather a statement that speaks of God's loving knowledge. Just as He knows the exact number of hairs on your head He knows every day of your life, the days you have already lived, and the days that are in your future. He knows every detail of each day you have lived and will live. He is deeply acquainted with everything about you; He knows you. God numbering our days has to do with God knowing you, and knowing you has everything to do with loving you.

God never limits life, but gives it abundantly. If someone dies, the will of God was violated and His full plan for a person's life did not come to pass. God knows the massive number of days that we can live on Earth, and that number is far greater than any man has ever lived, even those that lived before the flood.

Does this surprise you? Do you think God numbered the days of millions of aborted babies, that they were created with a meager destiny of living in the womb then dying, or was God's plan for their lives drastically cut short? Death is a reality, like it or not. Saddle up and do something about it.

"But aren't we destined to die?"

Another verse people like to tote in the face of resurrection power is Hebrews 9:27-28, assuming that it proves that man *must* die in life, but this verse proves the very opposite.

"Just as man is destined to die once, and after that to face judgment, so Christ was sacrificed once to take away the sins of many people; and he will appear a second time, not to bear sin, but to bring salvation to those who are waiting for him."

This verse is saying that, at birth, man is destined to die because of the inherent sin every human is born into. But when a person receives the sacrifice of Jesus that takes away our sin, the punishment of sin (death), is removed. This verse doesn't prove that death is an impossible event to avoid in life, one commissioned by God, but that Jesus overcame death. Jesus freed us from the punishment that sin brings from the enemy; death. If every man is destined to die, then what about Enoch, Elijah, and Jesus? They were taken away to heaven in various ways that didn't involve death.

Here is another angle on this verse. You already died once with Christ; You are not destined to die again. Christ was slain before the foundation of the earth so that you didn't have to. It was His destiny to die, not yours. It is true that it is *destined* that a man must die once, but scripture is clear that you died with Christ, co-crucified with Him on the cross, so why choose to die again?

"HOW CAN I PRAY FOR THE DEAD?"

In order for you to pray for the dead, you need to find someone that has died. This isn't easy in western nations because of the way we treat the dead. In other nations, the body stays with the family until it is buried, open for the public to view at anytime. But in the United States and much of Europe, it is a very sensitive issue that takes place behind locked doors and red tape.

Practically, you may want to begin to build a relationship with your local funeral director or coroner. Stop at car accidents and offer to pray for anyone that was hurt or killed. Keep your ear to the ground for anyone that dies in your extended family or friends. As long as you pursue dead raising through faith and honoring others, you will likely get an opportunity to pray to raise the dead. Get a persistence in your spirit, a perseverance for raising the dead, and it will be unavoidable. It is odd how often situations present themselves when we have our eyes opened to the illegality of people dying around us. The light goes on and we scan the horizon for opportunities to sow abundant life instead of accepting what seems impossible to change.

The reason most of us have not prayed to raise the dead is because we have never tried. God will give you opportunities, just be ready for them when they come by stoking the Fire within.

Some people do not like that I actually seek out opportunities to pray for the dead. But you aren't going to raise the dead till you pray for the dead to be raised. In order to raise the dead, you have to *find* someone that is dead. You aren't looking for a dead body, you are looking for someone to raise to life. Those that raise the dead aren't excited about death, but the fact that Jesus came to give abundant life and that they are commissioned instigators of it.

If someone dies and is taken to a local funeral home, honor and respect the family by asking for permission to pray for the deceased. Honor is not only the way the Kingdom of God functions, but it will also help you gain favor with the family so that you can pray to raise the dead. In America, typically you must have the family's permission in order to pray over the body, so honor the family. Be gentle, but honest.

You are called to be Christ to others. Jesus was compassionate, yet possessed power to change the circumstances. He was sensitive to those that were experiencing loss, but Christ never let His compassion be the last thing that He left a person with. Jesus' compassion always led Him into a manifestation of power. When you go to pray for the dead to be raised, remember that you are there to raise the dead, not to contribute to sadness. Sadness and grief on your part is illogical if you are there to raise the dead because if you were full of faith and believed that the deceased was about to be raised, you would be full of joy. Grief is a sign that a person has accepted the circumstances as unchangeable, thus anticipating loss rather than a gaining of life. In other words, grief in the wrong context is a sign of unbelief. The family is looking to you for the power of God, thus you must have faith when they do not. Though the nature of faith in the context of grief seems insensitive and brash, the family doesn't need a pat on the back but the miraculous power of God that changes impossible circumstances.

Once I received a phone call from a desperate man and woman that had just delivered a stillborn baby. They knew the baby was without life weeks before, but went through with the delivery in hopes that God would work a miracle.

The father was crying as he held the baby's body while I was on the phone with him. We would pray together for resurrection life, and he would check the baby for signs of life. To say the least, it was very intense. This man kept saying, "She is so beautiful, so beautiful".

My own wife was due any day with our son Jacob, thus I related to this man's situation very closely. I found myself crying as we prayed, overwhelmed by feelings of hatred for the devil and absolute horror of imagining my own wife and baby in the same situation.

The baby wasn't raised, and the parents had to bury their little girl.

I realized later that my ability to empathize with the father wasn't any help to him. He had called me because he needed to talk to someone that was full of faith, and I hadn't been that for him.

When people lose a loved one, though they may not say it, they are looking for someone that is militant in faith, someone that will see things drastically different than themselves, someone *offensively* full of faith. They are looking for someone that is violent in faith.

I am not endorsing a heartless attitude towards families that are experiencing loss. I am communicating that we are called to be a beacon of light and hope for those that are stuck in impossible situations. They are looking to you to have *faith*, not more sadness. Jesus wept at Lazarus's grave because of the unbelief of the people around, not because Mary was broken hearted.

"I FEEL BAD THAT I DIDN'T PRAY FOR MY LOVED ONE TO BE RAISED. I DIDN'T KNOW I WAS SUPPOSED TO!"

Many people, when hearing the message of raising the dead actually feel regret, condemnation, and even shame because they may not have prayed for their loved ones to be raised in the past. They realize that dead raising is a reality, and that if they had prayed for their resurrection, the loved one could be alive today.

If you struggle with regret, remember that regret doesn't exist in the Kingdom. God doesn't rewind history to see how things could have gone better if someone had performed better, and nor should you.

God doesn't hold you accountable for what you didn't know, and there is no condemnation for those that are in Christ (Romans 8:1). Don't let condemnation accuse you, for God doesn't accuse you. Now you know, so pray to raise the dead when you get the chance. Just pick up from here and go for it; Leave what is behind and press on towards Christ.

And if you pray and the dead are not raised, remember that God is pleased by faith alone, and you praying for the dead is a example of your faith, thus God is pleased with you for just *attempting* to raise the dead. He is not a performance God.

"HOW SHOULD WE PRAY TO RAISE THE DEAD, AND WHAT IF THEY AREN'T RAISED?"

You may be wondering how to pray when you get a chance to pray for the dead. The Dead Raising Team doesn't have a formula; we just invite the Spirit of God into the situation and then do what God says to do. Try not to have formulas in prayer. You don't have a set formula when talking to your friend or spouse, why would you when talking to God? Just do as you see Him doing, and pray from a place of faith.

If you have a desire to raise the dead and be a part of a group of likeminded people, contact us to start your own Dead Raising Team. God is starting teams all over the world, raising up people that desire to walk out the fullness of our commissioning as believers.

As for the person not being raised immediately, we come from a stance that you should keep believing. Period. Miracles aren't always instantaneous; sometimes they will be raised after you leave. And since Jesus raised Lazarus from *out of a grave*, we don't think it is too much to keep believing for the person's resurrection after an extended amount of time has passed.

Lastly, we have discovered that faith is found in the midst of a paradox, not in the manifestation of a miracle. The paradox is the knowledge of the will of God in one hand, and the unchanged circumstances in the other. Faith is when you are able to hold both firmly in your hands at the same time, fully acknowledging their existence, without allowing the reality of either to cancel the other out. If you are able to do so, the result is that you will always stay encouraged, and eventually, the manifestation of a miracle.

+ TAKE IT UP A NOTCH +

This section is probably going to get my family and I on more "heresy hunter" websites, but that is okay with us. I would like to formally thank the people ahead of time that do that kind of thing to us, because you are storing up reward in heaven for us. Keep it up! We love you, and bless you!

Lets take it up a notch. Not only will the people of God raise the dead, but they will begin to walk in such abundant life and resurrection power that whole morgues will be emptied out.

Dead raisers will walk into morgues as the power of Life exudes from them. Those that were dead will awake and need to be let out from their holding compartments. Coroners will give their lives to the Lord on the spot. God will be on display, and men will forget the name of the man that carried the power.

This is how we must think. We must shoot higher than we ever have before, much higher than what we could attain by our own strength. We need to reach beyond our grasp. Aim for the Heavens, far higher than you could ever dream of attaining. As we do, we will hit all the other things we need to do on the way up. Don't ever give into the lie that you are shooting too high, because nothing is impossible with God. If you are in faith, you shouldn't be thinking "rationally".

Emptying morgues is one thing, but what about graveyards? A time is coming very soon when men and women will enter graveyards, call forth a person, and they will crawl from their own grave.

You are probably thinking that I have lost my mind and are seriously considering being done with this book. I understand. If a few years ago I had read what I am writing, this book would have become starting fuel for my wood stove in under a minute. But hang in there; this is biblical.

In Matthew 27:52-53 God raised up men and women that had been dead for an extended amount of time, even years.

"The tombs broke open and the bodies of many holy people who had died were raised to life. They came out of the tombs, and after Jesus' resurrection they went into the holy city and appeared to many people."

This verse wouldn't be a problem if Jesus hadn't said that we would do greater things than even He did (John 14:12). But He did say it, so we are released to believe for totally impossible things such as clearing out graveyards!

Imagine it! A family loses the husband and father, and for ten years he is buried. One day, someone takes a risk, believes in the power of God, and holds their hand over a grave in prayer. Suddenly, a finger breaks through the surface of the dirt. A whole and healthy man crawls from the ground, raised from the dead. He goes back to his widowed wife, meets his children at the door, and is reunited with his family.

Are you uncomfortable or excited? How different is this from Lazarus, where Jesus intentionally *waited time* to raise him from the dead just so that it was even more of an impressive miracle than if He had risen him after two days of being dead. When dealing with dead raising, God is not concerned with time passing before He works His miracle. In fact, He *likes* showing off by waiting. It gives Him glory!

If you didn't already know, after four days without embalming liquid or low temperatures, a body will have already entered the stage of decomposing. This didn't seem to deter Jesus. And it shouldn't deter us. Nothing is impossible with God. After all, God can take a valley of bones and make them into an army that is alive and well. It is never too late.

"The blessing of the Lord makes a man rich."
Proverbs 10:22

"The enemy will hold back the church from walking in
her destiny in two main ways. First, he will try to raise up
tyrants. Second, he will convince the church that it is
godly to be poor." -Martin Luther

Solomon possessed the riches of the world. Joseph stewarded the wealth of the world power in his day. Jesus miraculously pulled a gold coin out of a fish's mouth. The Bible is full of examples of God handing wealth over to His servants. Does God still want His people to prosper, like He said in Jeremiah 29:11?

Yes, God wants to prosper you financially. First, let me say that I know the ground I am treading on is tender. For many in the Body of Christ, hearing that statement causes memories to rush back of fallen ministers, money spent irresponsibly, manipulative offerings, and 1-800 numbers on television. But that is not what I am talking about.

I am talking about people needing Jesus, and many won't know Him unless we tell them about Him. That costs money.

God desires to bless you so that you can be a blessing. God wants you to be rich so that you can be a source of provision to anyone that has need. He wants to you have more than enough so that His Kingdom can expand to every corner of the globe. He wants to you to be able to lend instead of having to be lent to. God wants to bless you so abundantly that nations take notice and acknowledge your God as *the* God (Ps. 67).

"I will give you honor and praise…when I restore your fortunes before your very eyes." -Zeph. 3:20

God desires to take you out of debt and out of the fear of how you will provide for yourself. After all, Jesus was the one to pray, "Forgive us our debts, as we forgive our debtors." God is all about freeing you from your debt! He desires to put you in a place flowing with milk and honey. He is escorting you out of poverty and into inheritance and abundant provision. Will you be courageous and take the land like Joshua and Caleb desired to do, or cower back and wander the desert for years until your unbelief has died?

+ THE ESSENCE OF THE CURSE +

Sometimes we may wonder why it is such a fight to live in abundance. Surprisingly, the very essence of the curse of sin that was attained in the garden by Adam and Eve revolves around finances and prosperity.

When Adam and Eve ate of the forbidden fruit, sin entered the world and manifested in two primary and immediate ways in the lives of the two garden dwellers: Eve was guaranteed to experience pain in childbirth and Adam was told that it wouldn't be easy for him to get what he needed from the earth. In other words, abundant provision became something that Adam would have to work extremely hard to attain. Adam and Eve suddenly found themselves distanced from their destiny of wealth and abundance, now face to face with poverty. The primary manifestation of the curse of sin for man was *poverty*.

The curse that was given to man when he fell in Eden revolved around *finances*. The curse gave birth to the manifestation of the law; that we must work or die. According to the law, if you didn't work, you wouldn't be able to eat. The way that translated into communities was the creation of money. Money is a form of representing work. But in Jesus, the law was broken. In fact, the curse started in a garden, and it ended in a garden. Just as God told man in the garden that it was by the sweat of his brow that he would survive, Jesus sweat blood in a garden and redeemed us back to being able to just be, rather than do. The curse also caused the ground to only produce thorns and thistles, but Christ wore thorns on His head in order to end the curse. Christ broke the curse of poverty when He died.

Though Christ ended the curse, some of us still think through the paradigm of a spirit of poverty. Poverty thinking causes us to believe that being poor is godly, makes us fearful of how we would misuse money if we had "too much" of it, and causes us to hold to bitterness from how we saw others misuse it in the past. But Christ died to take us out of this type of thinking and into the abundance that God first intended for us.

Does this mean that in Jesus we don't have to work in order to have our basic needs met. Yes! Romans 4:5 clarifies this point. Does it mean that we do not work for the Gospel? No! We work our tails off, because the time is short and there are souls that need to get into heaven. Apathy in our lives is not the correct response to Jesus' sacrifice, but our need to perform for our sustenance is shifted to grace.

You are in an age-old fight. It is a fight to get what you need; to have enough and more than enough. Adam knew the feeling. But in Christ, we are given abundant life and provision. The curse *is* broken, yet many of us still struggle against a spirit of poverty, just as many women still experience pain in childbirth though women have been set free from the curse.

So the question is, "If we have been set free from the curse, why do we still experience its affects?"

The answer is found in this chapter. Faith in what Christ has already done is what sets us free. Knowing God's will and promises about His desire to bless you financially will open the prison door to the cage of poverty that you have lived in. Your time of limitation is over, and it isn't going to change by cutting some ministry a huge check, but by stepping into Christ's finished work by faith. Our mindset must change from poverty thinking to the thinking of a son. Therefore, read on. You will be surprised at what God wants to give you.

+ A Tangible Power +

Typically, because of our reaction to how others have badly stewarded money in the church world, we devalue the need and blessing of money when within the walls of a church. We look forward to a raise at work, but we take on a more cautious perspective when we enter through the doors of a church. Everyone is trying to make money when they leave the context of church. This is because we inherently know that money is not evil, but means to obtaining what we need and want. You don't believe that money is evil at work (proved by your desire for a raise), so why would you believe that in a church context?

Did you know that it is ok to get excited about money? Money can be used for good or for evil, and to get excited about it doesn't mean that you worship it, but that you understand that it carries the power to change circumstances. God wants to get His church into a place where they honor the power that money carries, then steward it rightly.

It may surprise some of us to find that King David himself *liked* money. In fact, one of the desires of David's heart was to be financially prosperous. Though the verse is thoroughly quoted in church, it may surprise us to learn that Psalm 37 is written in the context of finances.

"Delight yourself in the Lord and he will give you the desires of your heart." Psalm 37:4

God knows the desires of your heart. He knows you want more money. Instead of wearing an appearance of resisting abundance out of reaction to other's bad stewardship of money, just embrace the desire you have for money. David had a deep desire for God to bless him financially, because he understood that money is a blessing, not a curse. Don't *love* money, but be honest with yourself that money is a blessing. Then delight in the Lord, put first the Kingdom, and receive what He gives you!

+ THE COMING SHIFT OF POWER +

God desires that the Church has the power in this world. Money is a form of power. Possessing it and using it correctly is spiritual warfare. The more money you have and steward according to His heart, the more power that is taken from the enemy and placed in God's hands.

Because money is power, some people may find it hard when God calls you to give. In giving, you are relinquishing a very tangible power that you possess and are giving it to God. God is raising up a people that can rightly steward the power that money provides without letting it distort their purpose, calling, or motive. He is raising up a people that give without hesitation when He speaks. If you want to be in the edge of what God is doing in the earth, give!

God is releasing a grace upon His people that will enable them to carry abundant resources without being destroyed by the blessing. The statement, "power corrupts" is true, but only when stated outside the realm of God's grace upon a man. When God's grace is enabling a man to carry the blessings that God desires to give His people, the man is safe.

There is a coming shift of power in the world. The people of God are about to receive that which God desires to give them in the realm of finances. The coming bride will be free from poverty, walking in power, full of love, and demonstrating dominion.

+ THE FEAR OF BEING CORRUPTED +

The stumblings of Israel always took place when they were in a place of abundance. Because of the blessings of the Lord, God's people would experience abundance in their finances and provision. Over time, they would become self-sufficient instead of acknowledging that it was God's blessing that caused their abundance. This pride would result in their fall, and they would then reap the consequences of their sin (which became poverty sooner or later). Then, when they had need again, they would humbly go back to God for mercy and favor so that their situation was restored. God would always respond graciously, accept them back, bless them again, and the whole process would start over again. Overall, you rarely see the people of God stumbling into sin when they were in desperate need. Their need put them into a place of constant dependence upon the Lord, thus they kept their focus upon Him and didn't stray away.

God doesn't want the blessings He desires to pour out on us to destroy us. He would rather wait until we are able to bear up under the weight and responsibility of blessings than give us good things prematurely that end up devastating us in the end. But God is also able to anoint a person with wisdom, humility, and integrity so that they are able to carry the blessings of the Lord. The Church *will* learn how to carry the blessings that God desires to lavish upon them. He is taking us past both a lack of character and the fear of being corrupted by money. He is taking us into the fullness of His desire; abundance. He is leading us into a place where we are so convinced of His desire to bless us that we actually *command Him* to do it;

" *And I will give thee the treasures of darkness, and hidden riches of secret places...Ask me of things to come ... command ye me.*" Isaiah 45:3,11 (KJV)

God doesn't want us in fear pertaining to the blessings of the Lord. Instead, He wants us in a place of recognizing what money can do on Earth, to command Him concerning it, and receive it in wisdom. Stewarding finances of great proportion is a large responsibility, but we will do it by His Spirit.

Joseph rightly stewarded the wealth that God entrusted to him by stockpiling the grain and food of an entire kingdom. He didn't view wealth as evil, so when it was given to him, he wasn't motivated by fear but faith. Joseph knew there would be a 7-year famine, so he put the wealth of the nation in the places God told him to put it. In doing so, *the nations of the world* came to him and were sustained, kept from total ruin. If a person wanted to, they could attribute the salvation of the entire world to Joseph, simply because he received wealth and stewarded it wisely, not viewing it through fear, but as a blessing.

+ A HIGH VISION +

Have you ever dreamed of providing for not just your immediate family, but whole cities? Have you ever dreamed of paying off the debt of entire countries in one day so that they can begin to live, build, and thrive again? Lets adjust our bearings, aim higher, and anticipate great things from Heaven pertaining to finances.

You are about to read something that takes a great deal of faith to grasp, but you made it this far through this book, so this should be just as palatable as anything else thrown at you so far.

Isaiah 61 is a fabulous portion of scripture, even quoted by Jesus to typify the nature of His ministry (Luke 4:18-19). We often quote portions of this chapter in church, intrigued by its wonder and direction, but unfortunately we usually don't quote the entire chapter. In doing so, we miss out on one of the most amazing promises in all of scripture.

In verse 6, Isaiah highlights that there will be a time when God's people will become a royal priesthood. That time is now (1 Peter 2:9). He then says something incredible, almost beyond comprehension.

"And you will be called priests of the LORD, you will be named ministers of our God. **You will feed on the wealth of nations, and in their riches you will boast.***"*

You may have missed it. Isaiah gives us a promise that the wealth of nations is ours for the taking. The wealth of the nations is no small thing. Lets put this into perspective.

America alone has trillions of dollars. This should give us an idea of what the "wealth of the nations" is when *one* country is worth trillions of dollars. God's statement through Isaiah does not have to do with one country, but is plural; "the wealth of the nations". The wealth of nations is quite a lot of money.

What does this mean? It means you have Heaven's approval to take all the nation's wealth, add it up, and deposit into your bank account. That is how much God desires, even promises, to give you if you step into His words.

Just think; all the gold in Europe, all the diamonds in Africa, all the crisp bills hidden away in Swiss bank accounts, all the finances reaped every day from the Middle Eastern countries because of oil, all of it; yours.

You can't call me crazy for bringing this to your attention. God said it; I just found it in the Bible. If you question this verse, then look at Isaiah 60:11, because it says the same thing. Men that have understood only a fraction of the revelation on these verses have built cities, changed countries, even become kings over nations.

+ A Different Way +

Typically the Church has been funded by Herself; those that make up the Body of Christ. This isn't an error, but the Bible sets forth a better way of gaining wealth for the purpose of expanding the Kingdom; getting money from those outside the Church.

There are many verses in the Bible that support the idea of not gaining wealth from the Body of Christ, but from those that do not know Christ. A few are:

"…The wealth of the sinner is stored up for the righteous." Proverbs 13:22

"And I will give you the treasures of darkness and the hidden riches of secret places." Is. 45:3

"You will eat the wealth of the nations, and in their riches you will boast." Isaiah 61:6

"...the wealth on the seas will be brought to you, to you the riches of the nations will come." Isaiah 60:5b

Israel took silver and gold when they left Egypt. They were holy thieves that plundered the wealth of the world so that they were enabled to fulfill the commission God had on their lives. God is okay with you taking from the heathen, that His kingdom may extend to the ends of the earth.

You have to understand, it isn't that we don't want others to prosper, but that we want money to go to the right things in the world instead of the wrong things. Money is power, therefore we must be ardent in attaining it so that it goes to the orphan, widow, mass crusades, country debts, and anointed ministries rather than the things that unbelievers may spend money on such as pornography (a 10-15 billion dollar a year industry[7]). It isn't that we don't want unbelievers to flourish and be blessed, it is that we don't want power (money) invested into godless arenas of life. The unbeliever isn't the problem; money invested into evil aspects of life is. This is why we are called to *take* the world's money, not with force or manipulation, but by receiving it when the Lord hands it over to us.

If we are going to walk in abundant wealth, we must dip into the world's bank account. Otherwise, we are just shifting money from place to place in the Kingdom. God wants us to look at finances from a global

---

[7] Hollywood is believed to make around 10 billion dollars a year. Hence, porn is believed to make much more money in America than Hollywood annually.

view. Money needs to be in the hands of the worldwide Church, all streams included.

The paradigm of getting money to fund the Gospel from *the world* primarily rather than the Church is not a new concept.

The Apostle Paul carried this understanding himself. He was a tentmaker that siphoned off of the limitless money held by the masses. Paul's tent making wasn't just a means of financial support, but a conduit through which he took power from the world and brought it into the realm of the Kingdom so that it could be stewarded correctly.

Paul realized that his needs could either be supplied by the world, or by the church. He didn't want to take from the power (money) that the churches he visited had, so he worked as a tentmaker. It wasn't that Paul wasn't willing to receive their hospitality and gifts, but rather that Paul wanted to contribute to the power that the churches had rather than take from them.

"Now I am ready to visit you for the third time, and I will not be a burden to you, because what I want is not your possessions but you. After all, children should not have to save up for their parents, but parents for their children." 2 Corinthians 12:14

"Surely you remember, brothers, our toil and hardship; we worked night and day in order not to be a burden to anyone while we preached the gospel of God to you." 1 Thes 2:9

"On the contrary, we worked night and day, laboring and toiling so that we would not be a burden to any of you." 2 Thes 3:8

Paul was a spiritual father to the churches that he visited. He understood that a parent's job is to give, not take. It would be foolish for me to expect my son to pay me when I teach him something, or for me to depend upon him for my financial stability. This is not to say that a father will not receive a gift given to him by a son that is honored to give, but that he doesn't depend upon such offerings.

"...because what I want is not your possessions but you. After all, children should not have to save up for their parents, but parents for their children." 2 Corinthians 12:14

Imagine it. Ministers with a father's heart that come and speak in a region, and rather than just talking about or praying for the breaking of debt, they actually *pay off debts*. God is looking for ministers that do not take from their children, but instead give to them, and on more levels than just spiritually. This will begin to happen as the Church steps into the wealth of the nations because ministers will have incredible amounts of money, capable and trusted to distribute it as the Lord leads like the Apostles did in Acts 4:34. Carlos Slim, the wealthiest man in the world according to Forbes in 2010, once said, "Wealth must be seen as a responsibility, not as a privilege. The responsibility is to create more wealth. It's like having an orchard; you have to give away the fruit, but not the trees."

+ WAS CHRIST RICH? +

Jesus wasn't poor, despite what people think. Jesus said, "The poor will always be with us", and He wasn't referring to Himself! Yet, did Jesus have lots of money? Scripture doesn't seem to give us that picture.

But poverty isn't determined by a number in a bank account; it is a mindset that is brought about by a spirit. Being rich isn't the point, having abundantly enough is. Though Jesus probably didn't have millions of gold coins stashed away (or did He?), He always had what He needed, plus some.

Once, Jesus and His posse needed to pay the taxes, so Jesus simply commanded the earth to give up some of its gold. As a consequence, a fish brought it to Him in its mouth. I know I am taking liberty with recounting of the biblical account of that story, but the point is that we never witness Jesus in a state of poverty. He always had what He needed, and even had an abundance.

Once, Jesus and His disciples needed bread, so He multiplied it to such an extent that there was more after feeding 5,000 than when they first began. There is always enough, and even more than enough with God. There is abundance. Abundance means "too much". It means that God overshot, and God loves to overshoot our need and reveal to us His ability to give us more than enough. He wants to break our poverty thinking by giving us *way* too much. Abundance is the attitude of the Father.

✝ SUPERNATURAL PROVISION ✝

Jesus portrayed an even better way than Paul when pertaining to obtaining provision; supernaturally. Jesus knew that His Daddy owned everything in the world. Anything Jesus needed simply needed to be asked for, and it was His.

God is still in the business of providing supernaturally for His children. He doesn't do so because we have been good girls and boys, but because we are His children and He loves us. Everything that is His is ours.

He is not like Santa, weighing our good acts against our mistakes to see if we qualified to get a present in our stocking or a piece of coal. He likes to give to us because He likes to give to us.

Supernatural provision is wonderful because it comes in the opposite spirit of a performance mentality. You can't say you "earned" or "worked for" a diamond worth 20,000 dollars that you found in a church service. Supernatural provision pushes the pride that comes from our ability to provide for ourselves out of the way and humbles us by grace. We find ourselves dependent upon God. Miracles are of the same nature: you *know* it wasn't you that made the impossibility bow.

It is becoming more and more common for diamonds and precious stones to show up in prayer and worship meetings. Gold dust is almost customary in meetings where the glory of God drops upon people. Just as a groom prepares and adorns his bride with jewelry and glorious gifts before they become one flesh, so is God raining down gifts upon His bride. It is a wonderful hour in history.

But gold dust, gems, and diamonds are just the beginning. God is watching His people to see how they respond to such manifestations of glory because He wants to release greater levels of it. He desires to release the "treasures of darkness and hidden riches of secret places" (Is. 45:3). If we begin to think we did something right to earn His blessings or wrongly steward the finances and the praise of man that comes from the manifestations of glory, He will wait to release more. But if we humbly keep our focus on Jesus, He can continue to pour out greater levels of glory. He doesn't want to destroy us with the blessing.

Gold bars will begin to show up when we least expect it. Angels may even drop off winning lottery tickets. Why not? You wouldn't be gambling; God would have bought the ticket!

I know of a young couple that, over a short period of time, found more than twenty diamonds in their apartment. Angels were dropping these precious stones off of significant size throughout their house. The couple would stay home from school, worship the Lord, then search their apartment to find new diamonds almost every day. It became such a well-known fact in the church they were attending that the couple opened their doors to anyone that wanted to come look for diamonds in their house. They had a rule that if you found it, you kept it. People were constantly walking through their house and searching the rug, drawers, and in couches for a new diamond. Many people found diamonds from heaven in this house, and the excitement and praise of God heightened in their church.

Imagine praying and worshipping in your car when suddenly you realize that your car is dragging its underside on the pavement of the road. You pull over to see what broke on your vehicle. Upon exiting the car, you don't see anything awry, except the fact that you now are driving a vehicle that looks more like a low-riding gangster car rather than your daily driver. Somehow, your car is bottomed out on the road, like an invisible elephant has just chosen your car for its seat. You glance at the shocks and springs and cannot find the problem. Puzzled, you open the back of your car to look for some tools so that you can jack the car off the ground to get a better look underneath. As you open the back of your car you are blinded as the sun reflects off of something metallic sitting in the back of your car. As your eyes adjust, you realize that somehow, in the middle of your driving to work, fifty gold bars materialized in the trunk of your car. Needless to say, you put in your two weeks and spend the rest of your life traveling the world, doing ministry, and giving to others that are doing Gospel work.

This can happen to you. When it does, sell the goods and fund the Kingdom. Don't lock the gold and diamonds away so that you can take them out once and awhile to look at them with friends; cash them in and give! Shovel it out as quickly as you get it! Store up an inheritance for your children, throw crusades in Africa and India, build orphanages all over the world, give to ministries that feed you, and take your wife on a hot date every week! Spend it well! I have seen these diamonds hoarded away instead of used to bring more souls into the revelation of Christ. Material items are not evil, but souls are more valuable than any material item in the whole world, so spend money in a way that makes Jesus smile. He wants us to use money to change the world into a place that reflects the likeness of Heaven.

+ RADICAL GENEROSITY +

Giving is a wonderful privilege we have as Christians. Unlike other religions, God's people are not *required* to give to His work, but rather do so because they genuinely want to. It is a joy to contribute to what God is doing on the earth. Do you give because someone other than God is telling you to, or because you really want to?

As we give, we are found by God to be faithful stewards. As we give, something unlocks in the heavenly realms and finances pour down upon us because we can be entrusted with more. He gives to us that we may be able to give. Doing so is a joy.

But in order for giving to become a joy, you have to know that you have a choice to do it or not. You need to know that you don't *have* to give to the Kingdom in order to be blessed. God will bless you even if you don't give because you are His child. Let it be clear; not giving to the Church will not result in your life being cursed. That lie has been around for centuries, and it is a lie that the Church has used to control the people that come within Her walls week after week.

Martin Luther noticed this in his day. Instead of the Church pulling people out of poverty, it added to it by taking the little money that the people had. Luther was furious about this and it was one of the main aspects of compromise in the Catholic Church that motivated Luther to bring about the reformation. Just as in Luther's day, verses are pulled out of the Bible today that instill fear into the listeners so that they give. Sadly, this kind of "reaping" works extremely well in that it rakes in the cash. However, God is raising up a people that give extravagantly not because they are manipulated or intimidated into it, but because they want the domain of the King to increase. They give because they love Jesus.

It needs to be said that the amount that we give to the Lord isn't His primary concern when it comes to giving. Generosity looks different for every person, and our ability to give generously reflects the state of our heart. The widow with two copper pennies taught us that someone can give little and it was beautiful to Jesus because her heart was one of radical generosity. The widow gave little because she had little. If she had possessed much, she would have given much. The facet of the Kingdom that is attractive to God is the heart that is filled with extravagant generosity.

What God is after is our hearts. Giving is a practical "measuring stick" into the state of our heart. We know something is arwy inside when the Spirit prompts us to give and we hesitate. Giving is *the* tangible aspect of surrendering the power that we have in our life to God and others.

God is shaping His people into a company of givers. He cannot give to the Body what He desires to give to them until they shovel it out as quickly as they get it. But that is exactly what the Church is becoming.

+ THE TITHE MENTALITY +

Did you know that the New Testament never talks about our need to give ten percent of our income? The tithe is derived from a formulaic, Old Testament thinking. Actually, if you want a formula to live by as to how much you should give, Jesus exhorted people to give everything!

The "tithe" mentality, though it regulated people's giving in the Old Testament, creates a problem in the thinking of new covenant Christians. The tithe generates a thinking that ten percent of a person's income is the Lord's, but the rest of their income (90%) is theirs to spend as they please. This is a problematic thought pattern because Jesus stressed the imperative of stewardship. *Everything* God gives us needs to be stewarded wisely, not just ten percent of our income. If we feel that we are only required to give ten percent of our income and the rest of our income can be spent in anyway we please, the majority of the Church's wealth will not be spent in a way that ultimately benefits the Kingdom in some way, but on Itself. For a person with a tithe paradigm, material items, while not wrong to have, begin to take precedence over the expansion of Heaven's reign on the earth.

You may be asking, "So if we aren't required to give ten percent, how do we know how much to give?" The answer is to become a people that give when the Lord speaks instead of being a people that follow an expired formula. With our ears open to the Voice of heaven, we release the power we have (money) to the places He tells us to sow. Be assured that He will challenge and grow our faith through the amounts that

He tells us to give. If giving isn't sacrificial to any degree, you probably aren't hearing the Lord in fullness. When He speaks it will carry peace, but it may challenge your faith because it is such a large number. If you have a spouse, separately ask the Lord how much you should give. You will be surprised how often you will both get the same number. My wife and I love to give for many reasons, but one reason is because we will both ask the Lord how much to give separately, and we usually get the same number. If we hear different amount, we give the larger number, trusting that He will take care of us. He always has.

Also, remember that the Bible never says that we must give to our local church. Give to the places you are fed. You will know them by their fruit, so give where there is fruit! If it happens to be your church, give, and give extravagantly! But if you are fed somewhere besides your church, give there! How will the rest of the five-fold ministry (Eph. 4:11) be supported if the majority of people's giving goes to the local church, which represents one-fifth of the five-fold (the pastor)? The prophets, apostles, teachers, and evangelists need to be supported as well, and because most churches do not offer paid positions to these offices, these ministries have been looked over and not heavily supported by the Body of Christ.

+ GOD PAYS WELL +

God is a God of promotion and increase. It is His delight to increase that which we already have. If being faithful with ten minas resulted in being given *ten cities*, we can deduct that a small portion of true faithfulness and stewardship goes a long way with the Lord. He loves to give extravagantly to us. He loves to give us raises, bonuses, and promotions!

See, you have to understand that God sees your work for the Kingdom and desires to reimburse you for your work. He is a good master, and doesn't pay cheaply. What you think to be a simple act of love and power is worth millions to heaven. Heaven doesn't pay badly. God desires to pay you well when you get to heaven, but also while on Earth too! The problem is that most people do not access the realm of "reimbursement" while on Earth.

Luke 10:7 says that the worker deserves his wages. God says that we *deserve* wealth. So, prophesy to your life and demand it! Take authority over the wealth in the world and make it your own! Say this prayer; "I command wealth to be mine!"

The only person that will limit the blessings that God desires to pour out on your life is you. He is ready. Can you receive? You don't need to pray or worship any harder to get wealth. You can't work yourself into this. You can't spiritually perform yourself into wealth because God already wants to give it to you and has given promises to you in the Bible about it. It is by faith. Don't muster it up. Let His goodness become a reality and know that He desires to bless you. Then, just receive it like a son or daughter.

Loved by Love
A Revealing of God's Affections For His Bride

Much of the Body of Christ does not know how to read the book of Song of Songs in a way that draws them closer to Jesus. If this pertains to you, know that you are not alone. Though in the past the Church grasped the depths of this book, its revelations have been largely lost by modern-day Protestantism. Because large portions of the previous chapters of the book you hold in your hands referred to the Song of Songs quite frequently, it seems shedding light about how to read Songs of Songs may help the reader. If this is you, buckle up and enjoy the ride.

The Song of Songs is one of the most profound books in the Bible. There is no book in the Bible that more accurately captures the emotions of God's heart towards man as the Song of Songs. There is an enormous release of power, confidence, and revelation that spills forth in the life of the believer that receives from the love that is captured in the verses of this book. It is fabulous.

Consequently, the Song of Songs is an amazing book to pray as it is read. If a person is able to personalize a verse in this book and allow it to become an interaction between themselves and God, there is no limit to the intimacy and revelation that they will obtain through that single verse.

This appendix is simply a result of making the Song of Songs an interaction between the Lord and myself rather than just reading the Bible as a textbook full of facts. The Bible's purpose is to lead us into an encounter with God, and that doesn't happen unless we interact with God through it.

I encourage you to interact with God through the verses in the Song of Songs rather than just read it. If you choose to do this, do so slowly, for this is a poetic book. Hamlet is rarely read quickly. Instead a line is read, then pondered. Poetry is an art of taking paragraphs of thought and beautifully putting them into a single line, the fullness of which will only to be discovered by those that will take the time to search for it. Song of Songs is best if read in the same manner. I would spend two or more hours interacting with the Lord on one verse before moving on. When I did this, the verse would open up to me like a gateway to deeper truths. It is as if each verse of the Song leads to its own world that you can explore and enjoy for all of eternity if you desire to do so.

The first read of the Song of Songs can be somewhat intimidating. Poetic language is usually somewhat emblematic and even cryptic. When I initially wrote this appendix it was a personal prayer to the Lord, and I wasn't intending anyone else to read it. Because of this, I did not explain what the symbols in Song of Songs represent. Therefore, if you get stuck because of the symbolic language, I recommend that you look at the prayers that I wrote. These prayers should help steer you back into understanding what is being said in the verse, because I spoke very simply to the Lord with the interpretation of the symbols already in mind.

Lastly, the prayers I wrote are only the beginning. Let God take you past what I prayed, into even deeper revelations of the beauty of Christ, and deeper revelations of the raw beauty that you, as His Bride, possess.

-Tyler Johnson

Key:
G: Bridegroom
B: Bride
D: Daughters of Jerusalem
W: Watchmen
H: Holy Spirit

Italicized- Scripture
Non italicized- Prayer

B: *"Let Him kiss me with the kisses of his mouth- for your love is more delightful than wine."*

Father, let Jesus come close to me. Intimately close. Let Him romance me. Jesus, you are better than any other lover I have ever had. You are gentler, more passionate, and more intimate. You make me feel comfortable and safe. Your words melt my heart. Your words are what feed me. You give me peace when you are near. Your love is truly more pleasurable than anything else in this world!

"Pleasing is the fragrance of your perfumes; your name is like perfume poured out. No wonder the maidens love you!"

Jesus, get so close that your fragrance rubs off on me. May your smell draw others in to You. But it can only rub off if You come close enough. This is my heart's cry. When You are close, I can understand why other Your lovers are so obsessed with You.

"Take me away with you- let us hurry! Let us run together! Let the king bring me into his chambers."

Lord, I want to be with You so badly because of who You are. I am tired of being without You, I just want to be alone with You. So let us go! Let us walk through rivers, search forests, explore our gardens, and simply be together. I want to get You alone. I want to be as intimate with You as possible. Steal me away. Lets go to the most intimate place You can think of and just enjoy each other. You are beautiful Lord. You are shockingly perfect. Lock the door behind us and let us forget the world as we sink into love with each other. I love to be in Your chambers, in this Secret Place, where nobody else is allowed to enter. Once I get this time with You, I can run with you in laboring for Your Kingdom. Loving You and being loved by You will empower me to love everyone else.

D: *"We will rejoice and delight in you; we will praise your love more than wine."*

As a body of believers we declare that we will delight in and love who You are, like she does. We want to have a relationship with Him where His love is better to us than anything this world has to offer. Jesus, we believe that You are worthy of all praise and wonder!

B: *"How right they are to adore you!"*

Anyone that sees You for who You are will praise you. I can understand why others admire You and love You so, because I have seen Your beauty. Those around me that are starting to love You are on the right track. A person is wise to see your beauty and then worship you for it. I agree with them and join in with the song that they sing of you, repeating over and over; Holy, Holy are You! You are gorgeous! Beauty is found in Your eyes!

"Dark am I, yet lovely, O daughters of Jerusalem, dark like the tents of Kedar, like the tent curtains of Solomon. Do not stare at me because I am darkened by the sun. My mother's sons were angry with me and made me take care of the vineyards; my own vineyard I have neglected."

There are things about me that are not desirable, and I do not profess to be perfect at all. But I am wondering if I am still beautiful, if only for the reason that my Lover finds me beautiful amidst my many faults. If He says that I am beautiful, then I am, wholly and completely. There are still a lot of places in me that are not yet healed and made beautiful by Your touch, Lover, because I have been too scared to look at those areas.

"Tell me, you whom I love, where you graze your flock, and where you rest your sheep at midday."

Lover, I seek after you. I need you. I need to feast upon Your beauty so that I can become beautiful. What I behold, I become. Will You tell me how to make my way to You? I want to come join the others that love You and rest along with them under Your care. You are not only my lover but my Leader and Protector as well. You are my shepherd and I desire to follow You.

"Why should I be like a veiled woman beside the flocks of your friends?"

I know that You desire to reveal to me how to make my way to You. You have taken me as Your own. I am no longer one who gives myself to other lovers, so tell me where You are so that I do not appear to be anyone else's.

G: *"If you do not know, most beautiful of women, follow the tracks of the sheep and graze your young goats by the tents of the shepherds."*

Before I tell you anything else, I want to tell you that you are stunningly beautiful. The very first thing I have to say to you is that you are beautiful to Me. You need to be grounded in this foundational truth before you can move into any deeper truths. I will continue to remind you of this truth until it becomes who you are; the Beloved. Before anything else happens, you must learn to Be Loved. About your question, I am eager to meet with you, so follow the path that your leaders are on who have gone before you. Listen to them, for they know how to find Me. Stay in the Body of Christ, amongst other Lovers of Jesus, Lastly, be faithful to those that I have given you to minister to, regardless of how big or small the number.

"I liken you, my darling, to a mare harnessed to one of the chariots of Pharaoh. Your cheeks are beautiful with earrings, your neck with strings of jewels. We will make you earrings of gold, studded with silver."

Hear me! I think you are beautiful. Right when I saw you approaching me, I was struck by how beautiful you are. Even if you are not sure that you are beautiful, be sure, because I say so and my opinion is the only one that matters. I desire to be with you more than you know. I love who you are. You possess strength and nobility that you don't know that you have. The Father, the Holy Spirit, and I will give you gifts that will make your beauty even more obvious to all who look at you.

B: *"While the king was at his table, my perfume spread its fragrance. My lover is to me a sachet of myrrh resting between my* breasts. My lover is to me a cluster of henna blossoms from the vineyards of En Gedi."

I want You to be drawn to me. I want to live my life in such a way that You cannot help but come from your Holy Place and ravish me with Your love. And likewise, I am drawn to you. The fragrance You carry makes me want to leave my life and enter into a romantic relationship with You, never to return again to the previous life I had. You are beautiful. You are what I want.

G: "How beautiful you are, my darling! Oh, how beautiful! Your eyes are like doves."

First, I cannot help but tell you again, I think you are beautiful, just as you are. I love to love you. Your job is to simply receive My love and out of that receiving, give back to Me the same love that I gave you. This is why I am called the Lover and you the Beloved. So hear Me! You are beautiful. My breath is taken from Me when I look at you. And your eyes! Oh your eyes. They give Me peace when I look into them. Your eyes reveal to Me your faithfulness because you aren't looking in any direction but towards Me.

B: "How handsome you are, my lover! Oh, how charming! And our bed is verdant."

I cannot help but echo Your cry back to You. You are beautiful as well! You are captivating! The place of intimacy with You is luxuriant and desirable, as if we were lying in thick, green grass, all alone. This is where I want to be; alone with You.

G: "The beams of our house are cedars, our rafters are firs."

I have many intimate places to take you that I have prepared for you, but for now, let us just enjoy the depths of this forest together. The canopy of the trees is like our ceiling, and the trees themselves are like the beams of a house. Lets just dwell together here with each other, lying in this bed of grass.

"I am a rose of Sharon, a lily of the valleys."

I am like a beautiful flower. I sense my heart coming alive like the way a lily blossoms in the warmth of the sun. But I didn't feel like this before. You are transforming how I see myself by simply being with You and gazing upon Your beauty.

G: *"Like a lily among thorns is my darling among the maidens."*

Yes! That is right! You are starting to understand. You are allowing my love to change the way you think and the way you feel. You are starting to let what I think of you affect you. I see you as a flower among thorns. No one compares to you. When I look across the earth, you are the one that stands out and that I see as beautiful.

B: *"Like an apple tree among the trees of the forest is my lover among the young men. I delight to sit in his shade and his fruit is sweet to my taste. He has taken me to the banquet hall, and his banner over me is love."*

Other desires do not compare to You. You are the greatest desire and Your love is most fulfilling. Also, You can't help but give it to me. It is in your nature to be generous. You do not know how to be anything else. So I pick of Your fruits of love and enjoy them. I sit in Your shade of protection and enjoy who You are. Thank you.

Everyone who looks at me knows that I am loved because You do not make it a secret. Though I am far from perfect, You are not ashamed to love me. You proclaim Your love for me everyday, declaring it to the angels and to the earth.

"Strengthen me with raisins, refresh me with apples, for I am faint with love."

Give me more of the fruits of Your love. I am addicted. The more of You that I get, the more of You I want. I am overtaken and overflowing with love, yet desiring for more. After knowing You intimately, I will always want You. I will always be hungry for more of You. I have been close to You, and it has made me intoxicated. I am inebriated with Love.

"His left arm is under my head, and his right arm embraces me. Daughters of Jerusalem, I charge you by the gazelles and by the does of the field: Do not arouse or awaken love until it so desires."

You hold me as intimately as possible. And it is all I want. Do not let go, do not leave. Stay here. And to other: Do not act as though you are in love with the Bridegroom when you are not. If you love Him, then give yourself, but if you are not, do not fake that you love to be close to Him so that everyone else is impressed.

"Listen! My Lover! Look! Here He comes, leaping across the mountains, bounding over the hills. My lover is like a gazelle or a young stag. Look! There he stands behind our wall, gazing through the windows, peering through the lattice."

Do you hear something? I do! I hear my Lord, my Lover, coming for me! Oh how exciting and wonderful it is to hear Him coming! He is coming quickly for me, even running to find me. There is a joyful urgency in the patter of His feet, and it is apparent that He does not like to restrain Himself from me. He loves to come to me. You come to me. I can hear Your love. I can hear You coming for me, despite the pearls and challenges it provides for You. There is no obstacle that You will not overcome in order to be near me. You do it all. I can simply wait on You, because it is Your work that enables us to be together, not my ability to draw near to You. You loved me first. You came for me. I don't need to do anything. I am free from performance, from the need to do anything for You. I receive Your gift of the Finished Work. He watches me when He arrives, and waits for the perfect moment to surprise me and throw Himself at me. I watch Him spy on me, and laugh as I see Him peer in at me in my hiding place.

B: *"My lover spoke and said to me, 'Arise my darling, my beautiful one, and come with me. See! The winter is past; the rains are over and gone. Flowers appear on the earth; the season of singing has come, the cooing of doves is heard in our land. The fig tree forms its early fruit; the blossoming vines spread their fragrance. Arise, come, my darling; my beautiful one, come with me.'"*

Jesus said to me "Get up and I will lead you into a new season of life. You have gone through harsh times in the past, but those times are over. I want to go even deeper and be even more intimate with you. I am calling you into more with Me. I will be close to you and life will be like the natural seasons of spring and summer. It will be a time of new life, of fruit, of beauty, of peace. Most of all, I will be near, more near than I ever have been before. Come, one whom I love dearly, and I will take you into this new season." I know that in order for this to happen I have to do as He says. He will not drag me into it. He wants me to choose Him just as He chose to pursue me.

G: *"My dove in the clefts of the rock, in the hiding places on the mountainside, show me your face, let me hear your voice; for your voice is sweet, and your face is lovely."*

My beauty, for whatever reason, may it be shame or a feeling of unworthiness or a fear of intimacy altogether, I sense you have begun to hide yourself from me. Please don't pull your heart away. You know what I think; I have told you many times before. You are beautiful, just as you are. You do not have to be anything special, for even in your faults I find you special because I made you. I am in love with you; please do not turn away from My invitation into deeper places of intimacy with Me. I am pursuing you; please don't reject My love, simply for your sake. In the spot of total exposure and vulnerability is the very time when it is most wise to fling wide the doors of your heart to Me. Sing to Me from your heart again. I miss it. Turn your face towards Me and do not look away, for I miss looking upon your beauty.

B: *"Catch for us the foxes, the little foxes that ruin the vineyards, our vineyards that are in bloom. My lover is mine and I am his; he browses among the lilies. Until the day breaks and the shadows flee, turn, my lover, and be like a gazelle or like a young stag on the rugged hills."*

Lover, I am scared. Part of me wants to do as You say, and part of me is scared to death of Your love. The part of me that wants to do as You say calls out for You to cleanse me. Take care of my shame, unworthiness, and fear. Take care of any darkness that is running free in my life and ruining me. But another part of me says that You're wanting to go too deep. Do you know the places of filth in my heart? Why would You want into my heart? I am scared to let You in. So although You had promise me summer and spring, I cannot do it. Until I am full of light and not darkness, I can't receive You. I feel like I need to be clean before I can approach You. Just as You came, please leave. Turn and go to the mountaintops without me.

"All night long on my bed I looked for the one my heart loves; I looked for him but did not find him. I will get up now and go about the city, through its streets and squares; I will search for the one my heart loves."

Oh no, what have I done? I am nothing without Him, and I have told Him to leave! While I know that He will never leave me nor forsake me, I also know that He is a gentleman and will not force Himself upon me, therefore His nearness is gone. I cannot sleep, and when I do, it is not fulfilling. Oh how I miss our intimate times. I miss being held by Him, I miss His sweet and loving voice. I miss His overwhelming beauty. I miss His affirmation and encouragement. What have I done? My shame has kept Him from me, though He has already bore it upon Himself. I wonder if I can go to Him as I am like He suggested? I have no choice but to search for Him. I know He will take me back when I find Him. But I must arise, just as He told me before, and go to Him. Once I find Him, I must go with Him where He leads. I must seek Him or I will just sit here in this place, regretful and depressed. Oh how my heart longs for Him. I should have just trusted and embraced Him instead of turning Him away.

"So I looked for him but did not find him. The watchmen found me as they made their rounds in the city. "Have you seen the one my

heart loves?" Scarcely had I passed them when I found the one my heart loves."

Jesus, when I lose You due to fear, all is lost. Sorrow sweeps over me and I desire with all that is within me for You to be near. I cannot sit still…I am compelled by desire to get up and search for You. You see my heart. You understand that I didn't do what You asked me to do because of fear and shame, not rebellion or defiance. You don't tell me that I have a heart of disobedience, but a heart that is not yet mature in love. You know that I want to obey You, but am having a hard time walking it out. Love has not developed enough in my heart to cast out all the fear that lies dormant there. While my love is not mature yet, You still see the goodness of my heart. You never speak to me as if I am evil. Thank you for seeing the true state of my heart. I am beginning to understand that You are most impressed by obedience that is motivated by love, not duty or obligation. I know You will captivate me with Your love to such an extent that I will want to obey You. You have told me that desiring to obey is the first step of obedience. Because of that, You are proud of me even in the midst of my shortcoming. You promise to finish the work You started in me; the work of love that is mature. The maturity of love will translate into an unwavering obedience in my relationship with You. I looked and looked for You but couldn't seem to lay my eyes on You nor hear Your beautiful voice. I even asked people who know You and know of the place where You dwell, but they did not offer much help. But, I believe that my actions will not cause us to experience distance forever, because I am now doing as You asked. Because I finally arose and obeyed, we suddenly reunite.

"I held him and would not let him go till I had brought him to my mother's house, to the room of the one who conceived me.

Daughters of Jerusalem, I charge you by the gazelles and by the does of the field: Do not arouse or awaken love until it so desires."

The moment I see You after not being with You, I cling to You. I am overjoyed that You are near and that I've found You. Next time, I hope to obey more quickly so that I don't miss out on intimacy with You. Immediately after finding You, I desire to take You to the most intimate place I can think of. I am not going to let go of You until we have established intimacy between us again. Being in relationship with You is a serious matter, and anyone that isn't sure that they are willing for You to make them uncomfortable with Your perfect, wonderfully intrusive, love should not come into relationship with You. You are grieved by luke-warm lovers who let You only so far into their heart. Your are saddened by people that say that they are in love with You but never allow for intimacy by shunning the uneasiness that real love creates. Your love unmasks, causing shame and feelings of unworthiness to come to the surface. It is not easy to let You love me, but is also the very thing that I yearn for.

H: *"Who is this coming up from the desert like a column of smoke, perfumed with myrrh and incense made from all the spices of the merchant? Look! It is Solomon's carriage, escorted by sixty warriors, the noblest of Israel, all of them wearing the sword, all experienced in battle, each with his sword at his side, prepared for the terrors of the night. King Solomon made for himself the carriage; he made it of wood from Lebanon. Its posts he made of silver, its base of gold. Its seat was upholstered with purple, its interior lovingly inlaid by the daughters of Jerusalem."*

The glorious Bridegroom comes out of the desert as a King with warriors all around Him, smelling of the most beautiful scents. He is the one true King. Because He travels with 60 warriors, it is obvious that His Bride would be safe with Him and under His leadership, for she would be with Him and under His protection.

B: *"Come out, you daughters of Zion, and look at King Solomon wearing the crown, the crown with which his mother crowned him on the day of his wedding, the day his heart rejoiced."*

Daughters of Jerusalem come and gaze upon the King. Gazing upon His Beauty was what changed me, and it will change you as well. You will begin to be more concerned of His desire than your own, but only after you gaze upon His beauty. You will become a people whose pleasure is fully determined by His being pleased.

G: *"How beautiful are you, my darling! Oh how beautiful! Your eyes behind your veil are doves. Your hair is like a flock of goats descending from Mount Gilead."*

Beloved, I love telling you over and over....you are beautiful. I do not say that out of pity because I feel bad for you, but because I really think so! I am shocked by how beautiful you are. I have made you exactly the way that I want to, so to me, because of the cross, you are perfect in my eyes now. You are who I want you to be, just as you are, even in the midst of your faults. Don't you see? I am in love with you! This is all I know to do, my bride, my sister. When you look past the veil and turn your eyes to Me, I am overwhelmed, excited, and filled with peace. Look at Me! I love to see your eyes! I love to see you look at Me, especially because you have to look through all the darkness of the world in order to do so, though you do anyways! I am so proud! I am captured by you. I love even your hair. It alone outshines the most beautiful things I created in nature. Do you realize that even your hair alone is more beautiful to Me than the created Earth? I love you that much.

"Your teeth are like a flock of sheep just shorn, coming up from the washing. Each has its twin; not one of them is alone. Your lips are like a scarlet ribbon; your mouth is lovely. Your temples behind your veil are like the halves of a pomegranate. Your neck is like the tower of David, built with elegance; on it hang a thousand shields, all of them shields of warriors. Your two breasts are like two fawns, like twin fawns of a gazelle that browse among the lilies. Until the day breaks and the shadows flee, I will go to the mountain of myrrh and to the hill of incense."

I love to take every detail of who you are and tell you how enamored I am with it. Every little part of you is enchanting to Me. You are exactly the way that I want you to be, right now. I am not driven to change you; I am driven to love you. Let Me accept you. Yes, I am making you more like Me, but today and everyday that follows there is complete acceptance of you by Me. Not only do I accept you; I love you. Not only do I love you; I like You. You are whole in my eyes. You will do great things in my name if you believe these words that I am telling you.

"All beautiful you are, my darling: there is no flaw in you."

Now I will simply say it, I see you as flawless, my lover. I have set the stage as to why this is true, now hear me as I say it again, I see you as one that is without flaw. You need to receive this and understand it in order for you to live the way I desire you to live.

"Come with me from Lebanon, my bride, come with me from Lebanon. Descend from the crest of Amana, from the top of Senir, the summit of Hermon, from the lions' dens and the mountain haunts of the leopards."

You have overcome the test of the mountaintop, a place of warfare with the enemy. You have walked in obedience, even when it was uncomfortable and challenging. You are victorious. You are becoming an overcoming Bride that will be stopped by nothing. Even the gates of hell will not prevail against you. If I am with you, nothing will defeat you. Shame is losing its grip on you. Now, I want you to come with me off the mountaintop and descend to the valley. You did well. Obedience makes Me feel trusted by you. Thank you, Love!

"You have stolen my heart, my sister, my bride; you have stolen my heart with one glance of your eyes, with one jewel of your necklace.

As you walk down into the valley with Me, let Me tell you how much I love you and am drawn to you. I am not sure if you understand the extent to which you ravish my heart, My bride, so I will tell you again in new ways. I tell you over and over because I have to…My lips cannot stay sealed when I am with you. Also, I tell you because you seem to forget over and over. In fact, everyday your heart forgets. So I sing this song to you again…I love you! When you simply glance at Me, love arises in My heart so vehemently that it makes My knees go weak. When you focus the affection of your heart on Me for a mere moment, all of heaven pauses in awe. I am the center and focal point of heaven, and everything that is happening here revolves around Me. When you glance at Me heaven stops, gasping in wonder because I stop, completely speechless in awe-struck love. My heart melts, conquered by you. No army in heaven and hell or on Earth can conquer me, no principality or chief power can overcome me, no beauty in existence has victory over My heart, but a simple glance of love from you overtakes My heart. One look from you and I am forever captured.

How could I ever leave you or forsake you if this is what you do so easily to Me? You have won me with one look, let alone all the times we have romanced each other. We have even stuck it out when things got tough. I would never leave you. I am unable to. Your kisses woo Me and bring Me near to you. I would give anything to get you even closer. Oh, how I love to come close to you and be received by you!

How delightful is your love, my sister, my bride! How much more pleasing is your love than wine, and the fragrance of your perfume than any spice!

I crave your love just as you crave mine. You told me near the beginning of our relationship that My love is better to you than any pleasure found on Earth. This is a secret stored away in heaven until this moment; it is the same for me. Your love is better to Me than any pleasure I have ever experienced. I created the earth and man, am worshipped by the cherubim, live in a city with streets of gold, and am constantly living in glory. These are all things that bring immense pleasure. I am enthroned in pleasure. Yet, all of these things pale in comparison to the pleasure I experience when you offer your love to Me.

Your lips, my bride, drip honey. Your lips drip sweetness as the honeycomb; milk and honey are under your tongue. The fragrance of your garments is like that of Lebanon.

Your words of love to me are delicacies to Me. Sometimes you wonder if I value your words of love to Me, let alone if I hear you when you speak. I do! Your words are immeasurably sweet to Me. I feast upon your words of love. They are cherished. Continue lavishing them upon Me, my bride.

You are a garden locked up, my sister, my bride; you are a spring enclosed, a sealed fountain. Your plants are an orchard of pomegranates with choice fruits, with henna and nard, nard and saffron, calamus and cinnamon, with every kind of incense tree, with myrrh and aloes and all the finest spices. You are a garden fountain, a well of flowing water streaming down from Lebanon."

You are the place I go when I want something wonderful that I can't find anywhere else. You are a secret garden, a private and pure fountain of love to Me. There is a reservoir of love in your garden that has been stored up as a result of the times you were alone with Me and drank of My love. Because of this, I love to enter this secret place of your heart and delight Myself in you. I drink of the Living Water that you have saved for Me and eat of the fruits of your love that you have cultivated over time. May I enter to eat and drink of the love you have stored up for me?

B: *"Awake, north wind, and come, south wind! Blow on my garden, that its fragrance may spread abroad. Let my lover come into His garden and taste its choice fruits."*

Yes, please come in. This is all for You anyways. I invite You in because I trust that You will not be critical of me, but will rather delight in who I am and what little I have to offer. I invite the Spirit to blow upon this humble garden that it may come to life and be pleasing to Him. It is His. Take it as Your own and do as You will with me. I lay myself down for You in vulnerability. I want You. Do as You please. Enjoy me. I am Yours alone.

G: *"I have come into my garden, my sister, my bride; I have gathered my myrrh with my spice. I have eaten my honeycomb and my honey; I have drunk my wine and my milk."*

I have done as you asked. I have taken you as my own in intimacy. I delighted in you and have been fed.

"Eat, o friends, and drink; drink your fill, O lovers."

Just as I have feasted upon You my bride, I desire all people to feast upon Me. This exchanging of love between us is reflective of what I want with every believer. I am the Bread of Life, and I am the New Wine poured out. My presence is sweet like honey, and I want every believer to be filled to the brim with Me.

B: *"I slept but my heart was awake. Listen! My lover is knocking: "Open to me, my sister, my darling, my dove, my flawless one. My head is drenched with dew, my hair with the dampness of the night."*

Though we had just loved on each other all night and it was now time to sleep, I tried, but couldn't sleep very well because I just wanted to be with Him again. Then I heard Him knock at the door of my heart and ask, "I want you to open yourself up to me again, you who I see as flawless. This time it is different though. You see, I have been outside in the dark night, alone and cold. This is what my life looks like many times. They even strung me up on a tree to die. Right now I invite you into the sufferings that you will take on because you are my lover. Come suffer with me, for me. I invite you into this part of intimacy with me.

"I have taken off my robe- must I put it back on again? I have washed my feet- must I soil them again?"

Unlike last time You asked something greater of me, this time I want to do as You say. I am learning that I can trust You. This time I am ready for obedience that leads to intimacy, but it seems You are asking for me to show that to You differently than before. I want to give You what You want, which I am demonstrating to You through the uncovering of myself to You. I don't know if I can do as you asked…it is cold and dirty outside. But I want it. Will You help me enough to get me started?

"My lover thrust his hand through the latch-opening; my heart began to pound for him. I arose to open for my lover, and my hands dripped with myrrh, my fingers flowing with myrrh, on the handles of the lock."

He helped me by breaking into my nice little world and removing me from a safe life so that I could be an abandoned lover of Him. I am now ready to embrace even death in order to obtain Him.

"I opened for my lover, but my lover had left; he was gone. My heart sank at his departure. I looked for him but did not find him. I called him but he did not answer.

Now comes the ultimate test. Though I obeyed Him, He still withdrew His presence from me. Can I believe that I did what was right and not succumb to confusion, offense, or condemnation? And will I live for Him even if it doesn't feel like He is near? He told that He could never really leave, so He must still be here. Will I still believe all the words of love that He spoke to me? Though I can see the purpose of this, I am still sad because I miss Him and want Him here. He must have been able to see my heart of obedience, because the suffering He invited me into has apparently started. My hunger for Him will not die as He is away, in fact, it will only grow stronger…. already I feel it evolving into an obsession and deep thirst in spirit. I have called out to Him in this desperation to have Him again, but He has not answered me. I am compelled to go out and search for him, to seek Him though I may not find him.

"The watchmen found me as they made their rounds in the city. They beat me, they bruised me; they took away my cloak, those watchmen of the walls!"

Nobody was helping me during this time. Even other Christians hurt me, wounded me, and took away my covering. Nobody was out to love or help me. I had to remember the words that He had spoken so many times before and believe them now. What were they worth unless in a time like this I hold onto them? Do I really believe Him? Why would this be happening if what He said was true? Nonetheless, I choose to believe He loves me and that He is good. I choose to believe that He has a good reason for this happening. I will not forget that this is a test, and I will stay faithful. I will not allow anything to come between us.

"O daughters of Jerusalem, I charge you- if you find my lover, what will you tell him? Tell I am faint with love."

If anyone talks or sees my Lover, simply tell Him that I miss Him. Tell Him that I haven't given up on Him, and His absence has made me desire Him more. I probably passed the test because I was faithful to believe He is good. I have stayed true to wanting Him even when He draws Himself away from me. Yes, I love you Lord. You are all I want. I have learned that there is nothing better than Your love.

D: *"How is your beloved better than others, most beautiful of women? How is your beloved better than others, that you charge us so?"*

Why is your Beloved so special to you? What stands out about Him so much that we should keep our eyes peeled for you? Why do you love Him so?

B: *"My lover is radiant and ruddy, outstanding among ten thousand. His head is purest gold; his hair is wavy and black as a raven. His eyes are like doves by the water streams, washed in milk, mounted like jewels. His cheeks are like beds of spice, yielding perfume. His lips are like lilies dripping with myrrh. His arms are rods of gold set with chrysolite. His body is like polished ivory decorated with sapphires. His legs are pillars of marble set on bases of pure gold. His appearance is like Lebanon, choice as its cedars. His mouth is sweetness itself; he is altogether lovely. This is my lover, this is my friend, O daughters of Jerusalem."*

I love to talk about Him, so good question. He shines. There is none like Him, even if you set Him in the middle of ten thousand other lovers, He easily stands out as the most desirable. Every detail about Him is perfect. He is completely pure, striking, gentle, wise, strong, romantic, and again I say, perfectly beautiful in every way. And not only is He my lover, but also my friend. I could talk about how wonderful He is forever: what I just said is only a small bit of what He is like. Desirable, isn't He?

D: *"Where has your lover gone, most beautiful of women? Which way did your lover turn, that we may look for him with you?"*

Your passion for Him has affected us. Now we want to know where He is so that we can find Him as well. We want to know where he is because of the way you talk about him…it is obvious that you love him very much.

B: *"My lover has gone down to his garden, to the beds of spices, to browse in the gardens and to gather lilies. I am my lover's and my lover is mine; he browses among the lilies."*

Another good question. I have just found Him and am about to go see Him, if you would like to follow me to this place. He is waiting in the place of intimacy for me, and I cannot wait to be held and spoken to by Him. He is always so gentle. We haven't been close to each other for some time, so I am excited.

G: *"You are beautiful, my darling, as Tirzah, lovely as Jerusalem, majestic as troops with banners. Turn your eyes from me, they overwhelm me. Your hair is like a flock of goats descending from Gilead. Your teeth are like a flock of sheep coming up from the washing. Each has its twin, not one of them is alone. Your temples behind your veil are like the halves of a pomegranate. Sixty queens there may be, and eighty concubines, and virgins beyond number; but my dove, my perfect one, is unique, the only daughter of her mother, the favorite one who bore her. The maidens saw her and called her blessed; the queens and concubines praised her."*

You are lovely my bride. You have stayed faithful to Me and waited on Me...and now as we come back together, you overwhelm Me. You have again conquered My heart, this time through your faithfulness despite the suffering. Your eyes of devotion, oh redeemed one, overwhelm Me when you are true to Me in times of testing. Do you see what you have done, oh beautiful one? Please see how much you mean to Me! There are many lovers, but you are unique. This is one reason why I love you. This is what makes you My favorite. You are different from everyone else. I love the way I have made you. That is one of the highest compliments, because it sets you apart from everyone else. I means that there is nobody like you in My eyes. You are the only place I can come get what you have to offer. The fruit that is found in your garden can be found nowhere else. Your love is a unique gift that only You can give Me. Nobody can love Me the way you do. I encourage you to be you; that is when I am most impressed by who you are. It is then that I can see Myself in you the most as well.

H: *"Who is this that appears like the dawn, fair as the moon, bright as the sun, majestic as the stars in procession?"*

I love to compare the bride's uncommon beauty to heavenly objects. I love to honor her, praise her, and build her up. She is becoming like Jesus more and more. She is starting to shine like He does. She is becoming beautiful like He is. She is majestic as He is, all because she has been with Him. I approve of this holy love affair. I will increase the love that the two of you have for each other, simply by revealing to her how beautiful He is.

G: *"I went down to the grove of nut trees to look at the new growth in the valley, to see if the vines had budded or the pomegranates were in bloom. Before I realized it, my desire set me among the royal chariots of my people."*

All of this testing has produced something new in my lovers heart. As I reflected upon the fruits of love being cultivated in her life, my heart was raptured at the notion of her love, and I was carried away in thought.

D: *"Come back come back, O Shulammite; come back, come back, that we may gaze on you!"*

Come back beloved, and be with us! We want to look upon you, because in being with Him, you have begun to take on His beauty! We know you are going out to meet the King, but we want you to stay here!

W: *"Why would you gaze upon the Shulammite as on the dance of Mahanaim?"*

Why would you spend your time looking at this average woman? Sarcastic remarks leave our mouth about her because she is so common in our eyes. We do not understand the love the King has for her.

G: *"How beautiful your sandaled feet, O prince's daughter! Your graceful legs are like jewels, the work of a craftsman's hands. Your navel is a rounded goblet that never lacks blended wine. Your waist is a mound of wheat encircled by lilies. Your breasts are like two fawns, twins of a gazelle. Your neck is like an ivory tower. Your eyes are the pools of Heshbon by the gate of Bath Rabbim. Your nose is like the tower of Lebanon looking towards Damascus. Your head crowns you like Mount Carmel. Your hair is like royal tapestry; the king is held captive by its tresses. How beautiful you are and how pleasing, O love, with your delights! Your stature is like that of the palm, and your breasts like clusters of fruit. I said, 'I will climb the palm tree; I will take hold of its fruit.' May your breasts be like the clusters of the vine, the fragrance of your breath like apples, and your mouth like the best wine."*

Why do you treat my beloved as an object or simple thing? Do you not see the details of her beauty? Beloved, do not listen to voices that do not echo Mine. Let Me affirm you once again. I love every characteristic about you. Every piece of you I made and enjoy. I love your personality and every thing about you, even the things you and others say are odd. I do not make mistakes. You are the way you are because I wanted you to be that way. Now, let me enjoy what I have made. For some reason you still think that what I have made isn't good, let alone beautiful...please, allow me to enjoy you. You are not in agreement with Me when you dislike, downplay, or disvalue anything about yourself. Allow me to enjoy what

I have made. You need to enjoy who you are as well. This cannot happen unless you receive what I am saying to you...that I love you exactly how you are.

B: *"May the wine go straight to my lover, flowing gently over lips and teeth. I belong to my lover, and his desire is for me. Come, my lover, let us go to the countryside, let us spend the night in the villages. Let us go early to the vineyards to see if the vines have budded, if their blossoms have opened, and if the pomegranates are in bloom- there I will give you my love. The mandrakes send out their fragrance, and at our door is every delicacy, both new and old, that I have stored up for you, my lover."*

I invite Your overwhelming, adoring, pleasure to rush over me. I am Yours. Lets escape from the many people and go be alone...lets spend the night together and wake up early to be with each other once again. I am eager to give myself to You. You have brought me through some hard times and because of that there are many fruits of my love that have developed for You in my garden... I am eager to give them to You.

"If only you were to me like a brother, who was nursed at my mother's breasts! Then, if I found you outside, I would kiss you, and no one would despise me. I would lead you and bring you to my mother's house- she who has taught me. I would give you spiced wine to drink, the nectar of my pomegranates. His left arm is under my head and his right arm embraces me. Daughters of Jerusalem, I charge you: Do not arouse or awaken love until it so desires."

I wish there was a way for us to relate so that I could show You affection in public and we wouldn't be disgraced....but the reality is that many do not understand when I love You to the fullest, in intimacy. Many don't understand intimacy with You. Intimacy is something that needs to happen behind closed doors, because many times, while in the midst of intimacy with You, I do things that seem odd to others. When You embrace me, I do not care how I look or sound to others. I lose control and am just a child, a broken person, a desperate-for-Your-love lover. I give up and stop trying to hold myself together, and others do not understand that. If you are not ready to let go of yourself and completely unveil yourself and lose control, do not take Him on as your lover. You will be shamed and scorned by man, but embraced by God Himself. If you are not ready to look like a fool for God, do not take Him on as your intimate lover.

H: *"Who is this coming up from the desert leaning on her lover?"*

In the distance there is someone coming up from the place of testing. It isn't clear if it is one person, or two. As they come closer, it is clear that it is the Bridegroom and His bride. The bride is tired, but has been faithful. She has learned how to rely upon the Groom, and how to lean hard into Him. That is why they are so close and appear to be one. He is becoming what she depends fully upon. They are becoming one in spirit. The Bridegroom is taking her out from the desert and into heavenly places where He will lavish her with rejuvenating love once again.

G: *"Under the apple tree I roused you; there your mother conceived you, there she who was in labor gave you birth. Place me like a seal over your heart, like a seal on your arm; for love is as strong as death, its jealousy unyielding as the grave. It burns like blazing fire, like a mighty flame. Many waters cannot wash it away. If one were to give all the wealth of his house for love, it would be utterly scorned."*

I will again take you to this place that you speak of; this place of intimacy. Repeatedly I will be faithful to do this, and each time I do, you will see yourself more and more as My inheritance. You understand now that I am your inheritance, but you are in the process of learning that you are My reward and inheritance as well. You are the gift the Father is going to give Me on My wedding day. You are learning to identify yourself as My lover, even to the point where I will be the seal over your heart. The only way into your heart will be through Me. Can you imagine that? All the affections of your heart will be directed at Me! Things that used to appeal to your heart and used to open it will not anymore. You will so identify yourself as my lover that you will be one who is marked by Me...you will carry My mark on your arm. All will know that you are Mine and I am yours so that nobody else can come between us...and rightly so because we are both jealous of each other's love. You see, my love is not only jealous for your love, but it cannot be quenched either. I must have you. No amount of water could ever put out the fire of love that I have for you, and nothing can change it nor move it. Nor can My love cannot be bought; I offer it freely. It is Mine to give to whom I desire to give it to, and I desire to give it to you.

B: *"We have a young sister, and her breasts are not yet grown. What shall we do for our sister for the day she is spoken for? If she is a wall, we will build towers of silver on her. If she is a door, we will enclose her with panels of cedar."*

There are others that need the revelation that You are their Groom and holy Lover. What do We do about them? They do not seem to know how to please You, and unless someone puts some time into them, they will never know You nor have the pleasure of loving You.

B: *"I am a wall, and my breasts are like towers. Thus I have become in His eyes like one bringing contentment. Solomon had a vineyard in Baal Hamon; he let out his vineyard to tenants. Each was to bring for its fruit a thousand shekels of silver. But my own vineyard is mine to give; the thousand shekels are for you, O Solomon, and two hundred are for those who tend its fruit."*

But I, on the other hand, bring Him pleasure; I am able to protect and feed others because I have drank deep of Him. I know who I am because He gave me revelation of how He sees me. He and I identify me as a receiver of His love and a bringer of contentment to Him. Jesus, I give everything to You that I have and am producing through this life! It is Yours, my King and Husband.

G: *"You who dwell in the gardens with friends in attendance, let me hear your voice!"*

Just as I delighted myself in your garden, you have learned how to delight of the fruits of the Spirit in my garden. You have learned how to spend long hours there, eating of what gives you life. You have learned how to dwell with Me and in Me. You are emanating the characteristics of what you eat and have allowed your ministry to others to flow out of that reality. Beloved, sing loud of your love for Me before others! I want to hear you sing of Me! Let Me hear your voice! Lavish your love on Me through your voice!

B: *"Come away, my lover, and be like a gazelle or like a young stag on the spice-laden mountains."*

I want to steal you away, right now, again. Come! Let us go to the place of intimacy and love each other! Though I have become accustomed to fruitful ministry to others, this is still my premier purpose in life, and my greatest joy. I will stay faithful to intimacy with You in the midst of promotion and blessing in ministry. Let us go now!

PARTNER WITH US

We are so excited about what God is doing in the globe today. People are being raised up in the place of intimacy with Jesus, lit on fire, then launched out to raise the dead and make disciples of nations. God is moving, and we are watching Him revive His Bride and prepare her for His coming.

There is a lot of work to be done for the Kingdom, and we would love your help. Jesus said, "To those that have, more will be given." We encourage people to sow into ministries that are producing fruit, and we believe that we are good soil to sow into, with abundant fruit. We desire to steward finances in a way that glorifies the King, touches the poor, and expands the Kingdom with every penny.

We dearly appreciate and honor our monthly partners. Would you consider becoming a partner with us? Take a few minutes and ask the Lord if He would give you the joy of sowing into this ministry. He likes to say yes!

Blessings on you,
Tyler and Christine Johnson

Become a partner with The DRT and
One Glance Ministries at www.OneGlance.org
or www.DeadRaisingTeam.com

STORIES OF THE SUPERNATURAL:
FINDING GOD IN WALMART
AND OTHER UNLIKELY PLACES
(Book)

A high witch is saved and healed in Walmart, a whole tribe comes to Jesus, blind eyes opening and cripples walking, the Dead Raising Team... These are just a few of the accounts you will find in this book of stories written by the founder of the Dead Raising Team. Each testimony consists of some sort of miraculous event such as a healing, a word of knowledge, or an encounter with supernatural Love. As you read this book you will not be able to avoid being challenged, entertained, encouraged, built up in your faith, and filled with desire for more of Jesus.

THE COMING
(Book, Fiction)

Have you ever felt a fair amount of suspicion when pertaining to the helplessness, hopelessness, and defeat that we have been told is inevitable in the end times? Have you questioned that destruction or avoidance will be your portion in those days? If so, you will resinate with the story of The Coming.

Scythe is one of the many that is living in the last days, but one of the few that still professes faith in The Eternal. He serves amidst The Chosen, a group of people not cowering and fearful in the end times, but overcoming and victorious. They are the last remnant of what used to be. Or so they thought. A heretic that has recently arisen, claiming to have greater truths than what Scythe's people grasp. The Seers have sent Scythe to confront and convert this heretic, and the conclusions he comes to about The Eternal surprise him. Everything he thought he knew is shaken. Will Scythe's discoveries shake you as well? Perhaps things are not as they appear....

THE POWER OF THE TONGUE
Dvd

Proverbs 18:21 says "Life and death is in the power of the tongue." This teaching highlights the right, and wrong, ways to use our tongue, exemplified through different examples in scripture. As we become people who steward the power of the tongue correctly, God is able to pour out His power upon His people in unprecedented ways upon His people.

SEATED IN HEAVENLY PLACES OF INTIMACY
Dvd

This experiential teaching discusses the many astonishing statements made by Jesus in the Song of Songs towards His Bride. Verse after verse, Jesus speaks words of affirmation and strength to His Bride, statements no believer can go without understanding. In closing the session, Tyler takes you into a visionary realm with Jesus so that you don't just hear what Jesus is saying through scripture but experience it as well.

POSSESSING A VICTORIOUS SPIRIT
Dvd

Destined to live as revivalists rather than survivalists, this teaching highlights the absolute authority that believers have over all evil; disease, witchcraft, and death. Tyler shares many stories of times when God prevailed in impossible situations.

DOES GOD KILL?
Cd/Mp3

Theologically challenging, deeply provoking, and incredibly encouraging, Tyler speaks on the practical aspects of God's goodness, especially highlighting on certain situations in the Bible that are read in an incongruent manner to the nature of God. God's inability to use death to accomplish His purposes is one of the main issues covered in this teaching, relating directly to our ability to believe for resurrection.

COMMISSIONED TO RAISE THE DEAD
Dvd

Given at the annual Spiritual Hunger Conference of the International Association of Healing Rooms, Tyler sets forth simple logic surmised from scriptures we have read all our lives, yet never followed. An impartation for faith to raise the dead rests upon this message.

THE FOUNTAIN OF LIFE
Cd/Mp3

In this teaching, Tyler speaks about the reality that through Christ's sacrifice death is made powerless, thus restoring humanity to its original state of abundant life. Not only expounding on the fact that we do not have to die, Tyler explains that it is not outside of our grasp to live for hundreds of years; we only need to start to believe for it.

AVAILABLE AT
ONEGLANCE.ORG

A while ago we were led by the Lord to train up others in the message of life and life abundant. Thus, Tyler began traveling and speaking on resurrection power, intimacy with God, and the goodness of God. In a short time we have seen many teams raised up and launched to go after the glorious command of compassion in Matthew 10:8 to "....raise the dead."

If you would like this thorough, in depth training in your city, whether to become a Dead Raising Team or just to get lit up with love and fire for God, contact us. You don't have to be a pastor to host one of these trainings. Tyler has dedicated much of his time specifically to these trainings, and has ways of handling the logistics and financial aspect that make it very attainable for anyone to pull it off. We want this to be available for anyone regardless of position or financial ability.

We have seen more fruit in the preaching of this simple, unmixed gospel of unrelenting goodness than anytime previously in life and ministry. The dead raised, the sick are healed, freedom and joy is released, and minds are renewed.

Change your city into a place where death is made powerless by the life that resides within you; host a training.

ABOUT THE AUTHOR

Tyler and his beautiful wife Christine live in Washington when they are not in the nations spreading a spirit of revival, revelation, and love. They impart faith to raise the dead, and an anointing to lead others into greater intimacy with Jesus. They lead the Dead Raising Team, travel the world speaking at churches and conferences, minister to the poor, love their kids, and are wildly in love with Jesus.

www.oneglance.org
www.deadraisingteam.com

Contact us at:
oneglanceministies@gmail.com
thedeadraisingteam@gmail.com

For all critical, discouraging, accusatory, religious, and altogether unhelpful emails, please write to:
wenevercheckthisemail@gmail.com

Any book with a chapter outline akin to the one that follows:

Chapter 1
Convincing God that He has some good in Him

Chapter 2
Reminding God of His promises and begging Him to fulfill them

Chapter 3
Only Pastors and World Famous Evangelists can raise the dead

Chapter 4
Finding a dead person without killing someone

Chapter 5
The anointing increases when your voice raises: How to yell your prayers

Chapter 6
If God doesn't use you to raise someone from the dead, check yourself for hidden sin

Chapter 7
Start fasting now, because you have a lot to catch up on in order to raise the dead

Made in the USA
Lexington, KY
02 June 2013